Contents

Tables

Figures

Acknowledgements

This evaluation project has required the help of a range of individuals and organisations. The evaluation could not have taken place without funding from the Gatsby Charitable Foundation. We are grateful to the Foundation for its continued commitment to the education of looked after children, and especially for the interest shown by Matthew Williams, Gatsby's representative on the project, in our work.

Members of the evaluation advisory group have provided ongoing advice and encouragement for the project, and we are grateful to David Crimmens, Harry Daniels, Carol Hayden and Sonia Jackson. We would also like to thank members of the Taking Care of Education Reference Group, in particular the chair Anne Sofer, for their interest and help. Within NCB we are grateful to colleagues in the Pupil Inclusion Unit for their contribution. In the research department we would especially like to thank Isabelle Brodie for carrying out much of the editing on the final draft. Thanks are also due to other colleagues at NCB and the University of Luton for the support they have provided in our work.

The three local authorities that participated in the evaluation, anonymised for the purposes of this book, deserve particular thanks. We are especially grateful to the Project Lead Officers for the considerable time and hard work they devoted to the evaluation, and to the IT and administrative staff who supported them in this. Carers, teachers, social workers and local authority officials were also kind enough to find time in busy schedules to be interviewed, often more than once. Finally, the evaluation has benefited enormously from the contribution of the young people who agreed to be interviewed. They deserve special thanks for their willingness to take part in this study and for sharing their experiences with us.

Rachael Harker

David Dobel-Ober

David Berridge

Ruth Sinclair

January 2004

Introduction

This book is concerned with the education of children and young people looked after by local authorities and living in foster and residential care. That this is an issue that continues to require attention may seem surprising, given the evidence suggesting that most looked after children recognise the importance of education and enjoy school (see, for example, Social Exclusion Unit 2003). However, despite many developments in policy and practice, the academic outcomes for this group continue to be poorer than for their peers. This absence of educational achievement at school has correspondingly negative implications for the later life chances of looked after children in terms of employment and income. Over recent years these issues have attracted growing amounts of attention from policy makers, and a number of programmes have been initiated to improve the educational outcomes for looked after children, though there is a lack of reliable evidence to enable evaluation of the relative effectiveness of these interventions.

The book stems from a development programme initiated by the National Children's Bureau (NCB), with funding from the Gatsby Charitable Foundation, to support local authorities in their efforts to promote educational opportunities and outcomes for looked after children. The *Taking Care of Education* development project aimed to support a small number of local authorities in deploying a range of good practice tools and techniques, policies and practices to improve the educational achievements of looked after children.

The Gatsby Charitable Foundation also provided funding for a detailed independent evaluation of the development programme carried out by the Research Department of the National Children's Bureau in conjunction with the University of Luton. The evaluation project began in September 2000 and aimed to develop an informed picture of the processes involved in establishing and maintaining a whole authority approach to improving the educational opportunities and experiences of looked after children and young people. This was done by carefully documenting local authority activity in terms of changes in policy and practice, alongside an analysis of the educational outcomes and experiences of young people who are looked after. This study therefore provides important new information about the educational progress of a group of looked after children and young people across time. Inevitably, it has not been possible to include at this stage of the study analyses of all the issues which might be examined – for example, the relationship between gender, ethnicity and the educational experiences of looked after children. These will be taken forward into the next three-year phase of the evaluation.

We begin by describing the policy and research context in which this project has operated. This has been a period of considerable change in policy relating to children looked after and children in need, and these developments have informed the way in which the project has unfolded. Chapter 2 describes the *Taking Care of Education* development programme, and the different ways in which the project was implemented in the participating local authorities. Chapter 3 focuses on the design of the evaluation and the composition of the young people's samples, while Chapter 4 examines the evaluation's findings regarding outcomes for looked after children in the three local authorities. Chapters 5 and 6 go on to discuss, respectively, corporate approaches to the education of looked after children and the nature of inter-professional working in the local authorities. Chapter 7 examines the different ways in which looked after children were motivated and engaged in different aspects of project activities. Chapters 8 and 9 consider findings related to the experience of young people, in school and in the care system, and the way in which this is perceived by young people, carers and social workers themselves. In Chapter 10, the key findings from the evaluation, together with their implications for research, policy and practice, are presented.

issues in conjunction with care placement decisions, foster homes are often in short supply – thereby restricting options of placement choice (Sinclair and others 2000).

Disrupted schooling

In addition to the potential disruption in schooling associated with placement instability, a number of other factors mean that looked after children's educational progress may be characterised by discontinuity and disruption. Initial entry into the care system, or movement within it, may require looked after children to change schools. Despite the requirement of the Joint Guidance to identify school places within 20 days, it is suspected that such a swift response is not always achieved (Jackson and others 2002) and missed schooling can cause children to fall behind in their education. Even when looked after children are provided with appropriate school placements, disengagement from education can arise due to poor attendance. A recent survey of young people looked after by local authorities in England found that 17 per cent of them reported regular truanting from school (Meltzer and others 2003). Looked after children are also over-represented in exclusion figures, being 10 times more likely than non-looked after children to be permanently excluded (Department of Health 2003b), and delays in securing alternative educational provision for excluded children can be experienced. Looked after children may be diverted away from mainstream schooling and offered alternative provision in pupil referral units (PRUs), which young people often perceive as stigmatising (Galloway and others 1994). Looked after children are also five times more likely to be allocated to special needs schools even if their difficulties are less serious than those of many children in mainstream schools (Gordon and others 2000).

The six key themes above, that are used to explain the underachievement of looked after children, appear to continue to be relevant for a number of young people. Somewhat disconcertingly, Fletcher-Campbell and Archer's very recent research (2003) into reasons why looked after children and young people do not attain GCSE examinations reinforced previously known

findings about the negative impact of placement instability, disrupted schooling, inadequate corporate parenting and low expectations.

Lessons from success

It should not be assumed that being looked after inevitably leads to poor educational outcomes. Indeed, in general, children who are looked after for longer periods do better educationally than those looked after for a shorter duration (Department of Health 2001b). Where looked after children have the benefit of such factors as supportive carers, stable care and school placements, successful peers, and opportunities to develop out-of-school interests, their educational attainment can be positive (Jackson and Martin 1998; Gilligan 2000; Martin and Jackson 2002). Some studies report children who feel their educational progress was enhanced through being looked after: that is, by being able to focus on their studies thanks to feelings of stability and safety in care placements; and by receiving enhanced support and encouragement from carers and teachers (Fletcher 1993; Lynes and Goddard 1995; Shaw 1998). In addition, where local authorities adopt a corporate parenting approach to the education of looked after children, including effective liaison between Education and Social Services departments, higher commitment to children's educational success is evidenced and young people are more likely to be maintained in school (Who Cares? Trust 1998; Vernon and Sinclair 1998).

The policy context

The introduction of the *Taking Care of Education* project, and its associated evaluation, arose within a context of increasing governmental concern over the comparatively poor educational attainment of certain social groups, one of these being looked after children. The Government expressed a firm commitment in *Opportunity for All* to achieving a more inclusive society where all citizens have the opportunity to achieve their potential (Department of Social Security 1999). *Opportunity for All* identified the eradication of child poverty as the key to tackling disadvantage. A major element of this policy was to ensure that all children get a high quality education, with particular emphasis given to supporting vulnerable children and young people, including looked after children. The *Opportunity for All* report is updated annually to reflect how various government departments are progressing towards the aim of reducing social exclusion.

General education policy has noted that the number of young people who become disengaged from education, who fail to achieve any qualifications and leave learning at the age of 16 is unacceptably high (Department for Education and Skills 2001). To combat this issue and enhance the educational opportunities of all young people, the government has introduced a plethora of initiatives, many of which are likely to impact upon the looked after population. The most significant of these initiatives are listed below.

Tackling school absence and exclusion

Improving school attendance and reducing exclusion is a key element of governmental strategy to address underachievement and disengagement amongst schoolchildren. Significant attention has been addressed towards discovering the extent of truancy and exclusion in English schools, as well as establishing underpinning causes and strategies to address the problem (Social Exclusion Unit 1998). Target-setting has been introduced at both school and local education authority level in an effort to reduce truancy and exclusion rates (Department for Education and Employment 1998). The government has also extended the use of legal sanctions enforcing school attendance and introduced further powers to hold parents accountable for young people who are persistent truants (Home Office 1998).

Education Maintenance Allowance (EMA)

As part of the government's commitment to improve participation in further education, the EMA offers weekly payments of £30 to young people enrolled on further education courses if they cooperate with the terms of a learning agreement. The scheme was introduced in pilot form in 2000 and a positive evaluation of the pilot (Maguire and others 2001; Maguire and others 2002) means that the EMA will be introduced nationally from September 2004.

Study Support
(Department for Education and Employment 1999b)

A strategy to promote learning activity outside normal lessons to improve young people's self-esteem, motivation and enable them to become more effective learners.

Education Action Zones
(Department for Education and Employment 1997a)

These are where local clusters of schools work in partnership with the local education authority, local parents, businesses and others to encourage innovative approaches to tackling disadvantage and raise standards.

Excellence in Cities
(Department for Education and Employment 1999a)

A programme to improve school standards in the most severely socio-economically deprived areas.

Sure Start
(Department for Education and Employment 1999c)

A cross-departmental strategy to provide more effective support services for young children and their families in socio-economically disadvantaged areas.

Connexions
(Department for Education and Employment 2000)

A new form of multi-agency support service aimed at young people aged 13–19 to enhance the coherence of support provided through the careers service, schools, Social Services, youth and education welfare services. The Connexions programme provides young people with a personal adviser to assist their effective participation in appropriate learning environments (school, Further Education college or training provision) and encourage them to remain in education. The strategy also contains the *New Start* programme to specifically target young people aged 14–17 who are disengaged from learning and at risk of becoming socially excluded.

Children's Fund
(Children and Young People's Unit 2000)

Provides funding to local partnerships who bring together voluntary organisations, schools, faith groups, statutory agencies and children and young people to develop a range of preventative services to address the needs of children and young people at risk of social exclusion.

This range of education-based policies designed to address social exclusion issues may also have some general impact upon the educational experiences of looked after children, particularly given that they tend to be over-represented in exclusion figures and many come from socio-economically deprived backgrounds. However, some commentators argue that current educational policy includes contradictory elements whereby those directed towards a more inclusive system are offset by an emphasis on high academic standards that may cause schools to focus on higher achieving pupils rather than those at risk of social exclusion (Blyth 2001; Gerwitz 1999).

Policy directly relating to the education of looked after children

In addition to general policy initiatives and strategies that could arguably have some impact on looked after children, the government has also shown interest in developing policies and practices that specifically target the education of the care population.

A joint Social Services Inspectorate and Office for Standards in Education report in 1995 (Social Services Inspectorate/Office for Standards in Education 1995) combined with a government commissioned review in 1997 (Utting 1997), drew attention to the continuing underachievement of looked after children and stimulated a government response (House of Commons Health Committee 1998; Ministerial Task Force on Children's Safeguards 1998). Subsequently, a range of policies was initiated that includes the promotion of the education of looked after children as a major aim. Of particular importance were the following policies.

The Quality Protects programme

The *Quality Protects* (QP) initiative (Department of Health 1998, 1999, 2001d, 2003c) was introduced to improve the management of services and outcomes for children in need, with particular emphasis given to those who are looked after by local authorities. QP is mentioned in the government's annual *Opportunity for All* reports as a significant element in addressing the needs of looked after children and aiming to improve their educational attainment. The QP agenda represents a significant progression in acknowledging the central importance of educational achievement for looked after children and young people's future development. Objective Four of the programme includes the need for looked after children to 'gain maximum life chance benefits from educational opportunities' and qualifies this as 'perhaps the single most significant measure of the effectiveness of local authority parenting'. Other QP objectives, for example those relating to placement stability, are also expected to have an impact on educational outcomes.

QP sets local authorities specific targets for rates of young people leaving care with GCSE qualifications, levels of school attendance and levels of school exclusions. Other targets, for example in relation to improving levels of placement stability, are also expected to have educational benefits. Local authorities are required to outline their plans for action with reference to meeting such targets and routinely record and report information on performance indicators relating to these. In general, local authorities are making progress towards these targets but the rate of progress is slower than expected (Robbins 2001; Social Services Inspectorate 2003).

Joint Guidance from the Department of Health and Department for Education

Of major relevance, in terms of advising local authorities as to how educational targets for looked after children might best be met, was the Joint Guidance from the Department for Education and Employment (now Department for Education and Skills) and the Department of Health (Department for Education and Employment/Department of Health 2000). The Joint Guidance provides direction as to how local authorities might fulfil their role as corporate parents to maximise looked after children's life-chance benefits from education. Six key principles of corporate parenting are outlined below.

Prioritising education
Recognising that education provides young people with access to better life chances and valuing and supporting their education is described as one of the most important contributions corporate parents can make to young people's lives.

High expectations – raising standards
Corporate parents are advised to expect young people to attend school regularly, to secure school places for young people without delay, to enable them to access homework and study support, to communicate high expectations and reward and celebrate achievement.

Inclusion – changing attitudes
Corporate parents should seek to challenge and change negative attitudes towards looked after children and young people and act to reduce the risk of discrimination against this group.

Achieving continuity and stability
Efforts should be made to increase the stability of school and care placements to ensure that young people's education is not affected by unnecessary disruption.

Early intervention

Corporate parents should act promptly to secure school placements for young people in cases of entry into, or movement within, the looked after system. Young people's educational needs should be carefully considered and effective advocacy should be available to ensure they receive appropriate educational support.

Listening to children

Children and young people should be consulted to discover their interests and experiences and to determine what engages and motivates them to succeed.

The Joint Guidance also emphasised the importance of effective cooperation between agencies involved in looking after children. This includes ensuring that there are focused educational plans for all looked after children; that information about the education and care history of looked after children is appropriately shared by relevant professionals; and that decisions concerning care-placement arrangements include satisfactory consideration and timely allocation of appropriate schooling.

The need for focused educational plans is underpinned by a statutory requirement that all looked after children have Personal Education Plans (PEPs) both to ensure access to services and support, and to establish clear goals for young people that can be used as a record of progress and achievement. The sharing of information about young people's progress is supported by the recommendation that all schools should appoint a designated teacher. The designated teacher role involves making sure that information about young people's educational progress is passed quickly to other agencies and professionals that need to know; and acting as advocate for young people in public care, making sure they can access services and support and that the school shares and supports high expectations for them. The guidance also recommends that the process of corporate parenting should be overseen by a skilled senior officer at local authority level.

The co-ordination demanded by corporate parenting
requires a skilled senior officer with a clear remit to
establish and enforce joint procedures and protocols and
provide a permanent resource for all involved in
corporate parenting: a champion for young people in
public care.
(DfEE/DoH 2000, Section 5.3)

The Children (Leaving Care) Act 2000

The Act (Department of Health, 2001a) represented significant progress in
the provision of educational support for young people aged 16 and over. It
introduces a statutory requirement that Social Services departments
encourage young people to remain in further and/or higher education and
provide financial assistance for expenses associated with their education and
training.

The responsible local authority must assist a former
relevant child (and may assist other care leavers) with the
costs of education and training up to the end of the
agreed programme, even if that takes the young person
past the age of 21, to the extent that his welfare and
educational and training needs require it.
(Department of Health 2001c)

All young people covered by the Act must have a Pathway Plan covering
education, training, career plans and support needed. The Pathway Plan
replaces any existing care plans and runs until the young person is at least 21
years of age. Young people should also have a personal adviser who helps to
draw up the Pathway Plan and ensure that it develops with the young
person's changing needs and that it is implemented effectively.

School admissions policy

In response to observations that difficulties could be experienced in securing
school placements for young people entering or moving within the looked

after system, the Department for Education and Skills amended the School Admission Code of Practice (Department for Education and Skills 2003) to recommend that admission authorities give 'top priority' to looked after children in over-subscription criteria. It is hoped that this amendment will reduce the likelihood of young people being without a school place.

The Social Exclusion Unit project

To reflect the government's strategic approach to tackling social exclusion, a cross-department body, the Social Exclusion Unit (SEU), was established in 1997. In 2001, the SEU was instructed to investigate the low educational attainment of looked after children. The SEU co-ordinated a series of consultations with a wide range of key stakeholders, including young people, Social Services departments, social workers, Local Education Authorities, teachers, foster carers, private sector providers, and other statutory and voluntary agencies (like Youth Offending Teams and Health Authorities). The consultation process was centred around the four key themes of: factors that affect the attainment of children in care; policy and practice that may work in raising educational attainment for this group; the impact and operation of *Quality Protects* and the Joint Guidance; and potential progression for policy in this area.

The main issues identified by this consultation were published (Social Exclusion Unit 2003) along with a separate report containing key recommendations for effective practice designed to accelerate the rate of improvement that has arisen under the auspices of the *Quality Protects* programme. This SEU project is also important in presenting evidence from local authorities about the progress of some other aspects of government policy, for example in regard to designated teachers and the use of PEPs, and in drawing together evidence concerning the context in which local authorities are working, for example in terms of workforce issues.

The SEU also commissioned an external research study into the costs and benefits associated with current policy and practice regarding the education of looked after children (Jackson and others 2002). The report suggested that substantial savings in public expenditure would be made if further efforts were made to bring the educational attainment of looked after children more in line with their non-looked after peers.

> If we could make coming into care a path to educational success as it is in some other countries, we would not only transform the lives of the children concerned but save immense amounts of public money. The cost of our past failure to educate children in care can be counted in billions.
> *(Jackson and others 2002, p.102)*

Clearly the *Taking Care of Education* project is couched within a policy context that firmly acknowledges the need to better address the educational needs of looked after children.

What really makes a difference to looked after children's education?

It is against this context that the government first introduced targets for local authority performance and introduced the Joint Guidance to advise authorities how such targets might be met. The Joint Guidance can be seen to draw upon the research evidence in encouraging local authorities to work to lessen factors that contribute to low attainment and promote those that may be linked to success. A central theme of the Joint Guidance is that more effective corporate parenting, with all that this concept entails, will enhance the educational opportunities and outcomes of looked after children. This rationale is shared with the *Taking Care of Education* project, which likewise aims to promote a 'whole authority', or corporate, approach to meeting the educational needs of looked after children.

However, the research base in this area is still relatively low, and to date there is no robust evidence to show that improvements in corporate parenting do lead to better educational outcomes for looked after children. Whilst it seems intuitively plausible to consider that more effective joint working and active promotion of the need to support looked after children's education are likely to result in improved experiences and outcomes, at present there is no research or statistical evidence to substantiate this view. The corporate parenting agenda is likely to have made at least some impact in most local authorities, and the trend is towards slightly improved educational outcomes at Key Stages of the National Curriculum, yet outcome indicators relating to looked after children's educational achievement reveal little improvement in performance over the last three years. The lack of clear progress may be partly due to problems with the outcome indicators themselves: different cohorts of young people are included in each year's figures and variations due to missing data and inaccurate data entry across authorities may influence the figures (Oliver and others 2001). Alternatively, it is possible that local authorities have simply not altered their practice sufficiently for any potential benefits of corporate parenting to be realised. Or it may be that policy and practice change takes longer than three years to begin to make a genuine difference to young people themselves. An analysis of outcome indicators alone cannot reveal what the underlying reasons for the relatively stable poor performance of looked after children might be. More in-depth analysis of what is happening within local authorities and what appears to genuinely make a difference to young people themselves is required.

The *Taking Care of Education* project had the unusual advantage of having a full-scale evaluation commissioned alongside it. The foresight of the funders in providing for such an in-depth evaluation is laudable. The evaluation programme enabled careful documentation to be kept of policy and practice changes arising over the course of a three-year period; alongside the perceptions of local authority staff and looked after young people regarding which changes appeared most effective in developing a whole-authority approach to promoting educational opportunities and outcomes for the looked after group. Hence, as well as examining the impact of the development project, the evaluation also provides an opportunity to ascertain how local authorities are responding to the general government agenda of improved corporate parenting and whether any elements of change do appear to make a difference to young people's education.

Summary

■ In comparison with the rest of their peers, looked after children underachieve in term of educational performance. They are over-represented in the population of children with SEN statements as well as amongst children who have experienced permanent exclusion. They are also largely under-represented in the population of young people going on to further and higher education.

■ Research into the educational failure of looked after children can be categorised around two broad areas: the negative influence of pre-care experiences associated with individual attributes; and the role of the care and education systems. Six main themes relate to the second area: inadequate corporate parenting, failure to prioritise education, inappropriate expectations, the care environment, placement instability and disrupted schooling.

■ In 1999, the Department of Health introduced the routine collection of records of educational achievement for looked after children. Since then, the gap between the performance of looked after and non-looked after children has remained broadly stable.

■ The *Taking Care of Education* development project aims to support three local authorities in deploying a range of good practice tools and techniques, policies and practices to improve the educational achievements of looked after children. The project started in September 2000. It has been fully evaluated by the NCB Research Department in conjunction with the University of Luton.

■ The government has expressed a firm commitment to achieving a more inclusive society where all citizens have the opportunity to achieve their potential. A particular emphasis has been placed on supporting and improving educational outcomes for all vulnerable children. In this context, the government has introduced a large number of initiatives aimed at enhancing the educational opportunities for all young people as well as for specific groups of vulnerable children. Most of those initiatives are likely to impact on the looked after population.

■ The Joint Guidance on the education of looked after children (DfEE/DoH, 2000) outlines six key principles: prioritising education; high expectations – raising standards; inclusion – changing attitudes; achieving continuity and stability; early intervention; and listening to children.

■ To date, there is very little research-based evidence to show that improvements in corporate parenting do lead to better educational outcomes for looked after children. The evaluation programme associated with the *Taking Care of Education* project has provided an opportunity to ascertain how three local authorities respond to the general government agenda of improved corporate parenting and whether any elements of change appear to make a difference to young people's education.

2. The Taking Care of Education development programme

The *Taking Care of Education* project was designed in response to the observation that a number of policies, tools and techniques had emerged that were aimed at improving the educational achievements of looked after children. However, the various approaches had not been collectively applied and evaluated and their transferability had not been tested. Therefore, the main aim of the project was to support a small number of local authorities in bringing together current knowledge, resources and ways of working that might improve educational opportunities and outcomes for looked after children. Sufficient funds were available to work with three local authorities by providing them with access to a range of resources to help strengthen their current policy and practice. Available resources were to cover staffing – a Project Lead Officer appointment in all three authorities and administrative support if necessary – funding for discrete project activities and assistance from the National Children's Bureau Pupil Inclusion Unit. There was, however, sufficient flexibility within this funding for the three authorities to develop the project in ways appropriate to their particular context. This chapter will describe the identification and selection of the local authorities, and the different ways in which the project was set up and implemented in each.

Identification of project authorities and appointment of Project Lead Officers

In July 1999, around 20 local authorities were invited to attend a seminar to introduce the project's aims and objectives and outline the application procedure for participation in the programme. Those authorities who wished to apply were required to complete a fairly lengthy audit of their current investment in educational provision and practice for looked after children. Thirteen authorities completed the NCB Current Investment Audit tool as part of a bidding process to gain access to the additional funding associated with the project.

Current Investment Audit details were examined by a panel of Gatsby Trustees and National Children's Bureau (NCB) staff, in conjunction with any recent Ofsted or SSI reports for the authority, in order to identify three local authorities that appeared to: a) be best able to respond to the challenge of the development project, and; b) offer it access to varied patterns of service development. In September 1999, the project sites were selected. For the purposes of this book, these will be described as Allborough, Wentown and Nettbury.

Decisions relating to the leadership of the project within each authority were an important part of the setting-up process. In November 1999, representatives of the Gatsby Charitable Foundation and the NCB met senior managers in each of the project authorities to discuss details of the project infrastructure, including the recruitment of Project Lead Officers and the respective roles of partner organisations. It was agreed that Project Lead Officers would be employees of the authorities with salaries claimed from the NCB at three-monthly intervals in arrears. The project authorities would be entitled to budget for around £62,000 per annum to cover the salary costs of the Project Lead Officer and an administrative support post if required. Following these meetings, NCB staff provided each authority with a standard job description and person specification for the Project Lead Officer posts that could be adapted to suit local needs. Each authority was informed that they should determine for themselves the salary level and where the Project Lead Officer would be situated in the authority's structure.

The three authorities took somewhat different decisions regarding the status and positioning of the Project Lead Officer's post. Allborough decided to spend most of the salary budget in ensuring that the post was a senior role, the equivalent of an Assistant Director of a department. This decision was based upon a view that a high scale position was necessary to attract candidates who were likely to have subsequent credibility with senior officers in Social Services and Education. In terms of positioning the post within the authority structure, it was decided that the Project Lead Officer would be an employee of the Education Department but would be based within the Social Services Department to emphasise the joint nature of the post. In addition, they were to be line managed by assistant directors from both Education and Social Services departments.

In Nettbury, the post was not given quite the same status as in Allborough, but it was judged to be necessary to allocate a senior management position to the Project Lead Officer. The Project Lead Officer was to be employed by the Social Services Department and line-managed by an assistant director within Social Services, with an assistant director from the Education Department also taking part in supervisory sessions to ensure appropriate input from both departments. Decisions about the accommodation of the Project Lead Officer were largely driven by the availability of office space, and an initial base in a Teacher's Centre was replaced by a permanent office in Social Services.

Interviews for the positions in Allborough and Nettbury were held in June 2000 and appointments were made in both authorities. In both cases the successful applicants had already been employed by the authority for a number of years and the Project Lead Officer posts were defined as secondments. In Allborough, the Project Lead Officer had been the head of the Special Educational Needs Service, whilst in Nettbury the successful candidate had been the authority's Social Inclusion Officer. Both Project Lead Officers were viewed as well-respected figures within the authority at the time of appointment.

In Wentown, senior officers were initially resistant to the idea of creating a Project Lead Officer post. It was felt that the authority was already making progress in relation to a corporate approach to the education of looked after children and that it would be possible to utilise project funds without the need to assign a designated officer. However, after discussion with NCB staff and the funding body it was agreed that a Project Lead Officer would be recruited. A decision was taken to create a post at a slightly lower level than in either Allborough or Nettbury. The post was to be positioned within the authority's Corporate Strategy Unit to emphasise that the education of looked after children was a corporate responsibility rather than the exclusive remit of either the Social Services or Education departments.

A low level of response to the original job advertisement in Wentown led to the post being re-advertised. An appointment was eventually made in July 2000. The successful applicant had a substantial amount of work experience in the voluntary sector working for an AIDS charity and The Children's Society and had also been employed as a part-time Policy Development Officer for Social Services.

Concurrent to the process of recruiting Project Lead Officers, a multi-disciplinary project Reference Group was established by NCB. Chaired by the NCB Chair the group was set up to include the head of the NCB Pupil Inclusion Unit, a representative of the Gatsby Charitable Foundation, representatives from the Department of Health and Department for Education and Skills, Local Authority Directors of Social Services and Education, and academics working in the area of the education of looked after children. The group was to meet on a quarterly basis with a major remit to review applications to fund specific projects and policy developments in each authority and approve the release of funds where appropriate. In fact, over the course of the project, difficulties were experienced in using the Reference Group to approve project funds and the decision was eventually taken to deploy the group's expertise in an advisory capacity to assist the Project Lead Officers' work, rather than serving as a funding scrutiny body.

At the same time, the National Children's Bureau Pupil Inclusion Unit was to continue working with the Project Lead Officers in a supportive role. The precise parameters of this were not clarified in the early stages, and this was to prove problematic later on (see Chapter 6). This issue was complicated by the fact that the lead member of the Pupil Inclusion Unit negotiating the project left just as it was about to properly commence, leaving the new post-holder to pick-up and develop the role. However, the sometimes rather ambiguous role of the Pupil Inclusion Unit raises broader issues about the need for a model of how the development work is to progress in a project of this type.

Development of project implementation plans

The *Taking Care of Education* project can be seen to have officially commenced in September 2000, when the three Project Lead Officers took up their posts and attended an induction day at NCB. The induction day focused on the Project Lead Officers' first major task: to develop a project implementation plan for their authority in conjunction with senior officers from Social Services and Education departments. The Project Lead Officers were advised that implementation plans should draw upon Current Investment Audit details to determine what new streams of activity and investment would further enhance the educational opportunities of looked after children, as well as what existing streams of investment and activity could be strengthened by the overall project strategy. Project funds would be released to support the implementation plans where there was clear evidence that activities undertaken could be sustained and effectively 'mainstreamed' at the end of the project should they prove to be successful. In addition, Project Lead Officers were advised that the Gatsby Charitable Foundation would welcome authorities investing their own funds, or those from other special grants, to support the overall aim of improving educational outcomes for looked after children.

In all three project authorities, Project Lead Officers developed their original implementation plans in consultation with those officers responsible for their line management.

There were three main strands to the development of implementation plans:

- identification of gaps and areas where current policy and practice could be strengthened, drawn from the NCB Current Investment Audit document
- consultation with a range of local authority personnel at both operational and strategic levels
- the need to integrate project work with government initiatives like *Quality Protects* and the Joint Guidance on the Education of Children in Public Care (see Chapter 1).

In addition, the Project Lead Officer in Nettbury undertook a fairly detailed literature review into the education of looked after children and used insights from this work to inform the development of the Nettbury implementation plan.

The nature of the project implementation plans was, therefore, informed by the specific context of the three authorities. While all three were small in size, they differed in respect to the nature of the looked after population and also in relation to the way in which certain services were delivered. Thus, for example, a significantly higher proportion of Nettbury's looked after population was living outside the borough than in Allborough or Wentown, and contained a higher number of children from minority ethnic groups. Nettbury also had a significant group of young unaccompanied asylum seekers. The authorities were also at different stages in respect to their thinking about the education of looked after children, though all had a reasonably good base on which to build. Wentown, in particular, felt that there was already a strong foundation of good practice with respect to the education of looked after children, exemplified by, for example, projects catering for children who were not attending school. Allborough had good systems in place for inter-professional working. Nettbury had policies in place that identified the education of looked after children as a priority.

It is also important to note that at the point at which the project implementation plans were being developed, various new legislation and other initiatives were just coming into play (see Chapter 1). While it was expected that the Project Lead Officers would make links with these, it was important that implementation plans should not duplicate work that was being developed under the umbrella of other initiatives and services. For example, in all three authorities the work of the new (at that time) Connexions service was expected to have an impact on mentoring and careers guidance. However, the timing of the *Taking Care of Education* project had the advantage that the Project Lead Officers could also influence the implementation of policy that was focused on the education of looked after children, such as the use of Personal Implementation Plans (PEPs).

Project Lead Officers presented their initial implementation plans to a meeting of the Reference Group in January 2001 and all plans were approved. The original implementation plans were revised and extended throughout the course of the project. The following sections provide details of the 'starting points' for each authority in terms of the development of the plans, the implementation plans themselves and the frameworks in place to support project implementation. We have organised the presentation of project activities contained in each authority's implementation plan around three main themes: i) promoting strategic change ii) influencing professional practice iii) directly supporting looked after young people's educational progress.

Project implementation in Allborough

In its approach to progressing the *Taking Care of Education* project, Allborough clearly set out to develop sustainable strategies that would enhance looked after children's motivation and help to raise their educational achievement. In the early documentation setting out its principles of implementation, the *Taking Care of Education* project is described as a 'change management project' that needs to influence practice in the widest possible context across the local authority. From the outset, it was acknowledged that, for the project to be successful, the Project Lead Officer would need the full commitment and support of the most senior officers in the departments of Education and Social Services as well as of the local authority's Chief Executive. The approach to project management and implementation also emphasised a commitment to inter-professional working, within as well as across services.

The framework established to manage and implement the project consisted of a project steering board, a Project Lead Officer, a core or executor group, a multi-disciplinary reference group and a number of inter-professional task groups. Figure 2.1 provides a pictorial representation of the framework to support project implementation in Allborough.

Figure 2.1: Schematic representation of project implementation framework in Allborough

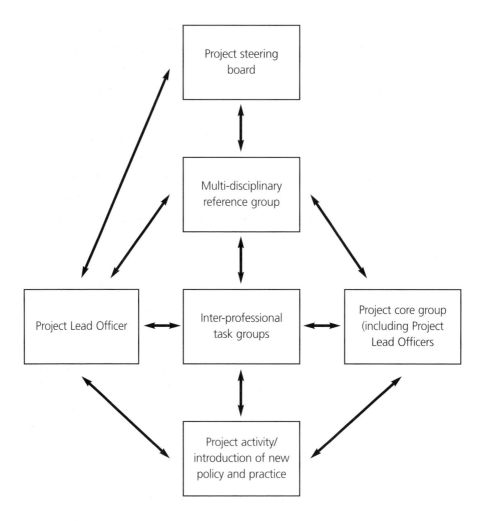

The Project Lead Officer was to play a central role in all parts of implementation. The Officer was employed by the Education department but housed and supervised within Social Services. The project steering board provided joint management and maintained overall responsibility for the project. The Project Lead Officer reported to the board on a three-monthly basis. The project steering board included the executive elected members attached to Education and Social Services, the directors and assistant directors of Education and Social Services, two senior officers representing the Health Authority, a school governor and a school head teacher. The board had overall responsibility for the project and identified broad target areas for project activity, approved implementation plans, monitored progress, adapted plans where needed and identified ways of jointly working through potential or actual barriers to progress.

A project core group, comprising the Project Lead Officer and two designated senior officers from Education and Social Services, allocated individual project activities to a range of inter-professional task groups and ensured that appropriate communication occurred both within and between these groups. The inter-professional task groups were charged with carrying forward the priorities identified by the project steering board, the core group and the multi-disciplinary reference group.

The multi-disciplinary reference group comprised approximately 25 members, representing Education and Social Services, the Health Authority, Youth Offending, Early Years, Leisure and Library Services. This group largely existed before the project as a sub-group of *Quality Protects*. The initial remit of the group was to identify departmental tasks within Education and Social Services and the Health Authority. It was easily assimilated into the project framework and became responsible for reviewing project progress through receipt of regular feedback from the inter-professional task groups. Regular reports from this forum were communicated to the project steering board.

As the *Taking Care of Education* project approached the end of its first three-year phase, the role of the Project Lead Officer in Allborough was reviewed. It was recognised that the framework in place had been efficient in bringing the initial system changes needed to improve educational outcomes for looked after children, but it was also acknowledged that more work should be directed toward children and young people at case level. It was agreed that in the future, the Project Lead Officer would need to work on two distinctive levels. Firstly, there was an identified need to work within the existing framework and to ensure that the efforts of the Local Authority to support the education of looked after children were maintained and sustainable in the long term. Secondly, the Project Lead Officer was to manage a small specialist team, working directly with individual young people. The team was to include an Education Welfare Officer, an Advisory Teacher and one or more Education Care Officers. It was envisaged that through this direct work with young people, the Project Lead Officer would be able identify barriers to young people's progress and find ways to deal with these at a corporate level.

The range of activites allocated to inter-professional task groups in Allborough were organised around 14 key priorities identified as being vital to promoting the educational opportunties of looked after children. These 14 priority areas in Allborough were:

- producing a statement of joint intent concerning the care and education of looked after children
- developing the Social Services and Education information-sharing system
- producing a glossary of terminology
- developing service-level agreement between Education, Social Services and Child and Adolescent Mental Health Service (CAMHS)
- ensuring access to appropriate educational provision for all looked after children
- ensuring all looked after children have Personal Education Plans
- empowering looked after children
- improving access to Early Years provision for looked after children
- promoting the professional development, and understanding of respective roles, of all professionals working with looked after children
- enabling residential staff to adequately support young people's education
- improving educational resources in residential centres
- targeting support for Year 11 students
- improving access to further education
- providing social and leisure activities for looked after children.

These priorities are presented below in sections relating to activities designed around three main themes of: promoting strategic change, influencing professional practice, and directly supporting looked after children and young people's educational progress.

Promoting strategic change

A number of project activities in Allborough were strategic initiatives designed to impact upon the authority's policy and practice by adopting a corporate approach to the education of looked after children. A major focus of these activities was to promote more effective inter-professional communication and to provide looked after children with access to appropriate educational provision.

Statement of joint intent

In September 2001, the Project Lead Officer developed a Statement of Joint Intent containing nine corporate principles underpinning the care and education of looked after children. The document outlined Allborough's commitment to improving educational outcomes for looked after children beyond the lifespan of the *Taking Care of Education* project. It was signed by the executive elected members and the Directors of Education and Social Services, and by the Chief Executives of two Primary Care Trusts and one Primary Care Group from South Allboroughshire Health Authority.

Social Services and Education information sharing system

Project funds were used to purchase *Business Objects*, an end-user reporting tool, as well as additional computers and a new server to allow a wider range of Education and Social Services teams to access the system. A data sharing protocol was developed and approved by the *Taking Care of Education* project board. The data system allowed the Special Educational Needs Support Service and the Advisory Teacher for Children in Public Care to access routine reports relating to looked after children and young people in Allborough. However, at the end of the first phase of the project it was not yet accessible to the full range of professionals for whom it was intended, nor was it producing information at the full level of detail envisaged. It was hoped that the system would be fully operational by September 2003.

The work surrounding the development of the joint system also highlighted the fact that monitoring the attendance and attainment of children placed outside the authority was being done on an individual – and time-consuming – basis. This has since led to recognition of the need to develop procedures with neighbouring authorities; and action plans to meet this aim were being considered for the next phase of the project.

Glossary of terminology

A directory and glossary of commonly used terms in the fields of education, social services and health was created and distributed in July 2001. The glossary is easily accessible to all staff working with looked after children and it is hoped that it assists in inter-professional communication.

Service-level agreement between the Education Service, Social Services and CAMHS

Allborough intended to agree a joint strategy for those looked after children who have emotional, behavioural and mental health needs. A draft service-level agreement was developed outlining a multi-agency approach to improving the quality of life and social functioning (including optimising educational opportunities) of looked after children and young people. However, barriers emerged when the agreement became a tangible proposition due to concerns that individual agencies may not have the relevant resources to enable the agreement to be implemented effectively, and at the end of the first phase of the project the agreement had yet to be finalised.

Ensuring access to appropriate, full-time educational provision for all looked after children

Changes to the Local Education Authority admission procedures in line with recent government policy have been agreed and will be in place from September 2004. Looked after children will be given 'top priority' in over-subscription criteria. Furthermore, Allborough agreed that if children were cared for in foster placements where foster carers' children attend a particular school, the looked after children would be treated as siblings. This was intended to improve the likelihood of a school place being allocated.

A project-funded Educational Welfare Officer was given the task of identifying some of the issues surrounding finding appropriate educational placements. The Educational Welfare Officer also became part of an inter-professional task group aimed at developing methods of working with young people considered 'hard to reach'. The group – attended by representatives from the Police, Youth Offending Service, Special Educational Needs Support Service, Connexions, Arts and Sports and Leisure Services – explored the possibilities of providing alternative activities for young people excluded from school (such as arts and motor mechanics) which might prevent them from becoming disengaged from education.

Ensuring all looked after children have a Personal Education Plan

A Personal Education Plan (PEP) review group was established, including representation from designated teachers, head teachers and social workers and consultation input from young people. The purpose of this review group was to examine the format, content, quality of information, and procedures concerning PEPs and provide recommendations for amendments to both format and content. The PEPs were therefore to be monitored and reviewed in conjunction with each young person's statutory placement review (see Chapter 5).

Empowering looked after children

A young people's reference group was established to inform, advise, influence and comment on progress and actions taken to improve the educational attainment of looked after children. In addition, project funding was used to appoint a part-time Youth Worker to promote opportunities for consultation and participation with looked after children and young people. One outcome of such work was the 'Allborough Young Achievers' Awards Ceremony' which took place in March 2002.

Improving access to Early Years provision for looked after children

The Project Lead Officer became a member of the Allborough Early Years Development and Childcare Partnership (EYDCP) Board and negotiated targets for looked after children to be included in the EYDCP plan for 2002 to 2003. The Project Lead Officer's involvement with the partnership is evident in a number of policy and practice changes in the Early Years area. Foster carers have been given access to Allborough's new Toy and Music Library since October 2002. A monitoring system was set up to update the Early Years Service on looked after children entering the care of the authority. Work on developing an Early Years PEP is underway. Training and awareness-raising for carers on Early Years issues is also in progress.

Influencing professional practice

Project activities in Allborough that aimed to influence professional practice included those aiming to improve inter-professional working and those designed to enable carers to support young people's education effectively.

Promoting the professional development, and understanding of respective roles, of all professionals working with looked after children

Initially, this priority centred on raising awareness of, and providing guidance and support to schools on the role of, designated teachers for looked after children. The approach was soon broadened to involve all professionals working with looked after children. A series of joint training events was organised for designated teachers, social workers, residential carers and school nurses, with plans for education welfare officers and foster carers to be invited to future training sessions. The joint training covered issues around the completion of PEPs, the role of the designated teacher and attachment issues for looked after children. A training session for school governors highlighting their role in supporting the education of looked after children took place in January 2003, and further, similar events were planned.

A separate course of training for foster carers was also delivered. The training programme aimed to empower carers in supporting the education of children in their care. Issues such as school admission, exclusions and appeal procedures, and special educational needs were addressed; and arrangements have also been put into place to enable foster carers to access the existing Early Years training sessions. In June 2003, the Paul Hamlyn Foundation agreed to fund work from the *Read On Write Away* project (ROWA) in Allborough. Work to promote reading and literacy skills amongst carers and looked after children was due to commence in September 2003. Additional support for residential carers was provided through a monthly educational forum designed to enable residential workers to receive regular information about educational issues and to share good practice in supporting young people's education.

Enabling residential carers to support young people's education adequately

Part of the role of the project-funded Education Welfare Officer was to provide support to residential centres both to improve young people's school attendance and assist residential staff in maintaining an overview of young people's educational progress. This work facilitated a number of changes in Allborough's residential centres. Wall charts for staff were placed in each centre outlining forthcoming school events and an allocated worker to attend each, as well as information on exclusion and admission procedures and a list of the Education Welfare Officers allocated to each school. Each residential centre also now keeps attendance sheets to record whether young people attend school or college.

Directly supporting looked after young people's educational progress

Some project activities in Allborough can be considered to provide direct support to young people through the enhancement of educational supports available in care placements and strategies to motivate their educational engagement and attainment.

Improved educational resources in residential centres

Key Stage study guides and educational software for personal computers were provided to residential centres in Allborough. The Library Services now deliver collections of books and magazines to each residential centre. Young people in the centres are also actively encouraged to join local libraries and have been provided with vouchers for free internet use in the libraries.

Targeting support for Year 11 students

The potential needs of looked after young people in Year 11 preparing for Key Stage 4 examinations are currently being assessed and possible support strategies identified. The range of supports that could be provided include: additional tuition in particular subjects; assistance in completing late course work; support in developing revision strategies; provision of revision guides and equipment required for exams; counselling to enable young people to deal with workload pressures, fear of failure and exam stress; and support to carers in approaching and discussing young people's needs with schools. The Education Psychology service has allocated resources to support looked after children in this area.

Improving access to further education, training or employment

Project funding was used to pilot a scheme to provide financial incentives for regular attendance amongst young people in further education. Since September 2002, young people have been able to benefit from an allowance of £30 per week for consistent attendance at a college of further education or school sixth form. A similar scheme will be introduced nationally and funded by central government through the Education Maintenance Allowance from September 2004.

Provision of social and leisure activities for looked after children

All looked after children and their carers in Allborough were provided with a Leisure Pass entitling them to free access or reduced rates to most sporting facilities run by the authority. Some consultation was also initiated by a Leisure Officer to assess the sports and leisure needs of looked after children, though problems were experienced due to workload and funding issues within the Sports and Leisure service. It was hoped that the planned reorganisation of the Sports and Leisure Service would facilitate progress in this area.

Project implementation in Nettbury

The Project Lead Officer in Nettbury was employed by the Social Services department and line-managed by an assistant director within Social Services, although an assistant director from the Education department contributed to supervisory sessions. This core group developed the project implementation plan for Nettbury and was responsible for overseeing project progress. In addition to this project implementation group, a project reference group was established – involving management staff from Education and Social Services, designated teachers, and Health Authority representatives – to discuss project progress and advise on future development. This was perceived as an opportunity to strengthen working relationships between group members from different agencies and discuss joint working strategies. However, the project reference group in this authority had no formal mechanisms for feeding into strategic or operational planning.

The framework to support project implementation in Nettbury is shown in Figure 2.2. The framework was much simpler than that in Allborough, with the Project Lead Officer taking responsibility for communication between staff associated with individual project activities, the project reference group and the project implementation group.

Figure 2.2 Schematic representation of project implementation framework in Nettbury

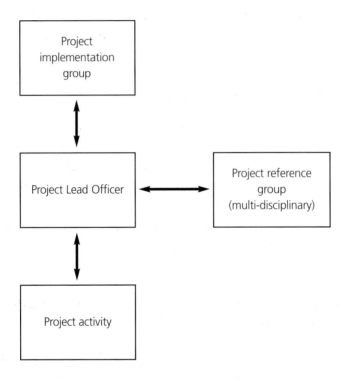

Project activities in Nettbury have focussed upon:

- producing a statement of corporate parenting principles for the education of looked after children
- improving information sharing
- making an ongoing commitment to training needs
- ensuring support from elected members
- developing and implementing Personal Education Plans
- improving inter-professional working
- enabling carers to support literacy and numeracy skills
- promoting the resilience and self-efficacy of looked after children

- improving educational resources in care placements
- acknowledging young people's achievements.

The following sections outline these activities under the three themes of promoting strategic change, influencing professional practices and directly supporting looked after young people's educational progress.

Promoting strategic change

A number of project activities can be classed as strategic initiatives designed to improve the authority's ability to provide a corporate response to the education of looked after children. A major focus of such activities was to raise awareness of the educational needs of looked after children and promote more effective inter-professional practice. It was hoped that the eventual outcome of these activities would be improvements in the educational experience and attainment of looked after children.

Statement of corporate parenting principles for the education of looked after children

The Project Lead Officer produced a statement of corporate parenting principles for the authority in October 2001. The statement was endorsed by the Education Arts and Leisure Committee, the Social Services Committee and the authority's Cabinet. The original aim was that the principles would be incorporated into the detailed planning of the Education and Social Services departments. However, this did not happen and, in the absence of such activity, the Project Lead Officer encouraged individual services and teams to produce statements describing how the corporate parenting principles of the authority were to be reflected in their operational practice. The services that produced such strategies included the:

- Educational Psychology Service
- Special Educational Needs Assessment and Provision Team
- Early Years Development and Childcare Services
- Education Social Work Service

- Leaving Care Team
- Family Placement Service
- Sensory and Communication Team
- Youth Service
- Youth Offending Team.

In addition, the *Nettbury Cultural Strategy* for 2003–2008, developed by the Arts and Leisure Service, included looked after children and children leaving care as priority groups.

Improving information sharing

Several changes in the collection, collation and sharing of information between key departments of Education and Social Services took place over the course of the project. Much of the change was attributable to the work of the Children's Quality Information Team within Social Services. However, the Project Lead Officer was seen to have contributed to this work by identifying where gaps existed in the accuracy and currency of information held. The Project Lead Officer also developed a questionnaire to collect information on an annual basis on children placed outside the authority.

In addition, the Project Lead Officer tried to establish a tracking process, whereby information available on the educational progress of Year 10 children could be used to identify those who may be in need of additional assistance well in advance of GCSE/GNVQ examinations. The aim was that field social workers could then explore whether there were any unmet needs or issues that young people felt could be addressed in order to support them better.

By the end of the first phase of the project, plans were being considered for a new electronic management system in Nettbury to further facilitate the sharing of information between departments. The Project Lead Officer was also a member of the Child Health Informatics Consortium, an inter-professional task group whose task was to explore strategies to share health information concerning looked after children in more effective ways.

Making an ongoing commitment to training needs

The Project Lead Officer organised a series of training sessions for social workers, residential and foster carers, designated teachers and elected members, which focused on the educational needs of looked after children. A core group of trainers from the departments of Education and Social Services has been established to ensure continuing staff development and training in this area. Plans were being made to organise the training programme around clusters of schools, to which carers, social workers and teachers would be linked.

Ensuring support from elected members

A cross-party Corporate Parenting Members Group exists in Nettbury and the Project Lead Officer was responsible for holding a series of briefing sessions with this group to highlight issues concerning the education of looked after children. The group also receives regular progress reports on all work designed to promote the educational opportunities of looked after children.

Developing and implementing Personal Education Plans

The Project Lead Officer led on the design and implementation of the authority's PEP pro-forma to ensure standardisation of response from social workers and schools and also developed a form for use with children under five years of age. The Project Lead Officer also provided considerable advice to social work staff regarding the instigation of PEPs and the level of liaison required with school staff, carers and looked after children. An audit of the content of the PEPs was undertaken by a project-funded Educational Psychologist. Project funding was also used to appoint a PEP coordinator.

Influencing professional practice

A variety of project activities can be described as aiming to alter the professional practice of management staff within the departments of Education and Social Services, as well as operational staff such as social workers, teachers and residential and foster carers. These include activities designed to facilitate more effective inter-professional working and those aiming to enable carers to support young people's education more effectively.

Improving inter-professional working

A series of multi-disciplinary training sessions for designated teachers, social workers, and residential carers was co-ordinated by the Project Lead Officer. The sessions also resulted in a document clarifying expectations for foster carers in supporting the education of looked after children and guidance for social work and teaching staff on the completion of PEPs. Meanwhile, the establishment of a multi-disciplinary reference group to oversee project activity represented an opportunity for senior and middle management staff to consider joint approaches to promoting the educational needs of looked after children.

Enabling carers to support numeracy and literacy skills

A number of training events were organised specifically for carers. These included the *Nettbury Book of My Own* scheme, *Reading Roadshows* and *Maths Count*. These focused on raising carers' awareness of the importance of encouraging children and young people to read as a leisure activity and to apply mathematical thinking in everyday contexts. It was hoped that project funding and input would in due course be replaced by support from the Education Department's Curriculum Advisers.

Directly supporting looked after young people's educational progress

The final strand of project activities in Nettbury can be seen to provide some form of direct support for looked after young people, either through practical resources in care placements, acknowledging and encouraging achievement, or enhancing resilience and self-esteem. It was hoped that these schemes would promote the fact that it is reasonable for young people to expect that they are provided with books, have access to computers and have someone exhibiting an interest in their educational progress.

Promoting the resilience and self-efficacy of looked after children

Five main project initiatives in Nettbury can be seen to aim to promote successful educational experiences for looked after children through enhancing their sense of resilience and self-efficacy. These five initiatives are outlined below.

A dedicated Educational Psychologist post was funded for one year in equal parts by the *Taking Care of Education* project, *Quality Protects* and Standards Fund from September 2001. The remit of the post was to undertake focused work with looked after children to promote resilience and enable them to fulfil their full development potential. The post was continued for an additional year, from September 2002, through monies taken from the Education Department's Standards Fund allocation and project monies.

A Youth Participation Worker, jointly funded by the project and Comic Relief funds, has also been undertaking direct work with young people to increase their participation in youth activities and their involvement with the Nettbury Young People's Forum. The worker has also encouraged a number of looked after children to enroll on the Duke of Edinburgh's award scheme. The original funding source for the post ends in September 2003. However, there are plans for the post to continue with funding from the Connexions Service.

In the summer of 2001, a free leisure pass for looked after children was piloted with project funding. The authority has re-negotiated their contract with the local Leisure Centre to ensure that concessionary leisure cards are issued to all looked after children from April 2003.

A week-long photography course for looked after children was held in the summer vacation of 2002. The course was funded by the *Taking Care of Education* project and involved the Arts and Leisure Service, residential and foster carers, the FE College and Kodak. The work of the young people who attended has been exhibited in various public areas on authority premises. The Arts and Leisure Service subsequently agreed to fund a similar course, in collaboration with an art gallery, during the half-term vacation of the 2003 Spring Term.

The final area of project activity intended to boost young people's self-esteem and resilience was a mentoring scheme in which trained adult mentors provided support for 11–16-year-old looked after children in foster or residential placements, primarily those living outside the authority. It was hoped that this scheme would subsequently be supported by a larger mentoring project.

Improving educational resources in care placements

Some project activities attempted to improve both the material resources and levels of encouragement available in care placements, for example training activities aimed at carers. The *Book of My Own Scheme* not only encouraged carers to support young people's literacy skills, but also enabled young people to purchase books, thereby adding to the availability of material resources to support their education.

In terms of material resources, project funding also enabled new computers with internet access to be installed in the Nettbury Leaving Care Base and the two residential homes in the authority. A commitment was made in the LEA Education Development Plan that the Information and Communication Technology advisor would visit the homes at least twice in the academic year to advise on how best to use the technology to support children's learning.

Project funding was used to enable the Library Service to establish libraries in the two children's homes, in consultation with residential staff. Funds were also used to produce information packs highlighting library facilities and opening hours, which are now distributed to all looked after children in Nettbury. In addition, an after-school club specifically targeted at looked after children of primary school age was established in one of Nettbury's libraries. The club is run on a weekly basis and provides a wide range of materials for creative work, access to computers, printers and photocopiers, as well as the entire stock of the library.

Acknowledging young people's achievement

The Project Lead Officer organised a celebration event for looked after children on behalf of Nettbury's Corporate Parenting Members Group, which was funded by the Social Services Department. Children were nominated by social workers in consultation with carers/parents and designated teachers, the criteria for nomination being that a child should have made progress or achieved success in examination results, attendance rates, behaviour at school or participation in school events.

Project implementation in Wentown

The Project Lead Officer in Wentown was employed by and housed within the authority's Corporate Strategy Unit. The post was jointly managed by assistant directors from Education and Social Services departments and an officer from the Corporate Strategy Unit. This group of three officers and the Project Lead Officer determined the implementation plan for Wentown. The role of the Project Lead Officer was to develop individual project activities by carrying out direct work or identifying other staff within the authority to take activities forward.

The framework for project implementation in Wentown, shown in Figure 2.3, represents the simplest implementation structure of all three authorities.

Figure 2.3: Schematic representation of project implementation framework in Wentown

The individual activities in Wentown included:

■ developing a whole authority policy on the education of looked after children
■ maintaining and expanding the database of looked after children
■ implementing and monitoring a data-sharing protocol
■ providing research evidence to support policy and practice development
■ improving inter-professional working
■ enabling carers to support young people's education
■ improving resources in care placements
■ acknowledging and encouraging achievement
■ promoting the resilience and self-efficacy of looked after children.

The following sections outline these activities under three themes of promoting strategic change, influencing professional practice, and directly supporting looked after young people's educational progress.

Promoting strategic change

A number of project activities in Wentown were strategic initiatives designed to impact upon the authority's ability to provide a corporate response to the education of looked after children.

Developing a whole authority policy on the education of looked after children

The Project Lead Officer took lead responsibility for the development of a corporate policy outlining the fundamental philosophy, principles and aims of the authority's approach to the education of looked after children. The policy was accepted at committee level and circulated throughout the authority. It included the contributions that named departments (Social Services, Education, Housing, Leisure Services, Environmental Health, Planning, Economic Development and Tourism, and the Engineers Department) would make to the improvement of the educational experiences of looked after children in Wentown. The individual departments were asked to include their respective contributions within their annual business plan to emphasise a corporate approach to the education of looked after children. There are plans to review the policy regularly and update the information relating to the relative contributions of individual departments where necessary.

Maintaining and expanding the database of looked after children

The Education Department database was upgraded using *Taking Care of Education* funds. The upgrade extended the range of information held about looked after children and allowed detailed historical data to be held. The database is not shared between the departments of Education and Social

Services but is managed by the LEA Special Projects team, which provides the Social Services department with regular information on looked after children.

Implementing and monitoring a data-sharing protocol

Information-sharing protocols, covering looked after children and care leavers, were developed by the LEA Special Projects team in negotiation with the Social Services Department. Although not directly involved in developing the original protocols, the *Taking Care of Education* Project Lead Officer was responsible for distributing them for consultation and re-drafting where appropriate.

Providing research evidence to support policy and practice development

Two major activities undertaken include investigations into the use of unofficial exclusions in Wentown schools and researching the support needs for looked after children to access further education. This stemmed from anecdotal reports that such practice was relatively widespread in Wentown schools in relation to looked after children and resulted in the LEA Special Projects team holding training sessions on exclusions for foster and residential carers. To research the support needs of looked after children in further education, a questionnaire was developed and distributed to staff in the leaving care team.

Influencing professional practice

Activities that aim to influence the professional practice include those designed to facilitate more effective inter-professional working and those aiming to enable carers to effectively support young people's education.

Improving inter-professional working

The Project Lead Officer had considerable input into the Department of Health/Local Government Association funded *Teenagers to Work* scheme

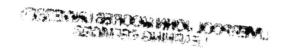

which ran in the summer vacation of 2001. The Project Lead Officer's contribution enabled young people to produce a video about the educational needs of looked after children. The video is used in training sessions with Social Services and Education staff and the Project Lead Officer ensured that all appropriate managers, staff and corporate parents saw the training video. The video shows young people describing a highly fragmented system of care and education and was used to stimulate debate regarding how different professionals might work together more effectively.

Also of significance in terms of promoting inter-professional working was the establishment of a work-shadowing scheme. Newly qualified teachers from three Wentown secondary schools were grouped with field social workers and residential carers to allow these staff the opportunity to work-shadow one another for at least five half-days a year.

Enabling carers to support young people's education

Project activities that have focused on raising carers' awareness of the importance of supporting young people's educational progress included developing literacy support schemes in residential centres and study-support resource packs for foster and residential carers. Project funding was used to second a secondary school teacher for one day a week, throughout the Autumn term of 2001, to analyse the availability of literacy support in residential centres. The teacher produced a report including a range of recommendations on how support could be strengthened. This led to a number of developments:

- work by the Library Service with the four residential centres to establish reference libraries
- training for residential staff by LEA Literacy Advisers on methods of developing and supporting young people's literacy skills
- identification of a staff education representative in each residential centre, with regular meetings held between representatives and LEA staff to discuss educational issues.

Project funds were also used to provide foster carers and young people with opportunities to receive complementary GCSE and SAT revision guides.

Directly supporting young people's educational progress

The final strand of project activities in Wentown can be seen to provide some form of direct support for looked after young people: either through practical resources in care placements to assist with their education; acknowledging and encouraging achievement; or enhancing resilience and self-esteem.

Improving resources in care placements.

Some project activities have attempted to improve both the material resources and levels of encouragement available in care placements. The previously noted activities aimed at enabling residential carers to support young people's literacy can also be seen to improve resources in care placements. As a consequence of this project, the Library Service in Wentown is using *Taking Care of Education* funds to establish adequate libraries in each of the authority's residential units.

The project also enabled the introduction of a pilot scheme to provide computers for children and young people in foster care. A total of 20 looked after children were given access to one of 17 computers in foster homes. Provision of a computer was linked to a training package whereby young people were given access to two hours of tuition each week. In addition, computers, scanners, printers and digital cameras were purchased for all four residential centres in the authority. The computers allow internet access and include educational software. The funding covers maintenance of the machines and software.

Acknowledging and encouraging achievement

Four main areas of project activity can be classed as designed to acknowledge and/or encourage achievement.

The Wentown Annual Awards Ceremony enables teachers, carers and social workers to nominate young people to receive recognition for progress in such areas as examination results, attendance rates, punctuality, behaviour at school, or participation in school events. The awards ceremony pre-dates the *Taking Care of Education* project but the contribution of additional project funds has expanded the ceremony into a larger and more high profile event.

The *Rewards for Revision* scheme uses project funds to provide monetary rewards for all young people passing GCSE or GNVQ examinations, with extra monies being given for achievement above predicted grades. The Project Lead Officer coordinates this scheme and ensures that letters informing cohorts of Year 11 exam-takers are distributed well in advance of exams. Those obtaining examinations receive their money along with a letter of congratulations from the Chief Executive of the Council and the Director of Social Services. The scheme is being monitored to determine whether the rewards have contributed to young people's revision motivation.

The funding of a dedicated worker for looked after children on the Wentown Vulnerable Pupils Panel arose from project activity. This Panel aims to identify and work with young people who are at risk of school exclusion. The dedicated worker liaises with looked after children to directly encourage them back into education and also acts as a point of liaison with other agencies involved in these young people's lives. A Saturday Club for looked after children in school years 5, 6 and 7 was established at a study centre in the local football club. The focus of the club is on developing and supporting literacy, numeracy and information technology skills in a relaxed and fun environment.

Promoting the resilience and self-efficacy of looked after children.

A series of outward-bound residential weekends for looked after children were organised by the Project Lead Officer. The weekends were attended by around 8–10 young people and focused on team building activities and fostering young people's personal development.

Summary

■ The *Taking Care of Education* project is a development project funded by the Gatsby Charitable Foundation. Its aims are to support a small number of local authorities in bringing together current knowledge, resources and ways of working that might improve educational opportunities and outcomes for looked after children.

■ In September 1999, three local authorities were selected and the project effectively started in September 2000 following the appointment of a Project Lead Officer in each authority.

■ Project Lead Officers were appointed at different levels of seniority in the three authorities. The most senior position was the equivalent of an education or social services assistant director.

■ All three Project Lead Officers initially worked on designing an implementation plan drawing upon the Current Investment Audit tool provided by the NCB (this had already been used in the process of selecting the project authorities) and on consultation with a range of local authority personnel at both operational and strategic levels.

■ Implementation plans identified gaps and areas where current policy and practice could be strengthened. The documents also ensured that project work would be linked to government initiatives like *Quality Protects* and the Joint Guidance on the Education of Children in Public Care.

■ All Project Lead Officers were encouraged to develop activities that could be sustained and effectively 'mainstreamed' at the end of the project, should they prove to be successful.

■ Project activities in all three authorities can be grouped under three main themes: i) promoting strategic change; ii) influencing professional practice; and, iii) directly supporting young people's educational progress.

3. The Taking Care of Education evaluation

The *Taking Care of Education* evaluation started in September 2000 and involved closely monitoring the developmental work taking place in the three project authorities of Allborough, Nettbury and Wentown. The research team included three research officers, one each attached to a given project authority to enable in-depth evaluation work to proceed. This chapter provides details of the main aims and its methodological design. The sections covering design include details of the types of information collected and the research methods used as well as ethical issues.

Aims and objectives of the evaluation

The main aim of the evaluation was to build an informed picture of the processes involved in establishing and maintaining a whole-authority approach and assess the impact of this on the educational opportunities and experiences of young people in public care.

More specifically the evaluation sought to:

- highlight the range of approaches used and project activities undertaken in each authority and investigate what appeared to work well
- identify barriers to implementation of the desired approaches within and between agencies
- identify any changes in the well-being of a sample of young people and in their attitudes to education and to school
- highlight any positive educational achievements for the young people and identify associated factors

- ascertain the views of young people on their education and care experiences and how they thought these might be enhanced.

Design of the evaluation

To meet the evaluation objectives, a range of qualitative and quantitative methods were used to examine both process and outcome of the *Taking Care of Education* development programme. The process study examined the developmental work within and between sectors of the local authority, as perceived by those involved. The outcomes study focused on educational attainments – both objective measures of attainment (National Curriculum Key Stage test results, GSCE results, attendance and exclusion rates) and subjective assessment by young people of the value of, and satisfaction with, their schooling and educational experience. Assessment was also made of the young people's general well-being and expectations for the future.

The evaluation was structured around four major, overlapping components which examined:

- policy and practice change
- key stakeholders' perceptions of policy and practice change
- educational outcomes for looked after children and young people
- the educational experiences of looked after children and young people.

Component 1: Policy and practice change

Policy and practice developments were monitored over the course of the development project in three main ways.

i) The most comprehensive monitoring form used was the NCB's *Current Investment Audit*. This tool includes a total of 81 items which relate to policies and practices a local authority might have in place to deal with the education of looked after children. The items reflect key elements that research and experience suggest are successful in promoting educational opportunities and outcomes for looked after children. The audit was initially completed by all three authorities in 1999, and the evaluation team requested that Project Lead Officers complete annual updates of the audit. Updated versions of the audit were completed in November 2000, November 2001 and November 2002. Audit forms were examined for apparent developments in policy and practice over each year of the project.

ii) Complete versions of the project implementation plans developed in each authority were made available to the research team. In addition, subsequent annual revisions of these plans, reflecting changes to plans associated with project progress and the identification of new areas of development, were examined.

iii) Regular communication between the research officer attached to each authority and the Project Lead Officer provided regular updates on all project activities. Where appropriate, members of the research team observed local project reference group and board meetings, and received minutes of all relevant meetings. Project Lead Officers also provided copies of all progress reports produced for their authority and for the NCB coordinated *Taking Care of Education* Reference Group.

These three strands of information were combined to furnish a detailed record of all project activities and any resulting changes in policy and practice. The evaluation team analysed and related this largely descriptive information to the experiences and perceptions of professionals and young people in the project authorities.

Component 2: Key stakeholders' perceptions of policy and practice changes

Throughout the course of the project, regular interviews were held in each authority with the Project Lead Officers and key personnel. The key personnel included a range of senior management staff from Social Services and Education departments, as well as elected members, whose roles predominantly dealt with the education of looked after children and who were involved in implementing project initiatives.

The first round of interviews was held in February–March 2001 with subsequent rounds taking place every six months, hence the most recent phase of interviews took place in May–June 2003. The number of personnel interviewed at each phase is displayed in Table 3.1, which also shows the frequency of individuals included in all stages.

Table 3.1: Frequency of key personnel included in each round of interviews

Authority	Interview round 1	2	3	4	5	Included in all rounds
Allborough	7	12	12	10	8	5
Nettbury	5	5	6	5	5	3
Wentown	6	7	7	6	5	4

Individuals who were included at all stages of the interviews were those with key responsibilities relating to project implementation, either due to line-management responsibilities for the Project Lead Officer or membership of a core group to oversee project progress.

The interviews asked personnel to identify all significant project-related activities, achievements and changes in the previous six months. They were also asked to assess how useful and successful they believed activities were and what impact they were having. Factors that facilitated and hindered project progress were also discussed, along with strategies to overcome any problems and recommendations for future project progress.

At each stage, all interviews followed a standard schedule across all three authorities although, where relevant, this was tailored to reflect knowledge of local project activity. The first three rounds of interviews consisted entirely of open-ended questions to seek general perceptions of project progress, without necessarily focusing on specific project activities and particular areas where the work may be having an impact. This was deemed appropriate for the phase of the project being assessed, as a number of project activities had not been running for a sufficient period for their impact to be evaluated. However, by the time of the fourth round of interview in October–December

2003 the project had been running for a sufficient period of time to enable legitimate questions to be raised regarding its impact. Hence the interview schedules began to include closed questions to rate the perceived impact of specific project activities, as well as the project's influence upon inter-professional practice to promote a whole-authority approach to the education of looked after children.

Component 3: Educational outcomes for looked after children and young people

The purpose of this component was to examine the local authority's overall record in respect of the education of looked after children and to note any changes during the evaluation period regarding attendance levels, exclusions, GCSE examination and National Curriculum test results. Educational data routinely collected for government 'OC2' returns were assessed to establish broad indicators of the outcomes for the young people and provide the backdrop to interpreting the perceptions of staff and young people as to the impact of project activities. Returns for the academic years covering 1999/2000, 2000/2001 and 2001/2002 were compared to ascertain whether any differences had arisen over the course of the project, as well as how the performance of the three project authorities compared to national trends.

Component 4: The educational experiences of looked after children and young people

Information was also gathered from a longitudinal study of a sample of 56 looked after children and young people across the three project authorities. The sample was followed-up over a two-year period in an effort to identify any changes in the young people's educational experiences, their attitudes to schooling and education and their general well-being. Where change had arisen over time, attempts were made to determine whether differences might be linked to project activity.

Recruiting the original sample

The original sample was recruited from a sampling frame of all young people looked after in the three project authorities, who: were between 10 and 18 years of age, had been looked after for at least three months, and were in a care placement within the authority or in a geographically neighbouring authority. Random quota sampling was applied to ensure that the sample reasonably reflected the overall looked after population in each authority in terms of variables such as gender, ethnicity, legal status and care placement.

Information about the evaluation and participation requests were distributed, via Social Services Departments, to 50 young people in each authority in February 2001, with the aim of recruiting at least 33 in each to take part in the evaluation project. The information about the project clarified that the researchers would like to interview young people on two separate occasions over a period of around 18 months. Young people who did not wish to take part were asked to return an opt-out response form to the researchers. They were advised that the local authority would provide researchers with contact details of all those who did not return opt-out forms. Young people who did not return an opt-out form were subsequently contacted by telephone to confirm their willingness to participate.

A total of 80 young people agreed to take part in the original round of interviews: 29 were looked after by Nettbury, 28 by Wentown and 23 by Allborough. These young people participated in their first interview during the period covering March to October 2001 and were informed that their follow-up interview would take place around 16–18 months later.

Strategies to retain the sample

The decision to restrict the sampling frame to young people who were looked after for at least three months aimed to improve the stability of the sample over time. Department of Health (2003a) statistics indicate that young people who have been looked after for at least three months are those most likely to remain in the care system for a considerable period. Hence, the sampling frame restriction aimed to maximise the possibility that young people would be looked after for a reasonable length of time. This would enable a more accurate reflection of the impact of any changes in local authority services on the educational opportunities of looked after young people.

As well as selecting a sample more likely to remain within the care system over the course of the project, strategies to reduce the likelihood of sample attrition due to lack of interest from the young people were also employed. A young person's Reference Group was established with volunteers from the sample in all three authorities. These young people then assisted members of the evaluation team in producing newsletters to update the young people's sample on project progress and in organising social activities to thank young people for their ongoing contribution to the project. Some of the reference group members also agreed to undergo a brief young researchers' training programme and subsequently helped to facilitate discussion groups with other young people drawn from the project sample. All of the young people who sat on a reference group and all those who attended social events remained within the sample and participated in follow-up interviews.

The research team also attempted to maintain an accurate register of contact details for all young people in the sample. At the time of their first interview, young people were given contact details for the researcher so they could notify them if their details changed in any way. Some young people in the sample were good enough to comply with this request and contacted the researchers to inform them of placement moves. In addition, Social Services staff in each authority were forwarded a list of contact details for the sample every six months and asked to notify the evaluation team of any known changes.

Requesting follow-up participation

In September 2002, having confirmed contact details with Social Services departments, letters were distributed to all members of the sample. The letters reminded young people that the evaluation project was continuing and they would be contacted within the next few months to arrange a follow-up interview. Young people were subsequently telephoned and their consent to participate in a follow-up interview was sought and, where given, a convenient date, time and venue were negotiated.

This procedure was adapted for a small number of cases involving young people who were no longer looked after and had moved out of the authority. For some of these young people a current telephone contact was not available, although Social Services departments frequently had a last known address. In these instances, interview questions were translated into a questionnaire format and this was forwarded to the young person's most recent address along with a freepost return envelope. In addition, three young people requested the opportunity to complete a questionnaire rather than be interviewed when they were telephoned.

Follow-up sample size and attrition rates

Unfortunately, the follow-up study was not able to retain all 80 young people from the original sample. The follow-up sample contained 56 young people: 20 from Nettbury, 19 from Wentown and 17 from Allborough. Table 3.2 displays the reasons for sample attrition in each authority and overall.

Table 3.2: Reasons for sample attrition

Local authority	Refusal	Over 3 'no shows'	No contact details	No phone contact	Lost to sample
Allborough	0	0	3	3	6
Nettbury	4	2	0	3	9
Wentown	3	1	3	2	9
Total	7	3	6	8	24

Table 3.2 shows that the most common reasons for attrition are that young people either refused to take part in a follow-up interview, or they were unable to be asked to participate as address and/or telephone contacts were not available. In Nettbury and Wentown, there were some instances of young people persistently failing to keep agreed interview appointments. In such cases a decision was taken to class the third occasion on which a young

person did not attend an interview, that is, a 'no show', as a refusal and there were no further attempts to contact the young person.

Obtaining up-to-date contact details for some young people in the sample proved problematic in Allborough and Wentown. In Allborough there were different reasons for this: in one case, a young person was known to have moved placement but their allocated social worker could not be traced to ascertain current details; in a second case a young person had been adopted and the adoption manager preferred not to contact the new family; and, in another case, a young person had left the care system some time ago and was believed to have moved out of the area.

In Wentown, the lack of contact details stemmed from inaccuracies in Social Services' records. Despite checking the accuracy of information in August 2002, when efforts to contact young people for follow-up interviews were underway, it emerged that a considerable proportion of contact details were inaccurate. The research team liased with Social Services staff in Wentown on several occasions to remedy this problem, but by February 2003 accurate contact details remained missing for three young people. Two of these young people were still recorded as looked after.

Ten young people (42 per cent) of the 24 lost to the sample were no longer looked after. In Allborough this concerned two of the young people for whom contact details were unavailable and one of those for whom there was no telephone contact. In Nettbury, two of the young people who declined a follow-up interview and two without telephone contact details were no longer looked after. Finally, in Wentown, two of the young people who refused a follow-up interview and one for whom contact details were unavailable had left the care system. Since over half the young people who refused to take part in a follow-up interview had left the care system, one can perhaps assume that these young people felt the study was no longer relevant to their situation.

Interview and questionnaire design

Interviews with young people, at both original and follow-up interviews, included a combination of closed and open-ended techniques. A series of standardised tests was applied at both stages to allow the possibility of detecting quantifiable changes in the young people's attitudes, expectations and well-being over the course of the project. Open-ended questions were also included in both interview schedules to ensure that young people felt that their individual opinions and perspectives were valued, and they were not always required to use the researchers' framework to describe their experience.

At both interviews, the majority of closed-ended questions were presented in a short questionnaire booklet divided into three sections: Sections A, B and C.

Section A was intended to assess attitudes to learning and school by combining the *Psychological Sense of School Membership* scale (Goodenow, 1993) with the *Attitudes to School* measure (Furnham & Rawles, 1996). The response format for all items was a five-point scale ranging from 'Strongly Agree' to 'Strongly Disagree'.

Section B contained the *Children's Future Expectation Scale* (Wyman and others, 1992) which comprises six items designed to assess young people's future expectations and aspirations. This measure is also scored on a five-point scale ranging from 'Strongly Agree' to 'Strongly Disagree'.

Section C aimed to assess the young person's current psychological well-being and included a combined presentation of the *Strengths and Difficulties Questionnaire* (Goodman, 1999, 2001) and an *Adolescent Self-Esteem Scale* (Rosenberg, 1979). The *Strengths and Difficulties Questionnaire (SDQ)* consists of 25 items that cover aspects of emotional well-being in addition to items concerning behaviour, ability to concentrate on tasks, social relationships and pro-social behaviour, all of which may be interesting variables to examine with reference to the impact of the development programme. The *SDQ* is completed by selecting from response options of 'not true', 'somewhat true' or 'definitely true'. These response options are the same as those used for the 10 items in the *Adolescent Self-Esteem Scale*, hence the two scales were presented in a combined section.

In addition to the questionnaire booklet, further closed-ended and a series of open-ended questions were asked of the young people. For closed-ended questions, young people were asked to describe how they believed their education was currently progressing using a 5-point fixed response scale, including options of 'very well' 'well', 'average', 'badly' or 'very badly'. They were also asked to indicate whether being looked after had made a difference to their educational progress using response categories of 'better', 'worse' or 'no difference' to indicate perceived effect. Finally, they were also asked to complete a checklist outlining a range of educational supports that might be available in their care placement.

For open-ended questions, young people were asked to explain their perceptions of their current educational progress and the estimated impact of being looked after on their education. They were also asked whether they could identify any individuals who were seen to have supported or hindered their educational progress and the manner in which they had done so. The interview also included questions about the young people's educational and career aspirations and factors that may enable them to achieve their goals.

The follow-up interview schedule included additional questions to establish young people's awareness of project-related activities and any observed changes in policy and practice designed to support their education. Where young people were aware of any activities or change, they were asked to indicate whether this had made a difference to their educational progress.

Interview procedure

All interviews with young people were held at their home address and most took place after school hours. In the majority of cases, interviews were held in private with the young person, although in a few cases carers were present at the interview. At interview, young people were reminded of the nature of the research, given assurances of the degree of confidentiality and anonymity afforded to them, and asked permission for the interview to be tape-recorded. Three young people were not willing to be tape-recorded and in these cases written notes of interview responses were made.

Key adults in young people's lives

For each young person included in the sample, the research team aimed to interview a carer and/or teacher regarding their perceptions of the young person's educational progress. Key adults were also asked about their own practice in supporting young people's education and whether local authority policy and practice might assist them in this role. In a small number of cases, usually where young people were in independent living and had left school, social workers were contacted in lieu of carers or teachers. This resulted in interviews being held with 37 foster carers, 12 residential carers, 18 teachers, four social workers and four parents.

Data analysis

Questionnaire data was entered into SPSS (Statistical Package for the Social Sciences) files and computational rules were developed to produce total scores for all the standardised scales used. Qualitative interview data was transcribed verbatim and entered into a NVivo qualitative analysis database. Interview responses were coded by question, with subsequent coding according to themes emerging from the data. Comparative analysis of data from original and follow-up interviews was undertaken. The selection of quotes contained in this book is informed by this analysis, and are representative of the data collected.

Composition of the young people's follow-up sample

Fifty-six young people took part in both original and follow-up interviews. This represents 70 per cent of the original sample size of 80 at the first phase of interviews. Both the first phase of interviews (T1) and the follow-up stage (T2) requested background information from the young person regarding their care and educational history and current placement. The background details collected allowed us to describe the sample in terms of variables like age, gender, ethnicity, care placement, placement moves, school attendance and experience of school exclusion.

The following sections describe the composition of the follow-up sample in terms of these variables, as well as providing details of the make-up of the original sample of 80 young people. This enables an estimation of whether certain groups are adequately represented in the follow-up sample.

Age

The ages of young people taking part in original interviews ranged from 10 to 18 years, whilst at the time of follow-up interviews the age of the sample ranged from 12 to 19 years. Table 3.3 displays the age groupings at the first interview phase (T1) and numbers completing a follow-up interview (T2). There are obvious differences in the proportion of young people from each age group that completed follow-up interviews. In general, it would appear that a higher proportion of young people aged 12 to 15 years at the time of the first interview also completed follow-up interviews. Attrition from the sample appears highest amongst those aged 16 or over at the time of their first interview. This is largely due to this age group containing the majority of those young people for whom accurate contact details were not available. In total, 10 of the 14 young people for whom address and/or telephone contacts were not available at follow-up were aged 16 or over. Reasons for the lack of accurate details are likely to be due to age-related placement changes as young people move towards independent living or, indeed, cease to be looked after; 6 of the 14 young people without contact details were no longer classed as being looked after.

Table 3.3: Frequency of young people by age group at initial interview phase (T1) and numbers who also completed follow-up interviews (T2)

Age at T1	Frequency at T1	Frequency at T2*
10	7	5 (71%)
11	8	5 (63%)
12	10	9 (90%)
13	7	6 (86%)
14	13	11 (85%)
15	9	8 (89%)
16	14	7 (50%)
17	10	4 (40%)
18	2	1 (50%)
Total	80	56 (70%)

*(percentage of T1 age group represented at T2 in parentheses).

Gender

The follow-up sample showed a relatively even gender distribution, with 30 males (54%) and 26 females (46%) taking part. These figures were relatively similar to the proportion of males to females at the first stage of interviews (52% male and 48% female).

Ethnicity

The ethnic composition of the follow-up sample was practically identical to that observed for the original sample. The majority of the follow-up sample, 77%, were classified as 'White–UK' (n = 43), with 12% (n = 7) classified as 'Black–British' or 'Black–Caribbean' and 11% classed as 'White–other European' (n = 6). The proportion of young people taking part in initial and follow-up interviews did not differ across ethnic groups, either for the sample overall or within individual authorities.

Care placements

At both stages of interview, the majority of young people were in foster placements, which reflects national and local trends for placement types. Figure 3.1 shows the sample percentages for different types of care placements at original and follow-up interviews

Figure 3.1: Percentage of young people according to type of care placement at original and follow-up interviews

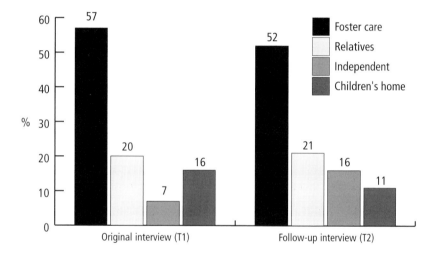

Whilst foster placements continue to be the most frequent placement type for the follow-up sample, there is some variation over time for the proportion of young people living independently and those placed in children's homes. The increase in independent living at follow-up is likely to be an age-related factor. It should also be noted that seven young people (12 per cent of the follow-up sample) were no longer looked after at second interview. Four of these young people were living with relatives and three were in independent living.

Placement moves

The majority of the follow-up sample had benefited from a stable placement: 37 young people (66 per cent) were living at the same address at the time of their follow-up interview. Of the remaining 19 young people who had experienced placement moves, 16 had experienced only one move, 2 had experienced two moves, and one had changed placement three times. The type of placement the young person was in at original interview appeared related to the stability of their placement. Figure 3.2 displays the percentage of young people in each placement type experiencing placement change or stability.

Figure 3.2. Percentage of young people experiencing placement stability or change according to placement type at original interview.

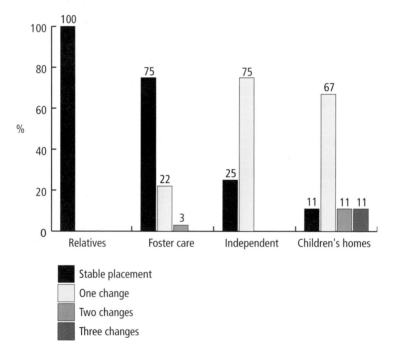

Young people placed with relatives or living in foster care at original interview were least likely to have experienced a placement move. Placement moves appear to be more frequent for young people in independent living and in residential care.

Time in most recent placement

The length of time young people had spent in their most recent placement ranged from one month to 13 years 4 months. The median average length of time in most recent placement was 2 years 2 months. It is also worth noting that, amongst the 19 young people who had experienced placement change, the average duration of the most recent placement was 11 months.

School and college attendance

Within the original sample of 80 young people, 64 (80%) were regular school or college attenders. Of these young people, 50 also took part in follow-up interviews (78% of the school-attending group). It is also worth noting that amongst the original interview sample of 80 young people, 9 young people were not attending school due to persistent truanting or undergoing an exclusion episode. Only 3 of these young people progressed into the follow-up sample. At the time of the original interview, 7 young people had already left school and 3 of these also took part in a follow-up interview. Of the follow-up sample, 49 (88%) were currently on roll at school or college. Table 3.4 displays the type of school of college attended by young people in the follow-up sample. Most young people were attending mainstream secondary schools.

Table 3.4: Frequency of young people enrolled at a school or college at follow-up interview

Type of school or college	
Secondary Mainstream	26 *
College of Further Education	14
Secondary Special School	5
Middle School	1
Pupil Referral Unit	1
Vocational training course	1
University	1
Total	49

* 16 community schools,10 foundation

The majority of young people (n = 45, 80% of sample) described themselves as attending school or college regularly. Four young people (7%) were not attending due to persistent truanting: one of these was on roll at a secondary school, with three young people enrolled at colleges of further education. Seven young people (12%) were no longer in education and described themselves as seeking employment.

Stability of school and college placements

Young people were asked to indicate whether they had experienced any school changes since their last interview. Twenty-six young people (46%) had not changed school or college since then. Where school or college change had been experienced this was mainly due to natural transitions: nine cases (16%) of primary to secondary transfer, six cases (10%) of secondary school to college transfer, seven cases (13%) of leaving school and one case (2%) of college to university transfer.

A total of seven young people (13%) had experienced a change of school or college that was not due to natural transition. Three young people had moved college through dissatisfaction with their course programme. Three young people had changed secondary school: one due to a care placement move, one due to transfer to a special school, and one due to a change in special needs secondary school that was closer to the young person's home placement. In addition, one young person had moved from a secondary school to a vocational training scheme.

Exclusions

At the time of the first interviews, a considerable proportion of young people, 34 of the sample of 80 (43%), reported that they had at some stage been excluded from school, either temporarily or permanently. These exclusions mainly occurred whilst the young person was being looked after. This highlights the importance for carers of understanding the exclusion process and being able to work both with the young person and the school in such circumstances. Seventeen of these young people (50% of those reporting experience of exclusions at original interview) also completed a follow-up interview. The remaining 17 young people reporting an exclusion episode at original interview did not take part in a follow-up interview: this represents 71% of the 24 young people who were lost to the follow-up sample.

During the follow-up interview, young people were asked if they had experienced any exclusion episodes since their last interview. Only four young people, 7% of the follow-up sample, had experienced an exclusion and all these incidents related to short-term exclusions. This is fewer than may have been expected.

Follow-up sample characteristics and sample attrition

The young people included in the follow-up sample appear to have experienced a relatively stable period, at least in terms of the maintenance of placements, between their two interviews. The level of stability in both educational and care placements amongst the follow-up sample appears to be an encouraging finding, in view of wider concerns about placement change and the disruption of educational placements (Social Exclusion Unit 2003). However, the attrition rate from the original sample of 80 young people is 30 per cent and we cannot ignore the possibility that this group of young people may have had markedly different care and schooling experiences to those progressing to the follow-up sample. Those young people for whom accurate contact details were not available at follow-up may have experienced a higher degree of placement change resulting in uncertainty regarding their whereabouts or telephone contact details. Likewise, those young people who refused to take part in a follow-up interview, or failed to attend a series of fixed interview dates, may represent a disaffected group as a result of turbulent care or educational experiences.

Indeed, it was possible to examine whether young people who did not take part in follow-up interviews differed from those who did at the time of original interviews in terms of responses to certain interview questions. Differences arose between these two groups of young people in a number of areas. Young people who did not take part in the follow-up interview had provided slightly lower ratings at original interview on standardised scales measuring self-esteem, attitudes to schooling and psychological sense of school membership. They also produced higher ratings of difficulties on the *Strengths and Difficulties Questionnaire*. Furthermore, a higher proportion of those who did not complete a follow-up interview, 29 per cent, had described their education as progressing 'badly' or 'very badly' at original interview compared to only 18 per cent of the follow-up group. Such differences lend support to the suggestion that young people who did not participate in a follow-up interview might represent a disaffected group.

Therefore, it must be acknowledged that the follow-up sample may be biased towards young people who have enjoyed relatively positive educational and care experiences. This is an important consideration to bear in mind when interpreting the findings from the young people's sample presented in subsequent chapters.

Summary

- The main aim of the evaluation was to build an informed picture of the processes involved in establishing and maintaining a whole-authority approach, and to assess the outcomes of this approach on the educational opportunities and experiences of young people in public care.

- Policy and practice developments were monitored over the course of the project through regular collection and analysis of all relevant documentation (that is, project implementation plans, NCB *Current Investment Audit* and minutes of all relevant meetings).

- Key stakeholders' perceptions of policy and practice change were collected during regular interviews with a range of senior management staff and elected members. Five rounds of interviews took place at six-monthly intervals.

- Educational outcomes were evaluated by using objective measures of attainment (that is, National Curriculum Key Stage test results, GCSE results, attendance and exclusion rates).

- A sample of young people was followed up over a two-year period in an effort to identify any changes in their educational experiences, their attitudes to schooling and education and their general well-being. Where change had arisen over time, attempts were made to investigate whether differences might be linked to project activity.

- Each young person who had accepted to take part in the evaluation project was to be seen twice at a two-year interval. Interviews included a series of open-ended questions and a series of standardised tests.

- For each young person included in the sample, the research team interviewed a key adult (parent, carer, teacher or social worker) in order to collect their perceptions of the young person's educational progress, as well as information about their own practice in supporting young people's education and whether local authority policy and practice might assist them in this role.

- Fifty-six of the 80 young people initially interviewed also took part in the follow-up interview. The 24 young people who did not take part in the second round of interview showed significantly lower levels of self-esteem and higher levels of difficulties in standardised scales than the rest of the sample. They were also more likely to have reported that their education was progressing 'badly' or 'very badly' than the rest of the sample.

- Despite strenuous efforts, the follow-up sample may be biased towards young people who have enjoyed relatively positive educational and care experiences. The views and perceptions provided by the sample of young people are, therefore, unlikely to be fully representative of the looked after population in each authority.

4. Outcomes for looked after children

A major question that the evaluation programme sought to answer was whether changes in policy and practice arising from the *Taking Care of Education* project, and the authorities' response to government initiatives, appeared to have any impact on outcomes for young people. The first stage in responding to this question involves determining whether there is any actual change over time in measurable outcomes. This was addressed in two main ways. Firstly, educational data routinely collected for government returns concerning the overall population of looked after children in each authority was assessed to provide a broad indication of any change in the proportion of looked after children reaching age-appropriate performance targets over time. Secondly, ratings provided by our sample of looked after young people regarding perceived educational attainment, general well-being and attitudes to education were also examined for changes over time.

Department of Health statistics

Since 1999, the Department of Health has routinely recorded information about the educational attainment of looked after children through standardised data collection forms. Educational data is collected through forms 'OC1' and 'OC2'. The OC1 return covers information about the educational qualifications of all care leavers aged 16 or over, irrespective of the amount of time they have spent in the looked after system. The OC2 return examines attainment at all Key Stages of the National Curriculum for children and young people who have been looked after for at least 12 months.

The evaluation team made a decision to focus on data from OC2 returns alone to assess the performance of the project authorities over time. The rationale behind this was that, since OC2 returns are restricted to young people looked after for at least one year, they are less subject to variation caused by young people first entering the looked after system shortly before examination periods. Focussing on those looked after for at least one year also increases the likelihood that policy and practice changes might have had some impact upon their educational progress (although admittedly, one year is a very short time to expect to have an impact on young people's education). OC2 returns enable us to examine educational attainment data at all Key Stages of the National Curriculum, whereas the OC1 only covers GCSE and GNVQ performance. Finally, OC2 returns enable an estimate of the performance ratio of looked after children compared to all school-age children to be examined at each curriculum Key Stage. Examining the percentage rates for looked after children without reference to the educational context for all children in each authority may not provide the most accurate indication of progress, as it may be that attainment rates for all children in each authority have risen or fallen. Therefore, it is of interest to compare percentage attainment rates for looked after children with those for all children in each authority and nationally.

The data presented in the following sections outlines the performance ratio of looked after children to all children for the three project authorities as well as national rates for all English local authorities. Performance ratios can range from zero to one and a performance ratio of, for example, 0.6 would indicate that where 100 per cent of all school-age children reach a given attainment target, 60 per cent of looked after children do so.

Educational attainment at Key Stage 1

Key Stage 1 tests of National Curriculum attainment are applied in Year 2 of schooling when children are aged 6–7 years old. The standard attainment targets at this stage are that children achieve Level 2 or above for tasks of Reading, Writing, Spelling and Maths. Figures 4.1a to 4.1d illustrate the percentage ratio of looked after children compared to all children reaching age-appropriate targets for each type of test. Table 4.1 provides information about the sample of young people from which these percentage ratios are drawn, including numbers with special educational needs, attendance and exclusion rates, and placement moves.

Figure 4.1a: Percentage ratio of looked after children to all children achieving level 2 or above on Key Stage 1 Reading task in 1999/2000, 2000/2001 and 2001/2002

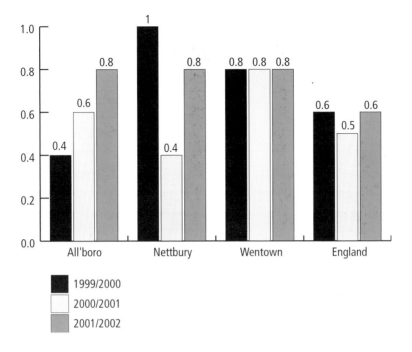

Figure 4.1b: Percentage ratio of looked after children to all children achieving level 2 or above on Key Stage 1 Writing task in 1999/2000, 2000/2001 and 2001/2002

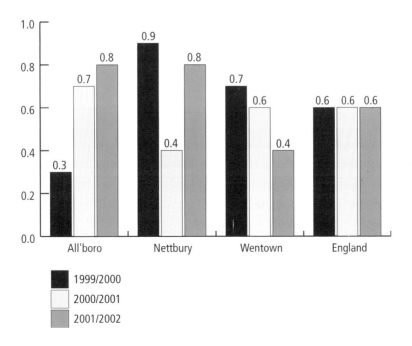

Figure 4.1c: Percentage ratio of looked after children to all children achieving level 2 or above on Key Stage 1 Spelling task in 1999/2000, 2000/2001 and 2001/2002

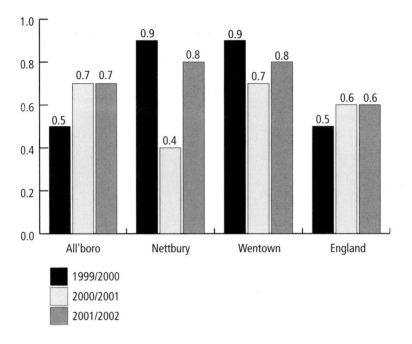

Figure 4.1d: Percentage ratio of looked after children to all children achieving level 2 or above on Key Stage 1 Maths task in 1999/2000, 2000/2001 and 2001/2002

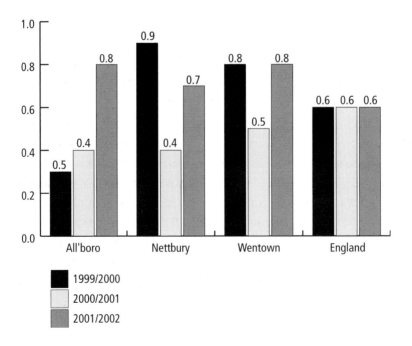

Table 4.1: Frequency of looked after children upon which Key Stage 1 task percentages are based and rates of special educational needs (SEN), attendance, exclusions and placement moves in 1999/2000, 2000/2001 and 2001/2002

Base	1999/2000	2000/2001	2001/2002
Allborough	11	15	12
SEN statements	4 (36%)	3 (20%)	2 (17%)
Over 25 days absence	0	0	1 (8%)
Permanent exclusion	1 (9%)	0	0
Placement move	1 (9%)	2 (13%)	3 (25%)
Nettbury	6	3	3
SEN statements	2 (33%)	1 (33%)	1 (33%)
Over 25 days absence	1 (17%)	0	0
Permanent exclusion	0	0	0
Placement move	1 (17%)	0	0
Wentown	10	6	5
SEN statements*			
Over 25 days absence*			
Permanent exclusion*			
Placement move*			

* Missing data

The figures for Key Stage 1 results suggest that the most consistent improvements in the performance of looked after children in relation to all children occurred in Allborough. On all Key Stage 1 tasks the performance ratio has increased over the past three years and the most recent levels are above the national level. In Nettbury and Wentown, a less consistent pattern emerges. Although on most tasks the most recent performance ratio is above national levels, there has often been a decrease in ratios for the academic year 2000/2001, followed by an increase to the same level or slightly below ratios reported for the academic year 1999/2000. In interpreting these results it is useful to review Table 4.1, which provides information about the cohorts of young people sitting tasks each year. As we can see the numbers are small, particularly in Nettbury and Wentown, and basing percentages on numbers less than 10 may explain why there is greater variation in ratings for these two authorities. In addition, the details from Allborough and Nettbury indicate that cohorts vary from year to year in terms of SEN rates, absence and exclusion rates, and experience of placement moves, and that these factors may have influenced test performance.

Educational attainment at Key Stage 2

Key Stage 2 tests are taken in Year 6 of schooling when children are aged 10–11 years old. The standard attainments targets at this stage are that children achieve Level 4 or above for tasks assessing English, Maths and Science ability. Figures 4.2a to 4.2c illustrate the percentage of children reaching age-appropriate targets for each type of tests. Details about the sample upon which percentages are based are shown in Table 4.2.

Figure 4.2a: Percentage ratio of looked after children to all children achieving level 4 or above on Key Stage 2 English task in 1999/2000, 2000/2001 and 2001/2002

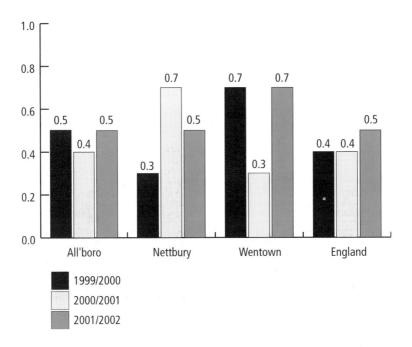

Figure 4.2b: Percentage ratio of looked after children to all children achieving level 4 or above on Key Stage 2 Maths task in 1999/2000, 2000/2001 and 2001/2002

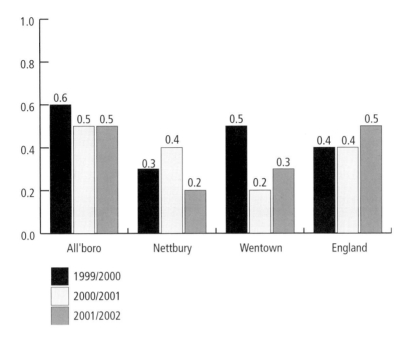

Figure 4.2c: Percentage ratio of looked after children to all children achieving level 4 or above on Key Stage 2 Science task in 1999/2000, 2000/2001 and 2001/2002

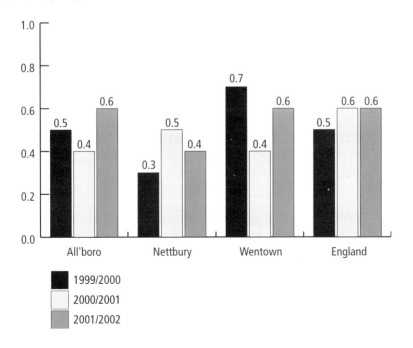

Table 4.2: Frequency of looked after children upon which Key Stage 2 task percentages are based and rates of special educational needs (SEN), attendance, exclusions and placement moves in 1999/2000, 2000/2001 and 2001/2002

Base	1999/2000	2000/2001	2001/2002
Allborough	13	25	25
SEN statements	4 (31%)	12 (48%)	7 (28%)
Over 25 days absence	0	3 (12%)	2 (8%)
Permanent exclusion	0	0	1 (4%)
Placement move	2 (15%)	2 (8%)	5 (20%)
Nettbury	4	7	3
SEN statements	3 (75%)	3 (43%)	1 (33%)
Over 25 days absence	1 (25%)	1 (14%)	0
Permanent exclusion	0	0	0
Placement move	1 (25%)	1 (14%)	0
Wentown	16	9	10
SEN statements*			
Over 25 days absence*			
Permanent exclusion*			
Placement move*			

* Missing data

There are no clear patterns of improvement or deterioration for each authority in terms of Key Stage 2 test results. In the case of Allborough there is some evidence of improvement in Science tasks, with more negative fluctuations in English and Maths tasks, but performance ratios tend to remain around national average levels. Such variation might be attributable to changes in rates of young people with SEN and those missing at least 25 days schooling, as well as numbers experiencing placement moves. In Nettbury, improvements are evident in the performance ratios for all tasks in 2000–2001, but this was followed by a deterioration in 2001–2002. In that year, the performance ratios are in line with national averages for England but remain well below national levels in Maths and Science. However, Table 4.2 shows that the base upon which the performance ratios are formed in Nettbury is very small and this may explain much of the variation in figures. In Wentown, there appears to have been a dip in performance ratios on all tasks in 2000/2001 followed by a rise in 2001/2002 to a level above or consistent with national figures on English and Science tasks but below national levels for Maths. It is difficult to hypothesise why this may have occurred without additional data regarding the Wentown cohorts being available.

Educational attainment at Key Stage 3

Key Stage 3 tests are taken in Year 9 of schooling when children are aged 13–14 years old. The standard attainments targets at this stage are that children achieve Level 5 or above for tasks assessing English, Maths and Science ability. Figures 4.3a to 4.3c illustrate the percentage of children reaching age-appropriate targets for each type of tests. The frequencies upon which percentages are based are shown in Table 4.3, along with the incidence of special educational needs, exclusion and attendance rates, and placement moves.

Figure 4.3a: Percentage ratio of looked after children to all children achieving level 5 or above on Key Stage 3 English task in 1999/2000, 2000/2001 and 2001/2002

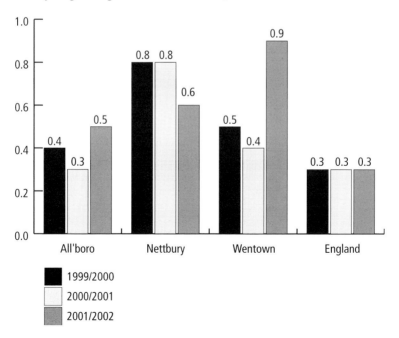

Figure 4.3b: Percentage ratio of looked after children to all children achieving level 5 or above on Key Stage 3 Maths task in 1999/2000, 2000/2001 and 2001/2002

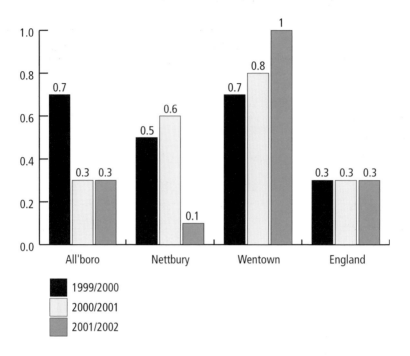

Figure 4.3c: Percentage ratio of looked after children to all children achieving level 5 or above on Key Stage 3 Science task in 1999/2000, 2000/2001 and 2001/2002

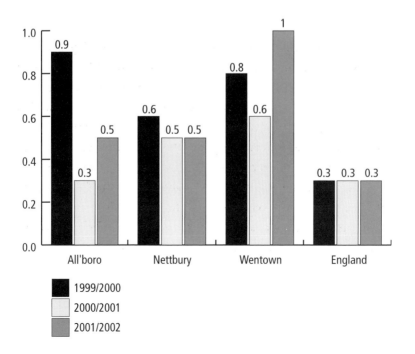

Table 4.3: Frequency of looked after children upon which Key Stage 3 task percentages are based and rates of special educational needs (SEN), attendance, exclusions and placement moves in 1999/2000, 2000/2001 and 2001/2002

Base	1999/2000	2000/2001	2001/2002
Allborough	17	27	30
SEN statements	5 (29%)	8 (30%)	12 (40%)
Over 25 days absence	4 (24%)	7 (26%)	5 (30%)
Permanent exclusion	0	1 (4%)	2 (6%)
Placement move	0	8 (30%)	4 (13%)
Nettbury	6	10	11
SEN statements	1 (16%)	4 (40%)	4 (36%)
Over 25 days absence	0	1 (10%)	2 (18%)
Permanent exclusion	0	1 (10%)	0
Placement move	0	2 (20%)	1 (6%)
Wentown	13	18	10
SEN statements*			
Over 25 days absence*			
Permanent exclusion*			
Placement move*			

* Missing data

The most marked improvement in performance ration for Key Stage 3 tests arises in Wentown where the proportion of looked after children reaching age-related targets is equal (1.0) to that of all children on Maths and Science tests and almost equal (0.9) for English tests. In Allborough and Nettbury there are fewer signs of improvement, with ratios remaining relatively constant for some tasks or decreasing over the three-year period for others. This may be related to differences in annual cohorts in terms of SEN rates, exclusions, placement moves and so on, as shown in Table 4.3. It is, however, of interest to note that with only one exception, all performance ratios collected in the three project authorities are equal or superior to national averages over the three years for which such data is available.

Educational attainment at Key Stage 4

Key Stage 4 tests are taken in Year 11 of school and include GCSE and GNVQ examinations. At this level, government indicators record the numbers of looked after young people achieving: 1 GCSE Grade A–G, 5 GCSEs Grade A–G, and 5 GCSEs Grade A–C. Figures 4.4a to 4.4c illustrate the percentage of children whose attainment falls within these indicator bandings. Table 4.4 provides additional information about the samples upon which percentages are based.

Figure 4.4a: Percentage ratio of looked after children to all children achieving at least 1 GCSE grade A to G in 1999/2000, 2000/2001 and 2001/2002

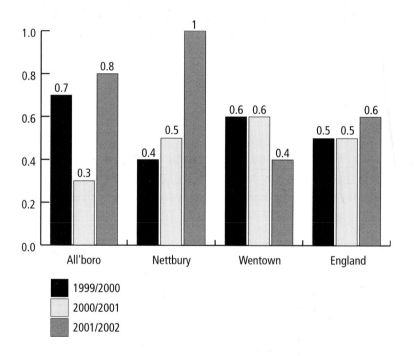

Figure 4.4b: Percentage ratio of looked after children to all children achieving 5 or more GCSEs grade A to G in 1999/2000, 2000/2001 and 2001/2002

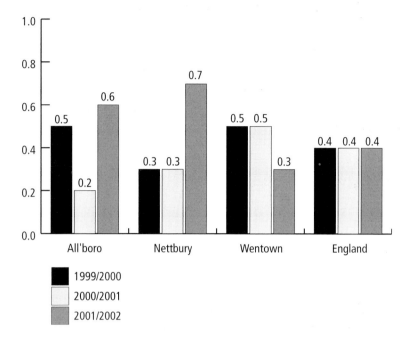

Figure 4.4c: Percentage ratio of looked after children to all children achieving 5 or more GCSEs grade A to C in 1999/2000, 2000/2001 and 2001/2002

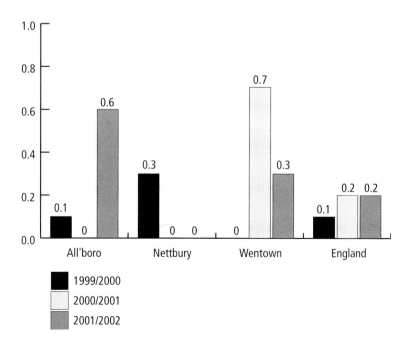

Table 4.4: Frequency of looked after children upon which Key Stage 4 task percentages are based and rates of special educational needs (SEN), attendance, exclusions, placement moves and percentage entered for exams in 1999/2000, 2000/2001 and 2001/2002.

Base:	1999/2000	2000/2001	2001/2002
Allborough	24	30	20
SEN statements	9 (38%)	15 (30%)	8 (40%)
Over 25 days absence	0	12 (40%)	3 (15%)
Permanent exclusion	3 (24%)	3 (10%)	1 (5%)
Placement move	1 (24%)	1 (3%)	3 (15%)
Percentage eligible entered exams	74%	41%	85%
Nettbury	13	10	15
SEN statements	3 (23%)	3 (30%)	3 (20%)
Over 25 days absence	3 (23%)	4 (40%)	0
Permanent exclusion	2 (15%)	0	0
Placement move	7 (54%)	4 (40%)	1 (6%)
Percentage eligible entered exams	46%	60%	93%
Wentown	19	9	20
SEN statements*			
Over 25 days absence*			
Permanent exclusion*			
Placement move*			
Percentage eligible entered exams	63%	67%	40%

*   Missing data

The most consistent improvement in performance ratios relating to GCSE attainment at grades A to G are to be found in Nettbury. There is a gradual increase over the three years in looked after children obtaining 1 or 5 or more GCSEs at A to G; and the numbers getting 1 exam pass in 2001/2002 are identical to percentage rates for all children. The improvement may be related both to the reduction in placement moves in more recent cohorts and the observation that more young people are being entered for examinations, as shown in Table 4.4. These improvements are, however, inconsistent with the fact that in 2000/2001 and 2001/2002, no young people obtained 5 or more GCSEs at grades A to C. In Allborough there was a dip in performance in 2000/2001 which could also be related to the percentage of young people entered for exams, with a higher proportion being entered in 1999/2000 and 2000/2001. In Wentown, performance ratios for GCSE grades A to G have fallen in 2001/2002 to below national levels. This may also be connected with a reduction in the proportion of young people entered for exams. However, the performance ratio in Wentown regarding young people obtaining 5 GCSEs grades A to C has increased over the past three years to an extent that places it above national levels.

Attendance and exclusion rates and placement moves

In addition to relating information regarding attendance, exclusion, and placement moves for the cohorts of young people included in OC2 returns at each Key Stage, it is also possible to examine overall rates for these variables as they apply to the total looked after population in each authority. Figures 4.5a to 4.5c provide information on overall rates for these variables.

Figure 4.5a: Percentage of looked after children missing 25 or more days schooling in 1999/2000, 2000/2001 and 2001/2002

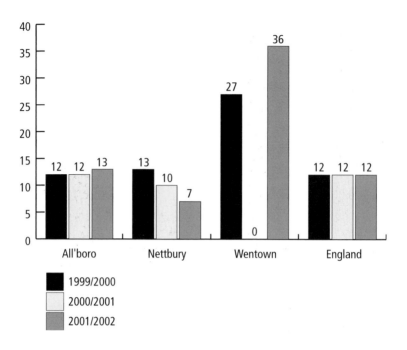

The percentage of looked after children missing 25 or more days schooling in Allborough has remained relatively constant over the three-year period and reflects national figures. In Nettbury, rates have followed a trend towards decreased absence and are currently below the national average. In Wentown, absence rates are well above the national average in both 1999/2000 and 2001/2002. (The missing rate for 2000/2001 is because the authority did not submit a return for this variable, rather than the rate being zero.)

Figure 4.5b: Percentage of looked after children experiencing a permanent exclusion in 1999/2000, 2000/2001 and 2001/2002

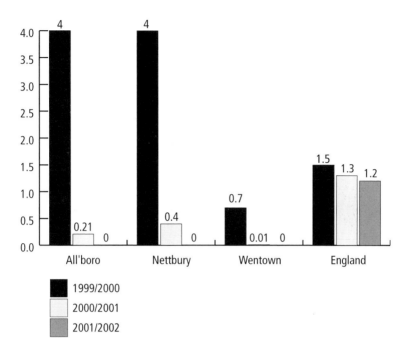

Reported levels of permanent exclusions for looked after children have fallen to below the national average for exclusions in all three authorities in 2001/2002. In Allborough and Nettbury this represents a substantial reduction, whereas in Wentown exclusion rates were less than the national average at the outset of the project.

Figure 4.5c Percentage of children experiencing three or more placement moves per year in 1999/2000, 2000/2001 and 2001/2002

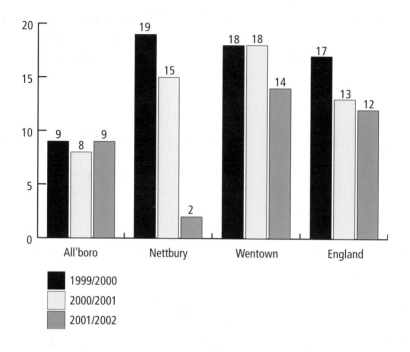

The change in prevalence of young people experiencing three or more placement moves is most pronounced in Nettbury, where rates for 2001/2002 have fallen well below the national average. The percentage of young people with three or more placements in Allborough has remained at a fairly consistent level below the national average for the three-year period. In Wentown, rates are above the national average, although they had begun to fall in 2001/2002.

It is difficult to draw any firm conclusions regarding outcomes for looked after children based upon OC2 return indicators. With the exception of figures for Allborough and figures for all three authorities at Key Stage 4, the numbers involved tend to be very small and, as such, poor or enhanced performance by just one or two individuals can result in large variations in percentage ratios. In addition, even where numbers are adequate to justify the use of percentage ratings, the cohorts sitting each Key Stage task do appear to differ in terms of experience of exclusion, placement change, absenteeism and rate of special educational needs. All of these factors may have some impact upon attainment and, as such, the validity of comparing disparate cohorts over time may be questionable. It may be that alternative outcome measures are required to determine whether project activities are making some difference to young people. The following sections discuss findings relative to outcome measures applied to the young people's sample for the project evaluation in each local authority.

Outcomes for the young people's sample

The 56 young people who participated in both original and follow-up interviews each completed a range of standardised scales at both stages of interview. This enabled us to compare scores yielded over time and so determine if any changes had occurred in reported psychological well-being, self esteem, attitudes to education and school, expectations about the future, and perceptions of educational progress.

Total scores were calculated for each of the scales used and were analysed for differences over time in the magnitude of scores. In addition, total scores for *Strengths and Difficulties Questionnaire* difficulty ratings were used to categorise young people's responses according to the expected scoring ranges associated with the measure, and an analysis of movement between scoring categories was undertaken.

The following sections report findings associated with the five standardised measures used: the *Strengths and Difficulties Questionnaire* (SDQ); the *Adolescent Self-esteem Scale* (ASES); the *Attitudes to Schooling Measure* (ASM); the *Psychological Sense of School Membership Scale* (PSSM); and the *Children's Future Expectations Scale* (CFES). In each section, ratings are shown for the overall sample, as well as being broken down by project authority. Presenting the ratings for individual authorities is intended to give a general impression of how young people in each authority respond to the measures over time. However, the numbers involved in the individual authority samples are very small and this increases the likelihood that chance fluctuations in ratings have arisen. Therefore, it must be stressed that examining ratings for the overall sample is a more reliable estimate of tracking change.

Strengths and Difficulties Questionnaire

The SDQ comprises 25 questions, 20 of which can be summed to produce a total difficulties score and 5 of which are summed to produce a pro-social behaviour score. Total difficulties scores and pro-social behaviour scores were calculated for questionnaires completed at both initial and follow-up interview stages.

SDQ difficulties scores

The SDQ difficulties score combines 20 items designed to assess the existence of problems in emotional symptoms, peer relationships, hyperactivity and behavioural conduct. Mean average SDQ difficulties ratings at initial and follow-up interviews are displayed in Table 4.5. The Table shows means for the sample overall, as well as for the sample divided into individual authorities where the young people were looked after. Mean ratings at follow-up were lower than at first interviews in all three authorities, and for the sample overall. The lower ratings indicate that fewer difficulties were reported at the follow-up stage.

Table 4.5: Mean SDQ difficulties ratings (and standard deviations, sd) at original (T1) and follow-up (T2) interviews in each local authority and overall

	Mean at T1	Mean at T2
Allborough (n = 17)	11.6 (sd = 6.0)	10.4 (sd = 4.6)
Nettbury (n = 20)	11.8 (sd = 5.5)	10.1 (sd = 5.6)
Wentown (n = 19)	14.1 (sd = 3.9)	13.0 (sd = 4.7)
Overall sample (n = 56)	**12.5** (sd = 5.2)	**11.1** (sd = 5.1)

A repeated measures t-test analysis found that the differences in mean ratings over time for the entire sample were significant ($t = -2.01$, $df = 55$, $p < 0.05$) indicating that significantly fewer difficulties were reported at follow-up interview. However, analyses of the individual authority ratings showed that although SDQ difficulties scores were lower at follow-up in all three authorities, the mean differences were not large enough to be of statistical significance. This may be due to the relatively small sample size in each authority.

As well as analysing overall scores for the SDQ, total scores were used to assign young people to categories associated with SDQ score ranges. The categories are normal, borderline and abnormal. In general populations it is expected that 80 per cent of young people's responses will fall within the normal scoring range, with 10 per cent as borderline and 10 per cent as abnormal. The observed percentages of young people in the overall sample classified as having normal, borderline or abnormal responses according to original and follow-up scales is shown in Figure 4.6 below.

Figure 4.6: Original, follow-up and expected percentages of young people classified according to SDQ scoring categories

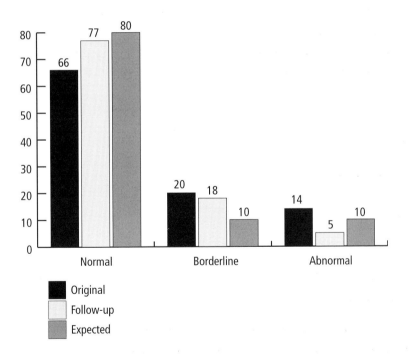

The figure indicates that over time, the proportion of young people with SDQ difficulties scores falling within the 'abnormal' range has decreased to less than an expected level. Whilst the proportion of young people classed as 'borderline' remains higher than expected, this has also decreased at follow-up. The percentage of young people with SDQ difficulties scores within the 'normal' range has increased to a level that is close to expected.

The percentage ratings do not specify the underlying changes responsible for the differences in categorisation over time. Table 4.6 clarifies the extent of movement between categories associated with young people's SDQ difficulties ratings over time.

Table 4.6: Movement between SDQ scoring categories over time

T1 Category	Same	Classification at T2 Positive change	Negative change	T2 Category
Normal (n = 37, 66%)	33	n/a	4 to borderline	Normal (n = 43, 77%)
Borderline (n = 11, 20%)	3	6 to normal	2 to abnormal	Borderline (n = 10, 18%)
Abnormal (n = 8, 14%)	1	4 to normal 3 to borderline	n/a	Abnormal (n = 3, 5%)

It is apparent from Table 4.6 that the majority of changes were positive ones, with 10 young people moving to within the 'normal' category from 'abnormal' or 'borderline'. Whilst there were no cases of young people moving from 'normal' to 'abnormal' categories, 4 young people had shifted in classification from a 'normal' range of scores to 'borderline', whilst 2 had changed from 'borderline' to 'abnormal'.

Overall, the findings relating to SDQ difficulties ratings appear to indicate improvements in psychological well-being for the majority of young people in the follow-up sample. The reduction in mean ratings at follow-up implies that young people are experiencing fewer difficulties stemming from emotional symptoms, peer relationships, hyperactivity and behavioural conduct. This is reflected in general increases in the proportion of young people whose SDQ difficulty ratings are classified as 'normal', and a reduction in the proportion classified as 'abnormal', both for the sample overall and for young people within individual authorities.

Unfortunately, it is difficult to determine whether these findings are connected to the presence of the *Taking Care of Education* project in the three authorities. The lower level of reported difficulties could simply be due to age-related maturational effects. The absence of a control group of looked after children from other authorities makes it difficult to rule out the possibility that this degree of difference could be expected to occur over time. Nor does previous research indicate what expected fluctuations in SDQ difficulties scores, or classification categories, over time might be for populations of looked after children. There is, however, some indication from research with other populations that SDQ ratings may be relatively stable over time. Goodman, Ford and Metzler (2003) conducted an 18-month follow-up study on 3, 965 children and adolescents involved with a national survey on the mental health of 5–15 year olds in Britain. They found little variation over time in SDQ difficulties scores and concluded that symptoms are unlikely to be transient. (Although it must be acknowledged that this study involved parental completion of informant versions of the SDQ rather than obtaining direct ratings from children and young people.)

A further consideration that should be taken into account when interpreting the SDQ results is that the instrument may have lost relevance to some of the young people in the sample. The SDQ is designed for use with young people up to the age of 16 years and a significant proportion (30 per cent) of young people in the follow up sample were over 16 by the time of their second interview. If questions were deemed inappropriate by these young people they may have been more inclined to respond in the negative (that is, by indicating that a difficulty was not present), hence deflating their SDQ scores at the time of follow-up.

SDQ Pro-social behaviour scores

Mean SDQ Pro-social behaviour ratings at initial and follow-up interviews are displayed in Table 4.7, which illustrates that mean ratings were slightly lower at follow-up in all three authorities, as well as for the sample overall. The lower ratings indicate less pro-social behaviour was reported at the follow-up stage. However, the differences in mean ratings over time were not substantial enough to be statistically significant, and therefore could have occurred by chance.

Table 4.7: Mean SDQ Pro-social behaviour ratings (and standard deviations, sd) at original (T1) and follow-up (T2) interviews in each local authority and overall

	Mean at T1	Mean at T2
Allborough (n = 17)	8.7 (sd = 1.7)	8.2 (sd = 1.8)
Nettbury (n = 20)	8.6 (sd = 1.8)	8.2 (sd = 1.6)
Wentown (n = 19)	7.4 (sd = 2.2)	7.2 (sd = 2.3)
Overall sample (n = 56)	13.7 (sd = 3.9)	14.9 (sd = 3.9)

There are no normative bandings associated with pro-social behaviour ratings for the SDQ, hence it is not possible to investigate changes in categorisation for pro-social behaviour scores.

Adolescent Self-esteem Scale (ASES)

The Rosenberg's Adolescent Self-esteem scale includes 10 items designed to produce a composite measure of self-esteem ranging from 0 to 20 – each item was scored from 0 to 2 dependent on response options of 'untrue' 'somewhat true' or 'certainly true'. Table 4.8 displays mean ASES ratings at each phase of interviews.

Table 4.8: Mean ASES ratings (and standard deviations, sd) at original (T1) and follow-up (T2) interviews in each local authority and overall

	Mean at T1	Mean at T2
Allborough (n = 17)	14.5 (sd = 3.4)	15.3 (sd = 4.0)
Nettbury (n = 20)	14.4 (sd = 4.3)	16.0 (sd = 3.2)
Wentown (n = 19)	12.3 (sd = 3.4)	13.3 (sd = 4.1)
Overall sample (n = 56)	13.7 (sd = 3.9)	14.9 (sd = 3.9)

In all three authorities, and for the sample overall, self-esteem ratings are higher at follow-up. The difference between means for the overall sample was substantial enough to attain statistical significance ($t = -2.1$, $df = 55$, $p < 0.05$) indicating that self-esteem ratings at follow-up interview were significantly higher for the sample as a whole. This finding appears to run counter to expected age-related changes. Previous research either indicates that self-esteem is likely to drop during adolescence, or remain relatively stable. The current finding is therefore of interest given that a number of project activities in the three local authorities were directed towards improving the resilience and self-esteem of looked after children and young people. Analyses within individual authorities did not reveal any statistically significant differences, which again is likely to be due to the relatively small sample sizes.

Attitudes to Schooling Measure (ASM)

The ASM contains 12 questions designed to assess young people's beliefs about the value of education and schooling. All items are scored on a five-point scale ranging from '1 = Strongly disagree' to '5 = Strongly agree', which allows for a minimum total score of 12 points and a maximum of 60. Table 4.9 displays the mean ASM scores for the responses of young people at both original and follow-up interviews.

Table 4.9: Mean ASM ratings (and standard deviations, sd) at original (T1) and follow-up (T2) interviews in each local authority and overall

	Mean at T1	Mean at T2
Allborough (n = 17)	43.7 (sd = 6.5)	45.5 (sd = 4.4)
Nettbury (n = 20)	42.9 (sd = 6.9)	45.2 (sd = 6.0)
Wentown (n = 19)	42.8 (sd = 5.4)	43.0 (sd = 6.2)
Overall sample (n = 56)	43.1 (sd = 6.2)	44.5 (sd = 5.7)

In all three authorities, and hence for the overall sample, responses at follow-up interview suggest that young people were placing greater value upon education, although this pattern is less pronounced for the Wentown sample. Although there is no previous research examining changes over time in the *Attitudes to Schooling* measure, there is some indication that young people's attitudes towards school and the value they place on education improve during secondary school. Hence, the current findings may reflect expected changes as young people in the sample grow older. Despite the apparent trend towards higher ASM ratings at follow-up interview, the differences between means were not large enough to reach statistical significance.

Psychological Sense of School Membership Scale (PSSM)

The PSSM comprises 17 items designed to assess a young person's sense of acceptance by, and belonging to, a school or college. Responses are scored on a continuum of 1 to 5 ranging from '1 = Strongly disagree' to '5 = Strongly agree', affording a minimum total score of 17 and a maximum of 85. Table 4.10 reveals mean PSSM ratings associated with original and follow-up interview responses.

Table 4.10: Mean PSSM ratings (and standard deviations, sd) at original (T1) and follow-up (T2) interviews in each local authority and overall

	Mean at T1	Mean at T2
Allborough (n = 17)	67.6 (sd = 11.1)	66.9 (sd = 9.5)
Nettbury (n = 20)	65.9 (sd = 7.3)	66.4 (sd = 7.4)
Wentown (n = 19)	61.6 (sd = 13.5)	61.3 (sd = 15.9)
Overall sample (n = 56)	64.9 (sd = 11.0)	64.8 (sd = 11.6)

In Nettbury, young people provided slightly more positive ratings for their sense of school membership at follow-up. None of the differences between mean ratings over time were substantial enough to be of statistical significance. Given that 54 per cent of the sample had changed school or college between interviews, examining changes in PSSM ratings may be inappropriate as many young people are referring to a different institution at follow-up. However, the fact that ratings do not differ significantly over time is perhaps useful in indicating that young people at least do not appear to suffer from a loss of their sense of belonging due to school or college transition.

Children's Future Expectations Scale (CFES)

The CFES is a six item scale that aims to assess how positive young people feel about their likely future educational progress and general well being. Items are scored on a continuum of 1 to 5 ranging from '1 = Strongly disagree' to '5 = Strongly agree', yielding a minimum total score of 6 and a maximum of 30. Table 4.11 shows the mean CFES ratings associated with original and follow-up interview responses.

Table 4.11: Mean CFES ratings (and standard deviations, sd) at original (T1) and follow-up (T2) interviews in each local authority and overall

	Mean at T1	Mean at T2
Allborough (n = 17)	25.5 (sd = 4.1)	26.1 (sd = 3.1)
Nettbury (n = 20)	25.3 (sd = 2.7)	24.5 (sd = 3.9)
Wentown (n = 19)	24.7 (sd = 3.3)	24.7 (sd = 4.5)
Overall sample (n = 56)	25.2 (sd = 3.3)	25.0 (sd = 3.8)

For the Nettbury sample there appears to be a slight reduction in future expectation ratings at follow-up. In Allborough, young people provided more positive ratings at follow-up, whilst ratings in Wentown remained stable. There is no previous research examining the likely stability of future expectation ratings over time, although reductions in adolescents' positive expectations for the future have been found to be associated with higher levels of problem behaviours and negative peer influences and lower levels of family support (Dubow 2001). Therefore, these finding may imply that young people in Nettbury are more likely, and young people in Allborough less likely, to have experienced difficulties between interviews. That said, the mean differences are somewhat small and none of the differences between mean ratings over time were substantial enough to reach statistical significance.

Conclusions relating to the standardised scales

It is encouraging to discover that young people report significantly fewer difficulties in terms of SDQ ratings and significantly higher ratings of self-esteem at follow-up. One explanation for such differences in ratings is that opportunities to benefit from more positive educational and care experiences over the course of the *Taking Care of Education* project have contributed to improvements in self-esteem and psychological well-being. However, this is only one possible explanation for the findings and the absence of an adequate control group means that any interpretation of these results must be treated with caution. Whilst there is some indication from previous research that our findings are not simply due to age-related maturational effects, such evidence is not drawn from looked after populations and the possibility remains that our observed changes are simple chance effects.

The remaining standardised measures did not involve any significant differences between ratings generated at each interview. In terms of *Psychological Sense of School Membership,* ratings were relatively similar over time and this may indicate successful transition between schools and colleges; young people certainly do not appear to have experienced a loss of belonging due to changing schools in terms of this scale. There is some indication of a trend towards improved attitudes to education and schooling in general, as measured by the *Attitudes to Schooling Measure (ASM),* although this may be an age-related effect. Finally, the slight fall in ratings for the *Children's Future Expectations Scale (CFES)* in Nettbury could indicate that some young people have experienced difficulties between interviews. Yet it must be noted that none of the differences between means on the ASM or CFES were substantial enough to reach statistical significance, hence any interpretation of the findings is necessarily speculative.

Overall, the findings revealed by the comparative analysis of standardised measures applied at original and follow-up interview are suggestive yet inconclusive. We cannot be certain that improvements observed in ratings of self-esteem, psychological well-being, and, to a lesser degree, attitudes to schooling, indicate that young people have developed a more positive outlook. It may be that the interpretation of the findings will be assisted by an analysis of qualitative accounts of young people's perceptions of their care and educational experience between interviews, which follows.

Estimates of current educational progress

The young person's interview began with a closed-question regarding how the young person felt their education was currently progressing. Response options were set at 'well, very well, average, badly, very badly'. An identical question was put to young people at their first interview, hence it was possible to compare responses over time. A total of 54 young people responded to the question on educational progress at follow-up interview; two young people from the Allborough sample believed this question was no longer relevant to them as they had left the education system. Figure 4.7 displays the results.

Figure 4.7: Percentage of overall sample describing their education as progressing Very Well, Well, Average, Badly, or Very Badly at initial (T1) and follow-up (T2) interviews

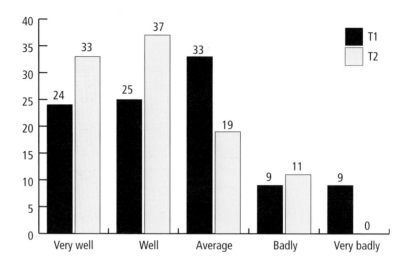

Cleary, the majority of young people felt they were performing at average or above average level at both stages of interviews. Whilst such ratings are obviously subjective, it was possible to compare some young people's perceptions of progress with educational data drawn from their most recent Key Stage test results. Data concerning Key Stage test results was available for 41 young people in the follow-up sample. Such data revealed that young people's perceptions were generally consistent with test results. The majority of young people who achieved the expected level of performance at Key Stage 2 or 3, or passed GCSE examinations, described their education as progressing 'well' or 'very well'. Those who had not achieved age-expected standards, nor passed a GCSE, tended to state that their education was going 'badly'.

Figure 4.7 also indicates some degree of improvement in perceptions of progress at follow-up interview with the proportion of young people providing above average ratings increasing: 70% said 'well' or 'very well' at follow-up, as opposed to 49% at original interview. None of the young people who believed that their education was going 'very badly' at original interview provided the same estimate at follow-up, although there is a slight increase in the proportion who feel it is going 'badly'.

It is also possible to treat estimates of educational progress as score data and seek to determine whether significant changes in global ratings have arisen over time. Table 4.12 displays mean educational progress estimates over time in each local authority and for the sample overall.

Table 4.12: Mean educational progress estimates (and standard deviations, sd) at original (T1) and follow-up (T2) interviews in each local authority and overall

	Mean at T1	Mean at T2
Allborough (n = 15)	3.6 (sd = 1.1)	4.5 (sd = 0.7)
Nettbury (n = 20)	3.0 (sd = 1.3)	3.8 (sd = 1.1)
Wentown (n = 19)	3.7 (sd = 1.1)	3.6 (sd = 0.9)
Overall sample (n = 56)	3.4 (sd = 1.2)	4.0 (sd = 1.0)

It is apparent that global ratings in Allborough and Nettbury and for the overall sample have improved at follow-up, whilst in Wentown ratings have fallen slightly. A series of repeated sample t-tests indicated that the magnitude of mean differences was significant for the overall sample ($t = -2.7$, df = 53, $p < 0.01$), as well as for the Allborough ($t = -2.2$, df = 14, $p < 0.05$) and Nettbury ($t = -3.4$, df = 19, $p < 0.01$) samples. This indicates that young people in Allborough and Nettbury, and for the sample overall, provided significantly higher estimates of educational progress at follow-up interview. There were no significant differences observed for the Wentown sample. However, it must be noted that, as with the previous results for standardised measures, the numbers involved when the sample is divided by local authority are very small and hence one might expect chance fluctuations in ratings to arise. Therefore, examining ratings for the overall sample is a more reliable estimate of tracking change.

The overall analysis of ratings, whether in terms of proportions in each category or scores, does not enable us to specify the exact type of changes in perception experienced by individual young people. By analysing individual cases it was possible to determine the frequency of shifts from one category to another. It emerged that 23 young people (43 per cent) had not changed their estimate of progress between original and follow-up interviews. The frequency of young people reporting stable ratings across authorities is shown in Table 4.13. The Table also displays the percentage of original ratings in each category that remained the same in the overall sample and individual authorities. Although again, reservations about the use of percentages with such small numbers must be noted.

Table 4.13: Frequency of young people reporting same progress ratings at original and follow-up interviews (percentage of original ratings of each kind for authority or overall sample in parentheses)

Rating	Allborough	Nettbury	Wentown	Overall
Very well	6 (75%)	3 (60%)	1 (20%)	10 (55%)
Well	0	2 (66%)	6 (100%)	8 (80%)
Average	2 (33%)	1 (14%)	0	3 (16%)
Badly	0	1 (33%)	1 (100%)	2 (4%)
Very badly	0	0	0	0
Total	8 (47%)	7 (35%)	8 (42%)	23 (43%)

Young people in Allborough appear to provide slightly more consistent ratings over time (47 per cent of rating remained the same), with young people in Nettbury showing the lowest levels of consistency over time (35 per cent). Overall, most of the young people reporting the same ratings of progress over time fall within the 'very well' and 'well' categories, and this is also apparent within individual authorities.

Fourteen of the young people continuing to describe their education as progressing 'well' or 'very well' provided explanations as to why their progress might have been maintained. The most frequent responses given for maintaining good educational progress concerned the personal qualities of the young person, or continuous support within care placements.

Six young people mentioned their own motivation and appreciation of the importance of education as an important factor in ensuring that they continued to do well. Their comments suggested that whilst they may have experienced difficulties associated with being looked after, their commitment to education had lessened the impact this may have had upon their progress.

> I've always liked school and I've always tried hard. I never really fell behind when I was taken into care, although I would say that it was a bit hard at first because I moved around a bit when I was first taken into care. The first foster placement I was in I didn't have a school place there – I was out for about a month – so I slipped back a bit, but then I made sure I caught up when I got back into school.
> *(15 year old, placed with relatives)*

A further five young people cited their care placements as contributory factors in enabling them to continue to do well. The provision of encouragement and support from carers were seen as key factors. Four of these young people had remained in the same foster placement over time, one had changed foster placement but had continued to receive appropriate support and encouragement from carers.

Finally, three young people believed that encouragement within school contributed towards their progress. All of these young people commented on commendation or rewards systems, which were not only appreciated for acknowledging young people's efforts but were also perceived as a motivational factor that could promote further progress.

Young people who continued to estimate that they were performing at an average level, did not provide any clarification of why this might be other than that their academic performance had always been of an average standard. The two young people who felt their education continued to go badly attributed this to falling behind with their school work due to poor attendance. Young people felt that their poor attendance stemmed from inadequate support for their education during initial entry into the looked after system or during subsequent placement moves.

> Right now I could be achieving something much better
> in school that can help me be what I want to be when I'm
> older, but because I missed a lot of stuff when I was
> moved about so much I ain't learning. I hardly
> understand maths but the class is so easy. I get picked on
> for being in the lowest class when I'm more than capable
> of being in a much higher class.
> *(16 year old, placed with relatives)*

The estimates of educational progress of a further 23 young people (43 per cent) had improved at follow-up interview. Table 4.14 indicates the types of positive shifts reported.

Table 4.14: Positive shifts in educational progress estimates between original (T1) and follow-up (T2) interviews

Rating at T1	Rating at T2 Allborough	Nettbury	Wentown	Overall
Well	1 to very well	1 to very well		2 to very well
Average	2 to very well	2 to very well	1 to very well	5 to very well
	1 to well	3 to well	5 to well	9 to well
Badly	1 to very well	2 to average		2 to average
				1 to very well
Very badly		1 to average	1 to badly	1 to average
		2 to badly		3 to badly
Total	5 (33%)	11 (55%)	7 (36%)	23 (43%)

The majority of positive shifts appear to involve movement from average ratings to those of 'very well' or 'well', with 14 out of the 23 positive moves occurring in this area. Most young people have moved only 1 rating point upwards, for instance from 'badly' to 'average' or 'average' to 'well', with only 1 case of a move of more than 2 rating points for the young person who moved from 'badly' to 'very well'. The highest proportion of young people whose progress estimates improved at follow-up interview is in Nettbury (55 per cent).

Of the three young people reporting moves from 'very badly' to 'badly', two did not clarify why their progress was not judged as negatively at follow-up. The other acknowledged the difficulty, but felt less badly about it since leaving school.

> I suppose it doesn't seem quite as bad because I've left now, so I'm not like thinking about how I'm doing worse than most other people. But I didn't get any exams so I'd still have to say it's bad.
> *(17 year old, independent living)*

The remaining 20 young people reporting positive changes from their original estimates of educational progress were able to clarify why they felt improvement had arisen. The most frequent explanation centred upon support available in care placements. Thirteen young people in both foster/relative care and residential care felt that the level of encouragement to succeed and the promotion of school attendance within placements had assisted their progress.

> Hard question. Being in a kids' home there is some pressure on you from the other kids not to bother with school, but then the staff did encourage me to stay in school and stuff. So on the whole I suppose it helped me to do better, 'cos they encouraged me to stick at it.
> *(16 year old, residential care)*

> It's just a lot calmer living here and my foster carers want me to do well so I'm trying.
> *(14 year old, foster care)*

It also appeared important that support was associated with a stable care placement and young people believed that being in a long-term placement was conducive to educational progress.

> I think things improved because of being in the same place. I had a fair bit of moving around at first, but then I got settled here and things definitely improved. It's just easier to think about school and stuff when you don't have to worry where you're at [in terms of placement].
> *(18 year old, foster care)*

Eight young people mentioned that the degree of support they received within school or college had enhanced their progress. These young people had experienced a change of school or college since their initial interview and preferred their current school placement. For six of these young people this was a transition from primary to secondary school, or from secondary school to college. In such cases young people appreciated the increased autonomy and responsibility associated with the new educational establishment.

> I'm enjoying school more now that I'm in the [secondary school] – the lessons are more varied and interesting and they seem to expect more of you, and they treat you like more of an adult.
> *(12 year old, foster care)*

> I'm doing better than last time I saw you because of being at college. I much prefer it to school because they treat you with more respect and expect you to work for yourself rather than just 'cos they've told you to do it.
> *(17 year old, independent living)*

Two young people had changed school or college during the academic year. One young person had changed college to take up what appeared to be a more interesting course and was subsequently pleased with the change and motivated to do well. The other had transferred from a mainstream secondary school to a special needs secondary school. The young person believed this to be a considerable improvement to his educational progress, despite the fact that he was unlikely to be entered for more than one GCSE examination within the special school setting. His perception of improvement appeared to be associated with a more comfortable atmosphere within the special school setting.

> It's better than last time because no one's nasty at [special school] and I don't get picked on so that makes me more settled and it's easier to concentrate.
> *(14 year old, placed with relatives)*

Six young people mentioned that age-related changes had contributed to their progress. Enhanced maturity associated with getting older was seen to enable young people to appreciate the value of education and apply themselves more fully to their studies. In addition, some young people felt that drawing closer to the school-leaving age emphasised the importance of working harder.

> I've just found that as I've got older I've generally become more interested in the lessons and subjects so I work a lot harder at them. Maybe it's because now I'm like thinking well I've got to take the exams next year so if I don't focus in now I'm risking messing up big time and wasting my chances.
> *(15 year old, placed with relatives)*

Finally, three young people had returned to their parental home since their original interviews, one of these being no longer classed as looked after. In these cases improvement in educational progress was attributed to returning home.

> Last year I was naughty, but this year I've bucked up my ideas and I'm learning more. I'm more committed now. It's all because I'm out of foster care now, I don't see my foster parents and I've forgot all about them.
> *(13 year old, placed with parents)*

Eight young people's (14 per cent) progress estimates indicated negative change. All of these cases related to young people who provided ratings of 'very well' at original interview. Table 4.15 displays the type of shifts from this category and indicated that more young people in Wentown than Allborough or Nettbury reported negative change.

Table 4.15: Negative shifts in educational progress estimates between original (T1) and follow-up (T2) interviews

Rating at T1	Rating at T2 Allborough	Nettbury	Wentown	Overall
Very well	2 to well	1 to well	3 to average	3 to well
		1 to average	1 to badly	4 to average
				1 to badly
Total	2 (14%)	2 (10%)	4 (21%)	8 (14%)

The three young people whose ratings shifted to 'well' had all experienced a slight drop in coursework or examination grades, which had led them to revise their estimates. The young person in Nettbury had progressed to college after obtaining 10 GCSEs although some of her grades had been lower than predicted. The two young people in Allborough were in Year 11 and believed that a degree of anxiety over forthcoming examinations had slightly affected their performance.

> It's gone down a bit because it is just a bit of pressure
> with GCSEs coming up, doing all the course work and
> that. I get average-ish grades – around a C to a B.
> *(16 year old, residential care)*

Two of the young people reporting a shift to 'average' (1 in Nettbury and 1 in Wentown) believed this was due to their own tendency to leave work until the last minute rather than any change in the level of support for their education. Of the remaining two young people in Wentown, one believed that low expectations on the part of teachers had prevented them being given adequate support for their education.

> When you're in care the teachers tend to have a low
> opinion of you and expect you to be naughty rather than
> someone who might be prepared to knuckle down if they
> were given a bit of an added push.
> *(16 year old, placed with relatives)*

The other young person had experienced placement change that involved a period in residential care, which was associated with reduced school attendance.

> When I was living in children's homes no-one else went
> to school so I started to think I didn't have to go as well.
> *(17 year old, independent living)*

The young person in Wentown, whose progress estimate changed from 'very well' to 'badly', had experienced difficulties within her current placement and arguments arising at home had made the young person argumentative and distracted at school.

To conclude, then, the findings concerning young people's perceptions of educational progress are generally positive. The majority of young people report sustained good progress at follow-up interview, or an improvement in their level of progress. A key feature for young people in explaining either improvements in progress or the maintenance of positive progress, was the degree of encouragement and support for education provided by carers. Young people mentioned carers emphasising the need for them to persevere with, and show commitment to, their education and communicating their desire for young people to succeed academically.

Such promotion of an educational ethos was frequently tied to the concepts of stability and security. Young people experiencing a rewarding, relatively long-term placement of at least 12 months, may be better able to build a relationship with carers and take account of encouragement in their education. Conversely, the four young people who reported experiencing difficulties, or little educational support, within their care placement or placement changes described their education as progressing 'badly'.

The frequent observations regarding stable support from carers and security of care placements may help to explain some of the previously outlined improvements in ratings for standardised measures. Improvements in young people's self-esteem and psychological well-being could be a natural corollary of living in a settled supportive environment. A number of young people attributed improvements in progress to their enhanced maturity enabling them to appreciate the value of education and the importance of academic success. Such comments were reflected in the apparent trend towards improved attitudes to schooling as recorded by the ASM. Many young people also felt that their current school or college was able to respect their developing maturity and provide them with greater autonomy in response. This was appreciated by a number of young people who had experienced transition from primary to secondary school or from school to college.

The findings regarding perceptions of educational progress also raise questions about differential levels of support provided for education in the individual project authorities. Although the majority of young people in Wentown did report that good progress was maintained or improved, slightly higher numbers of young people reported negative changes in their estimates of progress than those in Allborough and Nettbury. Unfortunately, only two young people in Wentown were able to clarify why they felt their progress had worsened, for one young person this was associated with a belief that teachers held low expectations of their ability and had not provided appropriate educational support, whilst for the other young person negative change was attributed to placement difficulties. The proportion of young people whose progress estimates improved at follow-up is higher in Nettbury than either Allborough or Wentown and this too raises questions regarding whether young people in Nettbury are better able to access support for their education. The majority of improvement in Nettbury was attributed to the provision of a stable, supportive care placement. However, it must be acknowledged that five of the young people from the Nettbury sample reporting improved progress were unaccompanied asylum-seeking young people. In part, their perception of improved progress was due to improvements in their English ability, which understandably had enabled them better access to the curriculum. The inclusion of these young people in the sample may have exaggerated the degree of improvement within the Nettbury sample.

Summary

- The cohorts sitting tests at Key Stages in any one year differ considerably in terms of experience of school exclusion, placement change, absenteeism and rate of special educational needs. All of these factors may have some impact upon attainment and, consequently, the validity of comparing disparate cohorts over time may be questionable. It is therefore difficult to draw any firm conclusions for looked after children based upon official indicators.

■ Alternative outcome measures were used to determine whether project activities have made some difference for the sample of young people selected for evaluation purposes.

■ Young people taking part in the evaluation project were asked to complete five standardised scales to determine whether any change had taken place in their reported psychological well-being, self-esteem, attitudes to education and school, expectations about the future, and perceptions of educational progress.

■ Two of the five standardised scales revealed significant progress between the two rounds of interviews. They indicate improvements in psychological well-being and self-esteem for the majority of young people in the follow-up sample across the three authorities. However, it is difficult to determine whether these findings are directly connected to the presence of the *Taking Care of Education* project in the three authorities.

■ Qualitative accounts of young people's perceptions of progress in their care and educational experience between interviews are generally positive.

■ A key feature for young people in explaining improvements in progress, of the maintenance of positive progress, was the degree of encouragement and support for education provided by carers.

■ Placement stability and security are closely associated with the quality of relationships between carers and young people and, therefore, with the availability and efficiency of the support and encouragements provided.

5. Corporate approaches to the education of looked after children

A major aim of the *Taking Care of Education* project was to promote a 'whole authority' or corporate approach to the education of looked after children. The need to develop an effective corporate response in this area is also emphasised in the Joint Guidance (Department for Education and Employment/Department of Health, 2000). As Jackson and Sachdev (2001) point out, there are two different dimensions to corporate parenting. The first of these concerns the need for local authorities to devise policies, procedures and systems to make sure that all relevant departments and staff within them work together for the benefit of looked after children and young people. This chapter concentrates on this area of corporate parenting by examining policy and practice at local authority level and highlighting any influence the *Taking Care of Education* project may have brought to bear. The second element of corporate parenting identified by Jackson and Sachdev (2001), concerns the everyday care and education of individual children. This aspect of corporate parenting is covered in subsequent chapters examining school, social work and carer practice.

The interviews held with key local authority personnel involved a structured schedule of questions in order to assess corporate approaches to the education of looked after children at local authority level. The interview also included questions regarding aspects of social worker, teaching and carer practice. When personnel were asked whether any aspects of the interview schedule could be seen as central to promoting improved outcomes for looked after children, the majority of staff across all three authorities described the corporate approach as the most important factor.

I think it has got to be the corporate approaches. I think if you have not got the basic framework and the political commitment right, you are always going to be struggling with the others.
(Allborough: Social Services Officer)

I think that good things can happen whether they are top down or bottom up but in terms of things becoming established, then probably the more corporate elements and the way in which agencies work together are more likely to lead to longer term improvement, rather than an enthusiastic designated teacher doing something, who may even disappear after a year.
(Nettbury: Education Officer)

The corporate commitment part is crucial, I think everything follows from there really, although the corporate side has to be seen to link with school and social work practice and the care settings so that carers, social workers and teachers are all working to the same aim.
(Wentown: Education Officer)

Interviews with key personnel were aimed at determining the extent to which the *Taking Care of Education* project was able to influence corporate approaches to the education of looked after children. Interviewees were asked to assess the performance of the authority in a given area by allocating a rating of 'very good', 'good', 'average', 'poor' or 'very poor'. They were then asked to rate the contribution of the *Taking Care of Education* project to the estimated level of performance using a scale of 'highly significant', 'significant', 'reasonable', 'limited' or 'no contribution'. The reasons underpinning such assessments were also explored with all interviewees. This chapter is structured around the responses given to questions about corporate policy and procedure in each authority and outlines the impact the project may have had on work in this area.

Policies relating to the education of looked after children

Key personnel were asked to assess whether they felt that the local authority included the importance of educational planning for looked after children in all relevant policy documents. The majority of staff in all three authorities described the authority's performance as good and believed that the project contribution to this work was highly significant. The influence of the Project Lead Officer in developing statements of corporate parenting practice, or whole-authority policies, was seen to have greatly reinforced existing commitments to emphasising educational planning for looked after children in a range of policy documents.

However in each authority, staff were reluctant to describe performance as 'very good', since they believed further work was required to ensure such corporate parenting principles were firmly embedded within policy statements of all relevant departments and services.

> It feels to me like we've got to have one or two cracks at this before people just build it into their thinking and it becomes part of the culture. That's not a criticism at all, because I think that's the inevitable process about turning around the way that people think.
> *(Wentown: Social Services Officer)*

There was some evidence that such mainstreaming of principles was underway. For instance, in Nettbury, a number of services and teams within the departments of Education and Social Services have produced statements describing how the corporate parenting principles of the authority are to be reflected in their operational practice. The *Nettbury Cultural Strategy* for 2003–2008, developed by the Arts and Leisure Service, also includes looked after children as a priority group in terms of ensuring access to the full range of activities available. In Wentown, the departments of Education, Social Services, Housing, Leisure Services, Planning, Economic Development and Tourism, Environmental Health and City Engineers have been asked to include the contributions they will make to improving the educational experiences of looked after children in their annual business plans.

The majority of personnel greeted these developments with enthusiasm and believed that the translation of general principles into individual department and service level documents would help to ensure that the principles became embedded in professional practice. However, interviewees were aware that written statements did not automatically translate into practice changes, and some staff suggested that additional support at management level was required to enable operational staff to build their practice around such priorities.

A skilled senior officer to promote corporate parenting

Personnel in all three authorities described performance as good in terms of the provision of a skilled senior officer to enforce joint working procedures and promote the importance of a corporate approach to the education of looked after children. In Allborough and Nettbury, the *Taking Care of Education* project was seen to play a 'highly significant' role in this area.

> I actually think that the project is highly significant in
> that we have got to 'good' in that particular area, which is
> because it [Project Lead Officer post] created a focal
> point at senior level for that work. I don't think we would
> have achieved it in the same way without Gatsby.
> *(Allborough: Social Services Officer)*

Personnel in both authorities believed that the Project Lead Officer played a major role in maintaining project momentum and facilitating policy and practice change. Descriptors such as 'vital', 'central to progress' and 'crucial' were all applied to the importance of having a dedicated Project Lead Officer to constantly promote a corporate approach to meeting the educational needs of looked after children.

Unfortunately, the Project Lead Officer in Allborough left the authority in September 2002. This had caused the majority of personnel there to appreciate fully the work of the Project Lead Officer in establishing effective frameworks to oversee the progress of the project. This had initially helped to maintain progress despite the absence of a lead person. All personnel interviewed believed that, the strength of the structures notwithstanding, there was a definite need for someone to drive the project and emphasise the importance of educational issues in the long term. The nature of the departments and agencies involved, their sometimes divergent agendas, and the practical problems of promoting joint working practice, all meant that strong leadership was required if a corporate approach was to be sustained.

In Wentown, a slightly different response was observed. Although all personnel commented on the importance of the Project Lead Officer role in maintaining project progress and promoting a corporate approach to the education of looked after children, some felt that the status of the post was not senior enough to effect maximum change.

> I think that [Project Lead Officer] is working in such a
> strange environment in a way because [they] don't have
> the status to push things. The post just isn't senior
> enough in some ways, to do some of the strategic things.
> *(Wentown: Education Officer)*

Nonetheless, the Project Lead Officer in Wentown was backed by a senior officer management group drawn from Education, Social Services and the Corporate Strategy Unit and these staff believed that this worked effectively to ensure that there was a collective responsibility for enforcing joint procedures and protocols.

Information collection and sharing

Numerous research reports have highlighted problems of information sharing between departments of Education and Social Services. These two key departments appear to find joint working and information sharing a difficult process (Audit Commission 1994; Firth and Fletcher 2001; Social Services Inspectorate/Office for Standards in Education 1995). This may be due to departments using disparate and incompatible paper- and computer-based systems to record information about looked after children which can prevent effective information sharing (Gatehouse and Ward 2002), or there may be a lack of accurate educational data (Fletcher-Campbell and Archer 2003). Even when information systems are compatible, ethical issues concerning client confidentiality can lead to protracted debate over the types of information to which staff in both departments should have access (Webb and Vulliamy 2001).

Local authority personnel in the current study were asked to provide their perceptions of the authority's capacity to collect and share accurate information for monitoring young people's educational progress. Their views on the contribution of the *Taking Care of Education* project were also sought.

Four main questions were asked relating to the authority's ability to:
- gather baseline statistics on looked after children's care and education history,and their progress beyond that baseline
- monitor the accuracy and extent to which the information held was up–to–date
- develop protocols for sharing relevant information between schools, Social Service and Education departments
- use information to inform practice and lead to action and improvement.

Information issues in Allborough

Table 5.1 displays the most frequently given response provided by key personnel in Allborough to the four questions regarding the authority's performance in relation to information collection and sharing and the project's contribution towards this.

Table 5.1: Staff perceptions of Allborough's information collection and sharing capacity and project impact in this area

Area of work	Rating	
	Authority performance	Project contribution
Gathering baseline statistics	Average	Significant
Monitoring accuracy	Average	Significant
Information sharing	Good	Significant
Informed action	Average	Reasonable

Central to any discussion of issues around information sharing in Allborough is the major effort made by the *Taking Care of Education* project to establish a database system and protocols for sharing information about looked after children across Education and Social Services departments. The majority of project funding available for the first year implementation plan was used to purchase an 'end-user reporting tool', called *Business Objects*, as well as additional computers and a new server to allow Education and Social Services teams to access the system. The purchase of the software was intended to allow a common interface between Social Services and Education databases. The approach relied upon the existing database structures and it was thought the new system would require little change to current processes or data recording procedures. It was hoped that the software would enable a wide range of personnel to have access to accurate and up-to-date information on looked after children's school and care placements, attendance and exclusion rates, and academic attainment.

The software was purchased in January 2001 with the view that the system would be fully operational by 31 March 2001. At the time, many staff in Allborough keenly welcomed this development and believed the project had enabled them to solve the issue of cross-departmental information sharing. Such optimism was unfortunately premature, and numerous delays were experienced in setting up the joint access system. By March 2003, progress had been made and the database was routinely able to produce reports for the Special Educational Needs Support Service and the Advisory Teacher for Children in Public Care, informing them of the identity of young people currently looked after in Allborough. However, the database is not yet accessible to the range of professionals for whom it was intended.

The problems encountered in developing the system were not technical issues, but were instead mainly due to organisational and personnel factors. Reorganisation of the Social Services department had hindered decisions regarding where computers would be housed and which specification would be bought. There were also problems in collating and preparing Education department databases for inclusion in the system. This stemmed from some individuals' reluctance to prioritise the task and view the need to share information as a central part of the authority's efforts to improve educational outcomes for looked after children. In addition, problems had been encountered where information from Education and Social Services databases did not tally due to inaccuracies in the data held in one or both of the databases. The strength of the system was dependent upon routine updates of both database sources but there was no agreement in place to ensure that such updating occurred in unison. The combined problems experienced caused some personnel to doubt the wisdom of attempting to develop the integrated system.

> I think we were too ambitious about being able to succeed in totally sharing information across the two agencies. I think we maybe should have come back to going down the route of improving the information that we have in Social Services, and developing the system we have here. Maybe if we'd focused on that a bit earlier than we have now we perhaps would have made a bit more progress with it.'
> *(Allborough: Social Services Officer)*

Delays were also experienced in developing protocols regarding what types of information would be shared between departments and what level of access would be afforded to different personnel. Much of this debate hinged around issues of confidentiality, but nonetheless the Project Lead Officer had been successful in reaching a final agreement to which both departments were willing to commit. This process was seen to have had a positive impact on inter-professional working and was expected to pave the way for future effective information sharing. However, the problems experienced with the joint database meant that much of the potentially communicable information had yet to be shared.

In terms of using information to inform action and planning for the education of looked after children, most personnel judged that improvements in this area were required. But, despite the problems encountered with developing the joint system, the majority of interviewees were optimistic that the system would soon furnish professionals from both departments with an accurate indication of looked after children's educational progress. At a general level it was felt that this would enable the authority to monitor their progress accurately against national and local educational targets for the looked after population. This was seen to represent a major improvement to the authority's information collection and sharing capacity at the outset of the project and, as such, the project's influence was judged significant.

> I think without Gatsby we wouldn't be there. So the contribution is highly significant to have got us from … poor to good. In terms of the specific resources that they have been able to put in, the IT resources, and so on, it has made a big difference. I think without Gatsby we wouldn't have made the progress that we have here.
> *(Allborough: Social Services Officer)*

In addition, it was hoped that the system would help develop more sophisticated use of individual level data to target support for young people more effectively.

> What I'm thinking about is the area of trying to make sure that in an absolutely systematic way between us we are able both individually and collectively, at any point in time, to say what young people are doing achievement based things and what help do we need to give them to achieve it … If I were to ask somebody to phone up a social worker for me in September about each of their young people, I want them to be able to tell me, 'Yes we think she'll get Spanish and Religious Education this year but it doesn't look like she's going to get her Maths, but this is how we could help her.' In a way that's my next target for the project.
> *(Allborough: Education Officer)*

It will be of great interest to observe the next phase of the project in Allborough to determine how the authority begins to work towards this aim.

Information issues in Nettbury

The most frequently given responses from Nettbury personnel to questions on the authority's performance and project contribution regarding information issues are shown in Table 5.2.

Table 5.2: Staff perceptions of Nettbury's information collection and sharing capacity and project impact in this area

	Rating	
Area of work	Authority performance	Project contribution
Gathering baseline statistics	Average	Significant
Monitoring accuracy	Good	Significant
Information sharing	Average	Limited
Informed action	Average	Significant

Toward the start of the *Taking Care of Education* project, personnel in Nettbury complained that the authority's information systems were very primitive. There was no way of producing an accurate list of the schools attended by looked after children, land othersone details of their attendance, attainment and any recorded exclusions. Over the course of the *Taking Care of Education* project this situation improved. The Children's Quality Information Team within Social Services had begun to collate information regarding children's care and educational history and information was shared with the Education Department. In addition, the Project Lead Officer had developed a questionnaire to collect information on an annual basis about children placed outside the authority.

All personnel interviewed appreciated a considerable improvement in the availability of reliable data regarding the schools young people attended and their most recent levels of attainment. Although this work had been driven by a senior officer within the Social Services Department, personnel commented that the project had played a significant role in highlighting the inadequacies of the previous data collection systems.

> [The Project Lead Officer] was instrumental in
> highlighting many of the gaps in the old databases and
> stressing that we needed much more accurate
> information to aid our planning.
> *(Nettbury: Education Officer)*

There was a general awareness that the improvements to data collection
procedures needed to be built upon to enable the authority to use
information effectively to inform action. Indeed, awareness of the need for
further development was responsible for most staff only judging the
authority's performance at an 'average' level in terms of collecting and
collating statistics. At present, available data provided only annual updates of
young people's attainment and attendance and it was hoped that this would
develop into more regular monitoring to track progress.

> I know we are only average on that because we do still
> have a scramble round finding stats because we don't
> have a real joined-up system. At least we know who we've
> got looked after now and their schools etc. So if you just
> mean who was there and what happened to them then
> yes we've got that. But if you're talking about base lines
> in terms of watching progress, we need a much more
> stringent system of regular updating and review.
> *(Nettbury: Social Services Officer)*

It is possible that a new electronic management system may be developed in
Nettbury to facilitate the sharing of information between departments. The
Project Lead Officer is a member of the Child Health Informatics
Consortium, an inter-professional task group to explore strategies to share
data more effectively on looked after children. The group has recently
produced a report containing specific recommendations on data
management.

There was already some evidence of information being used to inform action
relating to GCSE attainment. The observation that none of Nettbury's
looked after population in 2001/2002 obtained 5 GCSEs at grades A to C
had stimulated debate regarding what the authority might do to support
individual pupils who were approaching GCSE examination periods. The

Lead Officer also tried to establish a tracking process, whereby information available on the educational progress of Year 10 children could be used to identify those who may be in need of additional assistance in advance of GCSE/GNVQ examinations. The aim was that field social workers could then explore whether there were any unmet needs or issues that young people felt could be addressed to support them better. Unfortunately, this did not appear to happen, and there may be issues about the responsibility taken by team leaders within social services for following this through. The tracking process was carried out for Year 10 pupils in the academic year of 2000/2001, but has not been continued. However, it is hoped that the notion of tracking children's progress will become established through the use of Personal Education Plans.

Information sharing between Education and Social Services was seen to have improved through developing a method of recording and reporting educational information about looked after children. However, staff commented that there were no specific agreements or protocols to dictate such work at an authority level. A protocol did exist in terms of a 'change of circumstances' form to enable social workers to inform schools of changes in a young person's care status or placement but there were some concerns regarding the routine application of this document and the speed at which notification of any change was communicated to schools. Improving this system at operational level is likely to be an ongoing process somewhat outside the remit of the Project Lead Officer.

Information issues in Wentown

Table 5.3 shows the most frequently given responses provided by key personnel in Wentown regarding the authority's performance in relation to information collection and sharing and the project's contribution towards this.

Table 5.3: Staff perceptions of Wentown's information collection and sharing capacity and project impact in this area

	Rating	
Area of work	Authority performance	Project contribution
Gathering baseline statistics	Average	Significant
Monitoring accuracy	Average	Reasonable
Information sharing	Average	Reasonable
Informed action	Average	Reasonable

The majority of personnel considered the authority's performance to be at an 'average' level in all areas covering issues of collecting and sharing information about looked after children's educational progress. Much of the work in this area is carried out by the LEA Special Projects Group, which maintains a database including information about the educational experiences and attainment of looked after children. The group is responsible for producing an annual *Green Report* outlining key statistics concerning the education of looked after children, which is circulated to Education and Social Services staff throughout the authority, as well as to elected members. Whilst the production of the report pre-dated the *Taking Care of Education* project, project funds had been used to enhance the capacity of the Education department database to allow detailed historical data to be held. Improvements in the range of information that could be included in such reports were thought to have raised significantly the profile of the education of looked after children. Some of the more recent reports collated from the database were thought to have stimulated a commitment to improving inter-professional collaboration. In areas where looked after children appeared to be at an educational disadvantage, it was felt that personnel had begun to think more coherently about how they might develop joint solutions to improving the lot of looked after children.

> We had a print-out of 40-something children who had missed more than 25 day's schooling. So that was very hard-hitting and a lot of us round the table knew the names of those children so that was very powerful and I think it did galvanise all of us in terms of inter-agency working.
> *(Wentown: Social Services Officer)*

However, there were a number of concerns regarding the speed at which information became available and this caused most personnel to described the authority's performance as only 'average'. The *Green Report* tended to be circulated almost 12 months after data was collected and this resulted in a degree of frustration that the information could not be used in direct planning for current school cohorts. As in Allborough and Nettbury, personnel wished to see more timely educational data being used as a strategic planning tool to identify areas where resources could be targeted to improve educational experiences and outcomes for young people. Some personnel believed that the *Taking Care of Education Project* could have taken a stronger lead in promoting the need for timely information. Other than contributing funds towards an up-grading of the database, the project was not seen to have been particularly active in areas of information collection and exchange.

In fact, the Project Lead Officer had contributed to the development of information sharing protocols covering looked after children and care leavers. Although the protocols were developed by the LEA Special Projects team in negotiation with the Social Services Department, the Project Lead Officer was responsible for distributing them for consultation and redrafting where appropriate. The process of discussing the protocol development in itself was seen to have had positive implications for inter-professional communication but there were mixed feelings regarding the efficacy of such documents in enhancing the quantity and quality of routinely shared information at operational levels.

> I don't think that has had an impact, not necessarily. It's kind of incidental, it's a nice bit of writing on the case, it's a nice way of focusing agencies on issues and making sure that they are very respectful of data protection issues and the young people's rights to privacy and so on. I think that at practitioner level, I don't know that it is strictly speaking how people operate, they'll find their way around it to make sure that they know what they need to know.
> *(Wentown: Social Services Officer)*

The issue of staff failing to follow data-sharing procedures was seen to have repercussions for the quality of data. Although the capacity of the Education Department's database had improved, some staff wished to highlight that the quality of the data remained dependent upon effective cooperation and liaison between operational staff and the LEA Special Projects team. As with Nettbury, this is an issue which extends beyond the work of the Project Lead Officer to other managers and team leaders within the relevant departments. Despite the efforts of the Special Projects team to maintain effective communication with operational staff, delays in communicating relevant data and failure to report key information did arise. Some staff were concerned that, as a result, certain information contained in the database was out of date and inaccurate.

Focusing on educational matters in identifying care placements

The most frequent assessment in all three authorities was that performance in this area was 'average', although the project had made a 'significant' contribution. In all instances, the project contribution was seen to stem from general awareness-raising regarding the importance of education for looked after children. The project was seen to provide an additional imperative to focus on the education of looked after children to those stemming from the *Quality Protects* initiative and the Joint Guidance (Department for Education and Employment/Department of Health, 2000).

Although staff believed there was a genuine commitment towards seeking to identify educationally appropriate care placements, performance in each authority remained at an average level due to two main constraints on placement decisions. First, the urgency with which some placement decisions had to be made could prevent detailed consideration of a young person's educational needs. Second, a shortage of available care placements meant that an educationally supportive placement could not always be guaranteed. This was considered to be a particular problem in Wentown. It may seem desirable, therefore, to reduce the proportion of carers drawn from areas of social deprivation and/or with limited educational experience. However, such an argument would be somewhat naïve; in the face of a national shortage of foster placements, authorities may have to make use of foster care applicants from all sections of society. It may be more pragmatic to argue that significant attention should be directed towards the provision of training in educational issues for those carers with less educational experience. There is also scope for the development of alternatives, for example additional support and educational visitors might be offered to foster carers who lack knowledge and confidence in this area of work.

Staff were also asked to assess whether education was prioritised in the assessment, recruitment and post-placement support of carers. The general response across all three authorities was that performance in this area was 'average'. This was invariably described as a product of a shortage in foster care placements resulting in educational issues not always being paramount in the recruitment process. Although staff across all three authorities reported that the project had reinforced awareness that authorities should be considering such issues, practical circumstances meant that this had limited impact. At the same time, if problems with educationally unsupportive placements are to be avoided, consideration of educational issues at the point of recruitment seems of vital importance. Given that foster carers often report concern about educational issues (see, for example, Sinclair and others 2000), prospective carers might welcome guidance at an early stage about the authority's expectations in this area.

Involvement of elected members

Personnel in Allborough believed the involvement of elected members in promoting the education of looked after children was 'very good' and the project had a 'highly significant' impact in this area. Elected members there had shown a high degree of commitment toward raising the educational attainment of looked after children prior to the *Taking Care of Education* project and were involved in preparing the bid to participate in the project. Such commitment was seen to have been greatly reinforced by the central role elected members had been asked to play in the subsequent management of the project implementation plan.

> Absolutely, yes. It is. The involvement of elected members is good but what Gatsby has done has provided an explicit forum in the Board where it is not an optional thing, the elected members are tied very directly into the process. It is jointly chaired by the cabinet member for Social Care and cabinet member for Lifelong Learning. I think their engagement in it has been far greater because of that than it perhaps would have been without.
>
> *(Allborough: Social Services Officer)*

The involvement of elected members in Nettbury was generally described as good and the project was seen to have a 'significant' impact in this area. The Project Lead Officer had given briefing sessions on the education of looked after children to a cross- party Corporate Parenting Members Group in Nettbury. The group also received regular progress reports on all work designed to promote the educational opportunities of looked after children. Whilst the interest and enthusiasm of elected members in this area was not disputed, some personnel believed that such interest could take on a symbolic function rather than members fully understanding their own role in relation to corporate parenting and using their influence with senior officers.

In Wentown, the involvement of elected members was described as 'average' and the project was seen only to make a reasonable contribution in this area. The average performance was seen to be the result of changes to the political structure in Wentown. Originally, there had been a committee with a specific interest in the education of looked after children, which the Project Lead Officer was able to attend. A recent movement to a cabinet structure meant that this committee no longer existed, making it more difficult for the Project Lead Officer to communicate with members. It was hoped that, as executive members with responsibilities including the education of looked after children became more familiar with their remit, their involvement would improve. The Project Lead Officer was aware of the issues and further work in this area is being developed in the second phase of the project.

Securing school placements for looked after children without delay

All three authorities tended to be described as 'good' in terms of their ability to secure school placements without delay. In Wentown, this was seen to as due to local authority policy and practice in response to the Joint Guidance (Department for Education and Employment/Department of Health, 2000), with the main contribution of the project in this area being in terms of general awareness-raising. In Allborough and Nettbury, however, the *Taking Care of Education* project tended to be described as having a 'significant' impact on the authorities' ability to secure school placements without delay.

In Allborough, the Project Lead Officer's ability to strengthen relationships with head teachers and the added impetus of the project in raising awareness of the importance of promoting the educational opportunities of looked after children was seen to have enhanced head teachers' willingness to prioritise admission for looked after children.

> You can actually see some changes in schools. There's been a couple of meetings that I've been involved in where Heads have immediately recognised the issue and understood the issue. Whereas I think a few years ago there would have been an immediate sort of defensiveness about it – either saying that we treat these children the same as all the others, and seeing that as a virtue, or being concerned that these children get a precedence over others in the community and saying what problems that might lead to. But that appears to have shifted and I certainly haven't detected any further examples of that. I do think that much of that is down to the awareness-raising through the project, so yes I do think the project has [had] a significant impact there.
> *(Allborough: Social Services Officer)*

In Nettbury, earlier rounds of interviews with key personnel had indicated some concern over delays in establishing a school place for children whose entry or movement within the looked after system necessitated a change of school. As a consequence, the local authority changed the admissions policy for high schools to give looked after children the same level of priority for a school place as those with statements of special educational needs and medical needs. This policy has now been reinforced by the recent Department for Education and Skills' (2003) amendment to the School Admissions Code of Practice, advising admission authorities to give 'top priority' to looked after children in over-subscription criteria. This is a policy change that should also assist Allborough and Wentown to secure school placements with speed.

Maintaining a corporate overview of school admissions and exclusion policies as they affect looked after children

Staff in all three authorities generally believed that their authority showed a 'good' level of performance in terms of having a corporate overview of admissions and exclusion policies. In Wentown, this was viewed as the remit of the LEA Special Projects group and their work was described as effective in ensuring that an overall view of admissions and permanent exclusion data was available. Such information was regularly reported to the Corporate Management Team in Wentown. The *Taking Care of Education* project was not seen to have been making a contribution in this area. Despite the research instigated into unofficial/informal exclusions, some staff believed that this was inconclusive and suspected that such exclusions may continue to be an issue for a small number of looked after children. In Allborough the project was seen to have had a 'reasonable' input into the area, again through general awareness-raising that such information should be recorded and monitored. In Nettbury, most personnel described the project contribution as 'significant' given that the Project Lead Officer reported such information to the Corporate Parenting Members group and the Education and Social Service liaison group.

Ensuring that roles and responsibilities of corporate parents are clearly understood

Across all three authorities, personnel believed their authority was 'good' at ensuring that corporate parents were aware of their respective roles and responsibilities. The project's influence tended to be rated as 'significant' in all three. The significance of the role appeared to stem from the project's general ability to raise the profile of the importance of education for looked after children as well as from discrete project-related activities. In Allborough the framework surrounding project implementation was seen to support a clear understanding of relevant departments', services' and elected members' contributions to promoting the education of looked after children. In addition, work with head teachers, information exchanges with foster carers, and activities within residential centres were seen to have enhanced understanding of how different individuals could serve to support young people's education. Nonetheless, it was felt that performance in this area could be improved. Work within schools and training schemes for designated teachers had not been able to engage all of Allborough's schools and designated teachers. Likewise, the foster carer information exchanges were attended by relatively few carers and there was a desire to see more work being directed towards developing the role of foster carers in supporting the education of looked after children.

In Nettbury, the Corporate Parenting Principles developed by the Project Lead Officer were seen to have enabled a range of individual departments and services to develop clarity regarding their role. Information leaflets outlining expectations of foster carers in supporting the education of looked after children had been produced, alongside information packs for social workers and designated teachers. Training sessions around the Joint Guidance and wider educational issues had also been provided for designated teachers, social workers and foster and residential carers. In addition, the Project Lead Officer's work with elected members was seen to have enhanced their understanding of their role in supporting the educational needs of looked after children. Indeed, some staff believed that the authority's performance would have been poor in this area without the project's contribution. Nonetheless, some personnel believed that more work was required to ensure that statements of relative roles and responsibilities were clearly communicated to all relevant personnel.

> It's a different picture when we start using the word 'all' in there because I'm taking that as members, officers, head teachers, social workers, carers anybody who in any way provides some sort of service or overview. Although we've got statements and commitment I'm not sure how far down in every single team right across the board that we can say these are disseminated and understood.
> *(Nettbury: Education Officer)*

Although a positive start had been made it was suggested that more work was required to reinforce and extend understanding of all corporate parenting roles. A similar argument was forwarded in Wentown. The Project Lead Officer was praised for her efforts in persuading key departments to identify their contributions to the 'whole authority' policy and initiating a work-shadowing scheme between teaching and social care professionals. However, whilst awareness of roles and responsibilities was thought to have significantly improved as a consequence of such activities, most personnel believed that further work was required to genuinely embed such understanding.

Consulting with looked after children on educational issues

Personnel in Allborough generally reported that the authority was good at consulting looked after children. This was thought to have pre-dated the project, but nonetheless the project was considered to have made a significant contribution to the consultation agenda. The project's contribution involved the Project Lead Officer liaising with the local authority's Children's and Young People's Participation Officer to establish consultation groups with looked after children on educational issues. In addition, project funding was used to appoint a part-time Youth Worker to specifically promote opportunities for consultation and participation with looked after groups. However, some staff reported concerns that the participation officer post becoming vacant, combined with the lack of a

Project Lead Officer in Allborough, had reduced the level of consultation with young people. It was hoped that this situation would soon be rectified due to new appointments being made for both posts.

Staff in Nettbury and Wentown tended to report that their authority was 'average' in terms of consulting looked after children on educational issues. In Wentown, the authority's 'average' performance was based upon the view that an established consultation group for looked after children was poorly attended and there were no significant efforts to expand the range of consultation methods used. Although the Project Lead Officer was described as attending the young people's consultation group, the limited capacity of this group meant that the project contribution was judged only reasonable. The Project Lead Officer had also been involved in the development of a video concerning the educational experiences of looked after children, which was produced by the children themselves. Although this activity could also be seen to represent a mode of consultation, there appeared to be a lack of awareness of the issue and only one of the personnel interviewed mentioned the video.

In Nettbury, the project was seen to have made a significant contribution to this area through part-funding for a Youth Participation Officer. One remit of this role being to ensure that looked after children were included in consultation exercises. In addition, the Project Lead Officer was described as carrying out informal consultation with looked after children who attended project-related events and activities. Personnel in Nettbury felt that, without the project input, performance in this area would be poor.

> I don't think that it's specifically looked after children that we have not been consulting enough on, I think it's all children that we are not consulting enough on. In a way we are probably doing better with looked after children because of the youth worker post and [Project Lead Officer]'s informal consultations.
> *(Nettbury: Education Officer)*

Provision of designated teachers

The Joint Guidance introduced the recommendation that all LEA-maintained schools appoint a designated teacher for looked after children. Staff in all three authorities believed that they fully met this requirement and that all schools had a designated teacher. Indeed, in Wentown the LEA had introduced *Looked After Link Teachers* in all schools some time before the introduction of the Joint Guidance (Department for Education and Employment/Department of Health, 2000). In addition, most staff indicated that they were aware that their LEAs maintained an accurate list of who these teachers were.

In Nettbury and Wentown, interviewees felt that arrangements surrounding the identification of designated teachers were the responsibility of the authority and the project had not directed any work in this area. However in Allborough, personnel attributed a significant contribution to the project due to its continual emphasis on ensuring that elements of the joint guidance were in place.

There was one area connected with the designated teacher role in which personnel in all three authorities reported project contributions. This was the area of training provision for designated teachers. In Allborough and Nettbury, the level of training provided was judged to be 'good' and the project was seen to have made a significant contribution to this. In both these authorities, training for designated teachers arose as part of inter-professional training sessions involving teachers, social workers and residential and foster carers. Project Lead Officers had played a key role in the organisation of this training, and in Nettbury the Project Lead Officer had delivered the training. Indeed, there were concerns voiced by the Project Lead Officer in Nettbury that the authority had wholly relied upon the project to meet such training needs. This led to concern regarding the sustainability of the training.

In Wentown, designated teacher training was the responsibility of the LEA Special Projects. However, since the Project Lead Officer had been involved in some of the training events, the project was seen to have made a reasonable contribution to work in this area. The majority of personnel described the training as 'good'.

In all three authorities, recognition of the quality of the training was tempered by concerns over a relatively low level of attendance from designated teachers.

> The problem with the training is attendance and trying to get teachers along from schools that don't normally have looked after children. It's very hard. I know teachers are pressed for time and have a hectic workload, but I think something has to be done about encouraging greater attendance at these training sessions.
> *(Nettbury: Education Officer)*

In Wentown, some staff believed that low attendance levels could be due to previously noted concerns regarding designated teachers' awareness of their role.

> It all links in really. They might have training but if people don't know they're a link teacher they won't have been on it will they?
> *(Wentown: Social Services Officer)*

Similar problems were noted in Allborough and the authority had already begun to consider adapting their training programme to engage teaching staff more effectively. It was hoped that rather than holding large scale training events, training delivery might be focused around clusters of professionals working with the same groups of young people to address more specific issues and encourage more effective joint working. This may enable participants to feel more actively involved in designing more relevant training and, hence, promote better attendance.

Use of Personal Education Plans

The Joint Guidance on the Education of Children in Public Care (Department for Education and Employment/Department of Health 2000) introduced the statutory requirement that all looked after children should have a personal education plan (PEP). Performance in relation to meeting this requirement varied across the three project authorities. In Allborough and Nettbury, performance regarding the completion of PEPs was unanimously judged to be good. In both authorities, substantial problems were experienced in ensuring PEP completion but these had been successfully addressed: the rate of PEP completion had exceeded 80 per cent in Allborough and was 100 per cent in Nettbury. The *Taking Care of Education* project was seen as a significant factor in overcoming barriers to PEP completion. In Wentown, the project was not seen to have directed any work towards issues of PEP completion and, in general, the authority's performance was judged to be average. Staff could not provide an accurate indication of the proportion of young people for whom PEPs had been completed, but some suspected that this was likely to be as little as 50 per cent.

In Allborough, problems were experienced in engaging teachers in the process of completing PEPs. Area Union Representatives from the National Association of Head Teachers were concerned that the completion of PEPs placed an unnecessary additional burden on the already excessive workload of teachers. Sensitive negotiation between the Project Lead Officer and head teacher representatives eventually resolved this issue, and the Allborough PEP pro-forma was revised in response to the views of teaching staff. The Project Lead Officer also established a PEP review group to monitor the layout, content, and quality of information contained in the PEPs and suggest improvement where necessary. The review process was established to include representation from teaching staff, social workers and young people to ensure that the form continued to be seen as relevant and useful.

The strategy of the local authority regarding PEP completion was developed, in part, through discussion at project board meetings. This resulted in the introduction of a system whereby schools complete PEPs in consultation with children and young people,then forward completed forms to social workers so they can be passed to a Social Services Reviewing Officer in time for Care Plan Reviews. Reviewing officers monitor the number of PEPs completed and inform schools of the date for Care Plan and PEP reviews. In addition, schools are allocated additional funding to assist them with the PEP process and subsequent support for children and young people. The Education Department provides £150 for each looked after child or young person in foster care and £1,500 for those in residential care, the difference based upon the assumption that young people in residential care are more likely to require additional school-based support, so funding reflects more than the basic cost of administration surrounding the PEP.

In Wentown, the low completion rate was attributed to social workers' reluctance to instigate the PEP through a perception that it represented a bureaucratic exercise rather than a useful document that could improve educational support for young people.

> I think certainly with the assessment framework we have a
> tendency to want to do things to a level of quality rather
> than a paperwork exercise. Social workers are much
> more concerned with doing something that means
> something rather than just ticking boxes to say there's a
> PEP.
> *(Wentown: Social Services Officer)*

To some extent this argument may create a self-fulfilling prophecy. The limited level of completion may have prevented the authority from seriously considering how PEPs might be used to target additional support for young people and to develop strategies to ensure that recommendations contained in the PEP are acted upon. Without such planning in place, social workers may well be given the impression that the PEP had little value. This was certainly evident in the comments of some staff in Wentown.

> I don't think there is any indication yet that what goes
> into the PEPs is going to be acted on and I think that
> links back to the lack of enthusiasm about setting them
> up in the first place.
> *(Wentown: Social Services Officer)*

The authority was attempting to explore avenues through which to adapt the PEP procedure to reflect the needs of different young people and it was hoped that this would encourage social workers to view them as more relevant tools in care planning. The proposed system would see a three-tier level of planning in a '*POPs, HOPs and SHOPs*' scheme. Where young people were in stable supportive placements and appeared to be making good educational progress a POP (Perfectly Ordinary Plan) would be appropriate. If there were greater levels of concern a HOP (Higher Order Plan) would be produced, with a SHOP (Serious Higher Order Plan) being invoked for young people with complex needs. Whilst one might question whether introducing a new tier of bureaucracy is an appropriate response to addressing negative perceptions of the PEP process, the authority is at least showing commitment to addressing the issue.

In Nettbury, the project was seen to have made a significant contribution to the implementation of PEPS, but again the process of improving practice in this area had proved challenging. Indeed, the majority of interviewees commented that without the input of the Project Lead Officer it was doubtful whether many PEPs would have been completed. The Project Lead Officer led on the design and implementation of the authority's PEP pro-forma to ensure standardisation of response from social workers and schools and also developed a form for use with children under five years of age. They also provided considerable advice to social work staff regarding the instigation of PEPs and the level of liaison required with school staff, carers and looked after children.

In order to monitor the quality of the PEPs, an audit of their content was undertaken by the project-funded educational psychologist and the recommendations from this report are to be used to revise and improve current practice where appropriate. The audit of the PEPs revealed some instances of inappropriate target-setting, usually where targets could not be measured, and a degree of missing information. As a consequence, the Project Lead Officer coordinated a training session with social workers on issues of PEP completion. The educational psychologist also used the audit of PEPs to identify young people with complex problems who may need detailed support plans. In such cases, visits to the young person's school were made and – following discussion with teaching staff, social workers and young people – a report outlining potentially effective support strategies was produced. Where less complex issues were apparent, the educational psychologist liaised with social workers to clarify what support arrangements had been instigated as a result of the PEP.

Key personnel in Nettbury felt it was highly important that the audit and ongoing monitoring of PEPs continued to ensure that they were used properly to enhance the educational opportunities of looked after children.

> In themselves the PEPs are neither here nor there if
> we're not actually going to look at what's in them and
> find out what is going on – are the things mentioned in
> them actually happening? I think that's the positive thing
> about using [the educational psychologist] to review the
> quality of the forms. At least we're thinking about
> whether this is a useful form that we can use to support
> young people better.
> *(Nettbury: Education Officer)*

The review and monitoring of PEPs in Nettbury is likely to continue in the near future. Project funding has been used to appoint a PEP co-ordinator, who will work with managers of all services to ensure that PEPs are completed and that there is an understanding of the need to make good use of the action points and targets that they contain.

Summary

- Developing a corporate approach was described by interviewees as the most important factor when promoting educational outcomes for looked after children.

- Statements of corporate parenting practice, or whole authority policies, constitute an essential base on which individual department/service level documents can be built.

- The Project Lead Officers played a major role in maintaining project momentum and facilitating policy and practice change in all three authorities. The seniority of the post helps bridge departments' and agencies' different approaches and priorities and contributes to developing and sustaining a corporate approach.

- None of the three project authorities had been able to solve the problem of routinely sharing accurate and up-to-date information about looked after children's academic progress. Most problems seemed to stem from the poor accuracy and long delays in inputting data, rather than to technical difficulties in sharing the information between services.

■ The project is seen to have raised awareness of the need to consider educational issues when identifying care placements. However, the urgency with which some placement decisions have to be made and the shortage of foster placements available have contributed to limiting progress in this area.

■ Awareness-raising and regular monitoring were seen as positive factors contributing to maintaining a corporate overview of school admissions and exclusion policies as they affect looked after children. Delays when securing school placements have been reduced and improvements are expected to be reinforced when amendments to the School Admission Code of Practice come into practice in September 2004 (Department for Education and Skills, 2003).

■ Considerable progress has been achieved in ensuring that roles and responsibilities of corporate parents are clearly understood. However, further work needs to be done in order to embed such understanding in all agencies and all levels of staff.

■ Consultation with looked after children on educational issues has benefited from the project's contribution.

■ Designated teachers for looked after children are present in all LEA-maintained schools in the three authorities. However, some doubts have been expressed about the understanding and awareness of the designated teachers' roles and responsibilities. Specific training has been provided but attendance is an issue, in particular amongst designated teachers working in schools where no looked after children are placed.

■ The project is seen to have played an essential part in the introduction of Personal Education Plans (PEPs) in the two authorities where completion rates are high. Project activities contributed to the design, development, implementation and monitoring of PEPs.

6. Inter-professional working

The acknowledgement that different facets of children and young people's lives are inextricably related has led to increased calls for collaboration between different agencies and professionals working to address a range of social problems. The poor educational attainment of looked after children is one such issue. As previously noted, past research has shown that key departments involved in looking after children were not always successful in communicating effectively in order to share relevant information and co-ordinate services (Audit Commission 1994; Borland and others 1998; Roaf and Lloyd 1995). A major aim of the *Taking Care of Education* project was to promote and improve collaborative work within and between local authority departments and services so as to develop a whole authority approach to the education of looked after children. In addition, a key feature of the Joint Guidance (Department for Education and Employment/Department of Health 2000) is the need for local authorities to establish and enforce joint procedures and protocols to promote effective inter-agency collaboration.

There is a large body of research highlighting factors that support inter-agency work (Atkinson and others 2002; Atkinson and others 2001; Roaf 2002; Sloper and others 1999; Stobbs 1995; Webb and Vulliamy 2001; Wilson and Charlton 1997) and many of these are reflected in the Joint Guidance. This chapter outlines what these supportive factors might be and illustrates their relevance, in the three project authorities, to achieving collaboration in the education of looked after children. It also highlights barriers that have diminished capacity for joint working and illustrates some of the strategies adopted to deal with these.

Throughout this chapter the term 'inter-professional work' is used to refer to cooperative practice relating to the education of looked after children. A variety of other terms are used to describe the ways in which different agencies, disciplines and professions attempt to work together. This can mean that it is unclear whether different commentators are referring to the same thing. However, as Leathard (1994) sensibly points out, 'What everyone is really talking about is learning and working together' (p.12). Leathard argues that the phrase 'inter-professional work' is often the most useful term to capture the relationships and reciprocal operations between distinct groups of individuals working with others in specialist capacities. Using the term 'inter-professional work' acknowledges the changing structures within an increasing number of local authorities where Social Services and Education departments have merged into broader agencies. In such cases, there may be a temptation to assume that issues concerning inter-agency or multi-agency practice are no longer relevant. However, within such agencies, professionals from distinct cultures are still required to work collaboratively in the same manner as individuals from agencies with separate boundaries. The term 'inter-professional' can be applied irrespective of the organisational structure within an authority to cover instances of collaborative practice between different professional disciplines at both strategic and operational levels.

Commitment to joint working

Inter-professional work is thought to be enhanced where firm commitment to the importance of joint work, demonstrated by shared aims and objectives, is displayed by relevant staff at both strategic and operational levels (Atkinson and others 2002; Department for Education and Skills 2002a; Hudson and others 1997; Wigfall and Moss 2001). It is also argued that strong commitment from the most senior management levels is particularly important (Roaf 2002). During the first phase of interviews in the current evaluation, personnel in all three local authorities believed that strong commitment to inter-professional practice was already evident amongst senior management staff in both Education and Social Services departments. In addition, as noted in previous research (Rea Price and Pugh 1996; Stobbs

1995), firm backing from elected members was seen as significant in promoting inter-professional work.

> We have regular meetings between key elected members of the political structure with responsibility for Education and Social Services, and the chief officers of those departments, and a regular and automatic item on the agenda is always children in care and how we have progressed in, for example, sorting out service-level agreements.
>
> *(Allborough: Social Services Officer)*

Despite such evidence of commitment to inter-professional work amongst senior managers and elected members, at the outset of project activity, staff in all three authorities expressed concern that such commitment did not generally permeate to operational staff.

> There's quite a lot of joined-up thinking at the top, our difficulty is in getting it delivered on the ground.
>
> *(Wentown: Education Officer)*

The predominant explanation for the lack of inter-professional practice at operational levels was conflicting priorities within the workload of teachers and social workers. In keeping with the observations of Francis (2000), it was felt that the workload of social workers could prevent them from viewing educational issues as a priority over urgent placement issues and dealing with emotional and physical needs.

> Social workers are carrying too big a caseload and so they are not able to spend as much time doing the preventative work liaising with schools that you need to do to stop things like exclusions, poor attendance, and just falling behind from happening.
>
> *(Nettbury: Education Officer)*

Likewise, as noted by Jackson and Sachdev (2001), pressure on teaching staff to meet performance targets for whole school populations was not viewed as conducive to establishing and maintaining regular communication with social workers where looked after children were concerned.

> Schools have such a difficult job matching their own kind
> of performance indicators and tables and getting them to
> think of looked after children as anything more than an
> inconvenience is still a bit of a task.
> *(Wentown: Social Services Officer)*

Comment was also passed that there was not enough emphasis from senior
management, within individual departments of Education and Social
Services, on the need for operational staff to liaise with other professionals
regarding the education of looked after children.

> There is a gap between the strategic level and the
> operational level in both departments and that's
> something that needs working on. We can't necessarily
> expect operational staff to carry forward joint work if we
> haven't really communicated to them why it is so
> important and how they might do it.
> *(Allborough: Social Services Officer)*

It was observations of this kind that led Dyson and others (1998) to
comment that:

> good inter-agency cooperation, therefore, depends to a
> large extent on the capacity of large and complex
> organisations to put their own house in order and
> strengthen their own internal cohesion. (p.74)

However, the extent to which agencies are able to influence 'internal
cohesion' may vary. This is of particular relevance to inter-professional
approaches involving education services. Since the 1988 Education Reform
Act enabled schools to take responsibility for much of their budget, the
power of Local Education Authorities (LEAs) to achieve consistency across
schools in certain policy areas has diminished. Schools are often viewed as
autonomous units with very different policies on discipline, exclusions, and
levels of tolerance towards pupils with emotional and behavioural problems
(Webb and Vulliamy 2001). This has inherent difficulties for inter-
professional work in such areas, as LEAs may be unable to influence school
decision-making. The views of some staff in the current study certainly
suggested that the relative autonomy of schools could present barriers to
inter-professional working.

> The way the whole education system is set up now, the
> schools are like satellites. So you can't just go to one
> person and get things to filter out from there. It's quite
> difficult to build those relationships because it's often
> down to individual heads and governors.
> *(Wentown: Social Services Officer)*

Over the course of the project, joint working at operational levels was
thought to have improved. Two main reasons were given as explanations for
this change. First, statutory government requirements surrounding Personal
Education Plans (PEPs) had promoted joint work at operational levels.
Social workers and teachers were required to collaborate to complete PEPs,
and this had frequently necessitated joint training sessions to discuss the
requirements of compiling and maintaining PEPs. This confirms previous
observations that legal imperatives can help to overcome the challenges of
inter-professional work (Hudson 1987; Stobbs 1995).

Second, activities associated with the *Taking Care of Education* project had
promoted joint practice at operational levels. In all three authorities, Project
Lead Officers had initiated inter-professional training sessions amongst
operational staff such as teachers, field social workers, residential and foster
carers, school nurses and education welfare officers. Interviewees believed
such training would have a sustainable impact on levels of inter-professional
practice. In addition, involvement from individual schools had improved in
one authority due to project activity. The high profile of the *Taking Care of
Education* project, combined with the Project Lead Officer's inclusive
approach of consulting head teachers on matters of policy, had emphasised
the importance of inter-professional working; and staff believed that, as a
result, Allborough schools were exhibiting a greater commitment to joint
working to meet the educational needs of looked after children.

Whilst engaging schools in inter-professional practice may be a more
complex process due to their relative autonomy from LEA influence, the
evidence from this authority suggests that many schools are willing partners
in inter-professional work. It may require more effort to communicate and
establish working relationships with a variety of individual schools, but there
was no indication from the current study that schools were unwilling to
participate in inter-professional practice.

Structures to support joint working

Structures such as cooperative agreements, coordinating bodies and multi-professional groups have been found to facilitate inter-professional work (Cigno and Gore 1998; Stobbs 1995; Wigfall and Moss 2001). In the present study, the *Taking Care of Education* project was seen to contribute to such supportive structures. Project Lead Officers in all three authorities were instrumental in developing policy statements to emphasise the need for a corporate approach to underpin the work of all authority departments. Whilst many staff believed that these written statements helped to promote a whole authority approach, they were not seen as adequate mechanisms to ensure effective inter-professional practice. Backing up policy statements with frameworks to translate principles into practice appeared to be of importance.

The different frameworks to support project implementation in each authority, as highlighted in Chapter 2, were seen to influence the ability to support inter-professional working.

In Wentown, the Project Lead Officer met with senior management staff from Education, Social Services and the Corporate Strategy Unit to plan project implementation. However, there were no formal opportunities for inter-professional groups to meet at middle management or operational levels and some personnel felt this could prevent commitment to inter-professional working being translated into practice.

> It's little use getting people to agree to something in principle and then being surprised when they don't actually know how to put that into practice. We need to emphasise: 'Look, here are the frameworks within which you can actually begin to build this into the context of your planning and delivery.'
> *(Wentown: Education Officer)*

In Nettbury, in addition to a project implementation group of the Project Lead Officer and senior managers from Education and Social Services, an inter-professional Project Reference Group was established to discuss project progress and advise on future development. The group included service managers from the Education and Social Services departments, designated teachers and Health Authority representation. This reference group was welcomed as an opportunity to strengthen working relationships between group members from different agencies and to discuss joint working strategies. As with Wentown, though, the reference group in this authority had no formal mechanisms for feeding into strategic or operational planning, and some group members were frustrated that this limited their ability to transform ideas into action.

> I think there are some really interesting ideas developing out of the group but it's not got the capacity to have the strategic clout ... there's no real responsibility taken on from that meeting to get things moving within the departments.
> *(Nettbury: Education Officer)*

The approach to project management and implementation in Allborough appeared to have had a more effective impact on joint working. Personnel believed that the range of coordinating bodies set up to oversee project progress provided the necessary framework to ensure that the written commitment to inter-professional working was also evident in operational practice. The framework in Allborough consisted of a Project Steering Board including senior staff from Education and Social Services departments, elected members, a school governor, head teacher, and a Health Authority representative. The board approves project implementation plans, monitors progress and amends plans where necessary. An Executive Group consisting of the Project Lead Officer and senior managers from Education and Social Services then allocates project priorities to a range of inter-professional task groups charged with carrying forward the work. Representatives from the task groups met regularly in an inter-professional reference group, and progress reports arising from this forum were communicated to the project board. The establishment of this series of inter-professional coordinating groups was viewed by many personnel as crucial to ensuring the sustainability of a joint working approach.

> I believe that those sort of institutionalised systems and
> bridges between the services is the one big factor that we
> will be left with and I believe that will be for the good.
> *(Allborough: Education Officer)*

It was also felt that the framework engendered progress by making task
groups accountable since they must provide regular feedback to the project
board. In addition, the board's ability to modify implementation plans based
upon feedback from the task groups could result in a sense of ownership for
the project implementation plan amongst operational staff. Indeed, the use
of small inter-professional task groups may be the most effective way to
progress joint working. Roaf (2002) concluded that effective inter-
professional working is facilitated better by smaller inter-professional teams
than by creating large 'inter-agency agencies'.

The model of inter-professional practice in Allborough resembled the joint
working approach described by the Social Services Inspectorate (Department
of Health 2003c) in their analysis of Children's Services Plans, whereby inter-
professional groups develop plans towards which different agencies are
supported to work operationally. In addition, the approach can also be seen
to incorporate elements of a 'shared responsibility model' of inter-
professional practice (Dyson and others 1998) as formal communication at
strategic level is reinforced by inter-professional planning groups at service
delivery level, and these groups fed-back in turn to senior management.

Strong leadership

A great deal of the progress achieved in the project authorities was
attributed to having a dedicated Project Lead Officer to maintain a constant
drive towards the achievement of a whole authority approach and fulfil the
role of a 'champion for children in public care' as recommended in the
Joint Guidance (Department for Education and Employment/Department
of Health 2000). Many personnel believed this had enabled their authority
to progress more rapidly in a joint working manner than would be possible
without input from the Project Lead Officer.

> I think having someone with that privileged position of
> not having any day-to-day responsibilities other than to
> try to influence and change policy and practice, and
> promote the whole joined-up thinking approach, is a
> really good thing. Sadly, it's not something that local
> authorities can usually afford.
> *(Nettbury: Education Officer)*

The ability of the Project Lead Officer to promote joint working practice and achieve sustainable change, appeared to depend upon both the personal skills of the officer and their position within the authority. In all three authorities, Project Lead Officers were praised for their interpersonal skills and enthusiasm, and their ability to convince personnel of the importance of inter-professional cooperation.

The importance of a having an individual with a strong personality and 'passion' to drive inter-professional work was also noted by Coles and others (2000). However, in the current study, personality and leadership skills were viewed as necessary, but not sufficient, factors in promoting inter-professional work. The positioning of the Project Lead Officer's post, both in terms of status and structural position within the authority, was also seen to be an important factor in determining the degree of influence they had. In Allborough and Nettbury, the seniority of the position was specifically mentioned as a beneficial factor. In addition to the status of the Project Lead Officer's post, their position within the structure of the authority was also thought to be important. The Project Lead Officers were placed within Social Services departments, although they were line-managed jointly by assistant directors from Education and Social Services. This line management function was seen to ensure that Project Lead Officers could promote, to senior management staff in both departments, the profile of a whole authority approach. Their physical positioning within Social Services was seen as an additional benefit by enabling them to maintain daily contact with middle management and operational staff in this department. This was thought to have contributed greatly to promoting the need for inter-professional practice amongst field social work staff. In Wentown, the Project Lead Officer was placed within the Corporate Strategy Department of the authority to emphasise corporate responsibility for the education of looked after children. However, some personnel felt this positioning did not allow adequate influence within Education and Social Services and made the post appear peripheral to middle management and operational staff.

> It's really helped having [the Project Lead Officer] placed here, even if it's just by having someone called Lead Officer for the Education of Looked After Children making social workers think more about the educational side. But of course it's done much more than that because [the Project Lead Officer] is on hand to answer queries about education, tell people who they should be linking up with and that makes things much better I think.
>
> *(Nettbury: Social Services Officer)*

Perhaps because of the centrality of the role to the development of the project, Project Lead Officers could feel isolated in their work. Being a 'champion' and a 'catalyst' also poses particular challenges. The support structures available to them were therefore of significance. As explained in Chapter 2, the National Children's Bureau Pupil Inclusion Unit had worked with the authorities in the setting-up of the project, and was to have a continuing role in providing assistance to the Project Lead Officers in their work. Additionally, a multi-disciplinary Reference Group was established.

There appeared to be a lack of clarity in the way in which the roles of both the Pupil Inclusion Unit and the Reference Group were defined, at least from the perspectives of the Project Lead Officers. All three Project Lead Officers felt that this had diminished the amount of support available to them. This was particularly significant in the early stages, when the absence of a job description left them feeling somewhat adrift. When questioned about this during early interviews, disappointment was expressed that, despite being linked to the Pupil Inclusion Unit, there was little contact and they did not benefit from being part of a wider NCB network. This latter point was the source of much regret, in that all three were keen to find out more about practice in relation to the education of looked after children in other parts of the country. Equally, the role of the Reference Group was viewed with dissatisfaction, in that the Project Lead Officers felt it had not acted as the 'critical friend' they had hoped for. The way in which the

Reference Group was used to approve funding for the authorities also introduced some ambiguity.

This lack of clarity about the respective functions of the Pupil Inclusion Unit and the Reference Group were to some extent shared by these bodies, complicated by the fact that the person who had led the negotiations on setting-up *Taking Care of Education* with the local authorities left just as the project was about to be implemented. The new head of the Pupil Inclusion Unit also felt that the relationship with the Project Lead Officers had evolved in a way that was at odds with her expectations, in that the local nature of the projects in each authority seemed to limit the need for the Unit's direct involvement. Overall, then, it seemed that some of the strengths of the project – for example in terms of the flexibility surrounding implementation – had led to some confusion about both the needs of the Project Lead Officers and the role of the Pupil Inclusion Unit and Reference Group in meeting these needs. These problems might have been eased had some firmer ideas about the overall structure of the project and its development been in place from the outset. The time-limited nature of the project made the idea that this could evolve naturally somewhat unrealistic.

As the project progressed, some improvements were discerned in these relationships. There were some more meetings between Project Lead Officers and the Pupil Inclusion Unit and the former said that they could go to the Unit for information. The quality of discussion at the Reference Group meetings was also felt to have improved, and the Project Lead Officers welcomed the changes made to the arrangements for approving additional funding. However, as time moved on there was also simply a growing sense of acceptance on the part of the Project Lead Officers that they were not going to receive the amount and type of support they had initially hoped for. All three emphasised the challenges inherent in their work, and highlighted the importance of the support they received from the other Project Lead Officers.

Adequate resources

The promotion of inter-professional practice has various resource implications in terms of adequate time to develop and maintain joint working practices (Atkinson and others 2001; Stobbs 1995) and adequate financial resources to allocate to joint activities (Arblaster and others 1996; Sutton 1995). In all three project authorities it was felt that personnel rarely had sufficient time to devote to inter-professional practice. In keeping with the observations of Atkinson and others (2002), staff were described as frequently having to juggle a range of priorities, and constantly having to adapt to working towards new local and national initiatives. In both Education and Social Services departments, personnel reported there were limits on the time available to move beyond core roles to focus on joint work. In some instances, project activity could exacerbate this situation due to the time required to attend inter-professional meetings. Nonetheless there was a perception that, over time, joint working practice became a matter of course and the level of effort and input required lessened.

> Yes, fitting in additional working groups and so on doesn't come easy. The Gatsby project itself is of course increasing the workload, but I think there's now a fundamental understanding that it's something that is part of everyone's objectives. People understand it in relation to Quality Protects, the objectives for children's life chances for education to be given a higher priority, people understand it in terms of the need for schools to get results and so on. So working in this way can let you meet a number of agendas.
> *(Allborough: Social Services Officer)*

Such comments support the findings of Atkinson and others (2002) that where inter-professional work is in alignment with the targets and priorities of individual agencies, the level of cooperation is likely to be enhanced.

Problems associated with workload issues were compounded by staff shortages. This was particularly relevant to Social Services departments. Staff shortages were perceived to impact upon the success of inter-professional work in two main ways. Firstly, where the workload of existing staff increased because of personnel shortage, individuals were less likely to have the time and energy to devote to inter-professional collaboration. Secondly, the use of agency personnel to compensate for a lack of permanent staff reduced the ability to develop and maintain effective working relationships and communication with other professionals. Although the project could not be seen to lessen staff shortages, some personnel believed that it had lessened the impact of these by creating frameworks whereby liaison with other professionals was expected. Hence, new staff were immediately aware that there was an expectation to create and maintain inter-professional links.

Observations like those of Webb and Vulliamy (2001), that collaborative work could be hindered if agencies felt the need to preserve their own budgets, were also of relevance to the current study. Factors that improved this situation included service level agreements between key departments as well as the influence of the *Taking Care of Education* project. Combining project funds with contributions from key departments so as to deliver more extensive activities was seen to strengthen the view that joint funding could optimise individual departments' use of financial resources.

Effective working relationships

Ensuring that effective working relationships exist both within and between departments involves developing a clear understanding of the role and function of different agencies and individuals (Sloper and others 1999; Wilson and Charlton 1997), and establishing and maintaining regular communication (Atkinson and others 2001; Stobbs 1995). At the outset of the *Taking Care of Education* project there were concerns that, although individuals were willing to work in partnership, misunderstanding of roles and responsibilities could hinder progress. In keeping with observations from previous research (Carlen and others 1992; Hayden 1996; Hayden 1997), this could result in different agencies blaming one another for lack of progress in a given area. The project had helped to highlight instances where professionals arbitrarily attributed blame for lack of progress to other agencies and many staff felt that this helped issues to be addressed. The project's role of reinforcing the education of looked after children as a *corporate* responsibility was seen to have lessened the tendency to seek to blame other agencies for lack of progress.

Reflecting comments regarding commitment to inter-professional practice, concern was expressed that levels of communication between individual schools and operational staff in Social Services departments were in some cases limited. In part, this was attributed to variability across schools, but it was also felt that the Social Services system did not afford sufficient specialisation in educational issues or promote the need for effective communication and liaison between individual social workers and schools.

> The way the local systems work and how they're [social workers] supported and supervised, doesn't build up a team of social workers who are all clued up about this work and know about working with schools and linking in with them regularly.
> *(Allborough: Education Officer)*

A number of project activities had aimed at fostering a better understanding of the working of different agencies. Inter-professional training sessions and work-shadowing opportunities were seen to have contributed to further understanding of other professionals' roles and responsibilities. Echoing the findings of Wigfall and Moss (2001), joint training activities were highly valued by personnel in the current study as a means of crossing boundaries and developing trust between staff.

> The more opportunities you can take people from different agencies and get them in that setting together, the more chance you've got of understanding one another and actually moving things forward together.
> *(Nettbury: Education Officer)*

As noted in Chapter 5, Wentown's Project Lead Officer had set up a work-shadowing scheme, whereby residential and field social workers and teaching staff took up opportunities to shadow one another's working practice over six half-day sessions. The scheme was welcomed by a number of staff, who believed it would enhance understanding of each professional's working practice. However, while the authority reported positive feedback from those who participated, it proved difficult to keep staff on the scheme due to workload pressures. Of the original 12 staff (five designated teachers, four social workers and three residential cares), six had continued with the scheme, but only three had been able to complete the intended six half-day sessions of work shadowing.

Difficulties with attendance on training schemes were not specific to Wentown. As discussed in Chapter 5 in relation to designated teachers, the Project Lead Officers and other personnel in all three authorities reported disappointment in levels of attendance at training sessions from social workers, residential carers, foster carers and education staff alike. There appeared to be a perception that attendance was more likely from individuals who were already motivated to support young people's education and appreciated the need for joint working. The challenge for the authorities was to involve 'harder to reach' groups of professionals who perhaps did not appreciate the relevance of the training to their role. This may be a particular problem in relation to schools that admit looked after children only very occasionally.

> The problem with the training is attendance and trying to get teachers along from schools that don't normally have looked after children. It's very hard. I know teachers are pressed for time and have a hectic workload, but I think something has to be done about encouraging greater attendance at these training sessions.
> *(Nettbury: Education Officer)*

> I know there have been gaps, I know there have been occasions when people have been scheduled to attend training and haven't. So as long as there are examples of that then, yes the training is good but we are not complacent about that. There are still groups of carers that we need to encourage to come along.
> *(Allborough: Social Services Officer)*

Strategies to address these issues were being developed in all three authorities. In Allborough, proposals were underway to organise smaller scale inter-professional training forums organised around school clusters, so that professionals working with the same groups of young people could discuss issues of particular relevance to their needs in supporting young people's education. It was hoped that making the training more relevant would encourage more people to take up training opportunities. In Nettbury, the Project Lead Officer had also considered organising training using school clusters. In addition, the Project Lead Officer suspected that the inter-professional training held with teachers and social workers in Nettbury may not have been as productive as desired. There was a sense that the limited understanding of educational issues amongst social workers and the restricted understanding of the care system from an education perspective caused some staff to become defensive and rigid in relation to their own professional boundaries. In such a context, the idea of promoting joint work and understanding of respective roles was not easily achieved. To address this, a strategy of holding separate training sessions for teachers, social workers and carers on issues of joint working was introduced. Having delivered training to enable an understanding of the constraints under which each profession operates, the training will then be delivered in inter-professional groups. In Wentown, the Project Lead Officer revised the work-shadowing scheme into an intensive two-day programme. It took place late in 2003, this time attracting 11 participants.

Additional factors appeared to undermine the significant efforts made in all three authorities to promote more effective working relationships and inter-professional communication. There was evidence that certain staff were resistant to the changes in working practice associated with movement towards a joint working approach.

> One of the issues that we are coming up against is 'We have always done it this way, we can't manage looking at it any differently.' I don't think there is a practical problem at all, I think it is about changing hearts and minds.
>
> *(Allborough: Education Officer)*

The *Taking Care of Education* project was thought to contribute to 'changing hearts and minds' by continually promoting the importance of a corporate approach. Many personnel reported that the project had begun to convince even the most reluctant members of staff of the merits of inter-professional collaboration. Nonetheless, factors such as organisational restructuring or staff changes could still represent barriers to effective joint working relationships. Staff turnover had occurred in all three authorities and, in two, major departmental restructuring had involved changes of personnel in key posts. Whilst this did not affect commitment to inter-professional collaboration, it could result in a moratorium whilst new working relationships were established.

> Departmentally there's no wavering of commitment at all but clearly when you have got new individuals coming into different roles then work has to be done to ensure that relationships are sustained. Rebuilt is not quite the right word, but established with new people in new roles so that people understand working practices.
> *(Wentown: Social Services Officer)*

It was accepted that the project could not in itself prevent or avoid the disruption associated with departmental restructuring and staff change. Encouragingly, though, the continuity provided by the project and the Project Lead Officers could serve to act as a continuing reminder of the importance of an ethos that promoted joint working amidst these changes.

Information sharing

Joint working is thought to be more effective where inter-professional communication includes sharing accurate and up-to-date information (Atkinson and others 2002; Hallett 1995). This is reflected in the Joint Guidance (Department for Education and Employment/Department of Health, 2000) by the inclusion of the statutory duty that local authorities establish protocols for sharing relevant information. The importance of effective information sharing in terms of promoting the welfare of looked after children has also been highlighted by the Social Exclusion Unit (2003) and the Green Paper *Every Child Matters* (2003).

Developments in this area in each of the project authorities are obviously reinforced by the Joint Guidance but, as noted in Chapter 5, the *Taking Care of Education* project was seen to have enhanced significantly the authorities' ability to respond to the information needs of different groups of professionals. Project Lead Officers had contributed towards developing information-sharing protocols agreed by Education and Social Services. However, as in Webb and Vullimay's (2001) study, ethical issues concerning client confidentiality had caused much debate over the types of information to which staff in both departments should have access. Negotiating the complexities of issues like client confidentiality and access to information had lengthened the process of developing protocols.

> There has been a good deal of confusion about what data Education can share with Social Services – are we allowed to share it, should we share it, or should we just hold it and give it when Social Services wants it for their own SSI returns etc? People weren't sure of the implications for confidentiality and data protection so it took a while to sort that one out.
> *(Wentown: Education Officer)*

Such comments would suggest that there is a need for more direct government guidance to indicate how joint systems should operate and what forms of information need to be routinely shared.

Personnel in all three authorities acknowledged the need to make progress from simply having the capacity to share information; to using it in a constructive manner to target resources appropriately and provide effective support for looked after children's educational progress. It will be of great interest to continue to monitor information-sharing systems in the three authorities as the project progresses into its next phase. It seems likely that the strength of information sharing will depend upon convincing operational staff of the importance and utility of regularly collecting and reporting information about the educational progress and care history of looked after children. One way to achieve this would be to ensure that the outputs of the system are meaningful to school staff and social workers and enable them to highlight swiftly any apparent deterioration in progress so that remedial action can be considered.

Summary

■ The study indicates that strong commitment to inter-professional working – even when originating from the most senior managers and backed by legal imperatives – is not sufficient to bridge the different approaches and priorities of services without the use of additional inducements such as financial resources or staff input. It is, nonetheless, regarded as an essential foundation on which to build inter-professional practice.

■ The existence of joint meetings and structures and the capacity of such forums to influence strategic decision-making and carry forward operational plans, appear necessary to the translation of principle into practice. Small inter-professional groups accountable to a coordinating body appear to be the most conducive to efficient inter-professional working.

■ Lack of understanding of respective roles and responsibilities amongst services; resistance to changes; staff turnover and service restructuring; as well as insufficient staffing, appear to have been some of the main barriers to inter-professional working. The project's constant promotion of the importance of a corporate approach seems to have contributed to minimising and overcoming the effects of such barriers.

■ The project has contributed significantly to improving information-sharing in all three authorities. The two main issues highlighted by the evaluation programme are the ethical difficulties surrounding sharing confidential information between departments and the importance of keeping up-to-date and accurate data.

■ A great deal of the progress achieved in terms of promoting joint working was attributed to having a dedicated Project Lead Officer. The personal skills and enthusiasm of the post holders were seen as necessary but insufficient in term of promoting joint working. The influence of the Project Lead Officers was clearly related to their seniority and structural position.

■ Heavy workloads and staff shortages limit the time available to inter-professional work, but there is a perception that, over time, joint working practice can become a matter of course and the level of effort and input required lessen.

7. Motivating and supporting looked after children

> Motivation to learn is a competence acquired through general experience but stimulated most directly through modelling, communication of expectations, and direct instruction or socialisation by significant others (especially parents and teachers).
> *(Brophy 1987)*

The relationship between motivation to learn and academic success is well documented, with higher levels of motivation being associated with higher levels of attainment (Meece and McColskey 2001; Tomlinson 1993; Wentzel 1997). Children and young people who lack motivation to learn do not tend to view themselves as basically competent and their ability to engage with educational activities and challenges can be greatly diminished (Lumsden 1994).

If one accepts Brophy's definition of motivation to learn as an acquired competence it is plausible that the individual and combined effects of pre-care disadvantage, distress of leaving home and entering the looked after system and subsequent limitations in compensating for disadvantage, serve to de-motivate looked after children and contribute to educational failure. In promoting educational success, therefore, a key issue may be determining which factors appear to motivate looked after children's ability to learn and become involved with education. This chapter focuses on what these factors might be.

Interest and encouragement

Research indicates that some looked after children and young people believe their educational progress was enhanced through teachers and carers taking an active interest in their education and providing positive encouragement (Fletcher 1993; Lynes and Goddard 1995; Shaw 1998). A detailed study of factors contributing to educational success amongst looked after children found the most frequently mentioned factor was receiving positive encouragement from significant others (Jackson and Martin 1998; Martin and Jackson 2002): the significant others mentioned being foster carers, residential carers and parents.

The current study lent support to such findings. Twenty-three young people (42 per cent of the follow-up sample) reported improvements in their educational progress and 18 young people (32 per cent), whose reported progress was maintained at above average levels, tended to attribute their success to the receipt of encouragement and interest in education from carers.

> I still get a lot of help with homework and support and interest and so I make the effort to do it and I don't know, I just pay more attention in school and everything. Because I'm settled here big time now I've got enough energy in the morning to actually get up and look forward to school and bring work back to do at home [foster placement] that I didn't when I was at home with my Mum.
> *(12 year old, foster care)*

> Staff did encourage me to stay in school and stuff. So on the whole I suppose it helped me to do better, 'cos they encouraged me to stick at it.
> *(16 year old, residential care)*

Conversely, young people reporting deterioration in their educational progress, or maintained poor progress, cited the absence of effective support from carers as a major explanation for their poor achievement.

> When I was living in children's homes no one else went
> to school so I started to think I didn't have to go as well.
> The staff didn't seem interested in whether I went in or
> not so I just drifted.
> *(17 year old, independent living)*

> One of the places I ended up in was just disgusting,
> absolutely filthy, I got a real shock that they could expect
> children to be put there, but I was dumped there for a
> couple of months. It really was unbelievably bad and
> there was no way I could sit in there and do homework
> and stuff. Plus the carer, if you can call them that, didn't
> even bother to notice if you went to school or not.
> *(18 year old, independent living)*

Showing a positive interest in young people's educational progress was not
restricted to carers. A number of young people believed their education had
benefited from the increased range of individuals taking an interest in their
development, including carers, teachers and social workers.

> Better because when I was at my parents they would just
> give in on me, they'd give up, I put them through a lot
> and I did that at first with some of the carers. But I've
> had some really nice people who are out there you know,
> carers, social workers, teachers, all these people taking an
> interest and who've just like stuck with me and kicked me
> into action, you know.
> *(18 year old, residential care)*

> Yes, I think it's better because I'm in care just because
> I've got a lot more people looking out for me and trying
> to help me to get a good education.
> *(14 year old, foster care)*

Acknowledging achievement

Fletcher-Campbell (1997) emphasises the value of acknowledging and celebrating the achievements of looked after children. Recognition of achievement does indeed appear to be a key factor in motivating young people to learn and engage with school activities (Alderman 1999; Pisapia and Westfall 1994).

Young people in the current study appeared well aware of the positive impact that recognition of their efforts and achievements could have upon educational progress. Where carers were seen to provide praise for behaviour and attainment this could serve to promote further success.

> When I've done well she's [foster carer] really proud.
> The other day I got two commendations and then I
> told her and she was like 'oh, that's really, really good!'
> That makes me want to keep doing my best.'
> *(12 year old, foster care)*

Without such recognition of effort and attainment young people commented that it was easy to become disillusioned with education and disengaged from their studies.

> Just knowing that there is someone there who takes a bit
> of notice if you do something well, or even bawls you out
> if you've gone off the rails. I think that makes all the
> difference. Otherwise it gets too easy to think 'Well, if no-
> one else is bothered, what do I care?'
> *(17 year old, independent living)*

As well as acknowledging young people's efforts through verbal praise, some young people greatly appreciated the opportunity to earn rewards from their carers as an added incentive to apply themselves to their studies.

> My foster carers help to support me, they're good at
> encouraging me to revise and study, they're like 'If you
> want to get your exams, it's up to you to work at it.' They
> try and get me to work harder at my homework too,
> taking more time and doing it carefully. If I work hard

> they give me rewards, like they have paid for me to go to
> see football matches and things, that helps me try better.
> *(15 year old, foster care)*

The motivating force of being rewarded for achievement was also apparent
from the school experiences of some young people who had benefited from
commendation systems.

> School helps me work hard really. I've got some
> commendations which is a sticker, but it's more than a
> sticker, and it's like saying very well done sort of thing if
> you do a really good piece of work or something. I've got
> five so far and if you get 40 then you get a voucher but I
> haven't reached that yet, but I want to try.
> *(12 year old, foster care)*

In addition to the practice of individual carers and schools, the *Taking Care
of Education* evaluation was also able to gain insight into the impact of
corporate attempts to reward and acknowledge young people's
achievements. Project funding was used in all three authorities to initiate or
expand activities designed to celebrate young people's success.

All three project authorities held awards ceremonies for looked after
children that enabled their achievement to be recognised in areas such as
improved attendance, punctuality, behaviour, and academic performance.
Almost all young people included in the follow-up sample were aware of
these ceremonies and there was unanimous agreement that the events were
most enjoyable. In addition, the majority of young people also commented
that they might well serve to motivate further progress.

> Yes I have had an award for educational achievement
> from Nettbury Social Services. I went along on the day
> and saw the mayor and we had a party thing. It was really
> good. I'll probably work harder this year to try and get
> another one.
> *(15 year old, foster care)*

Fletcher-Campbell (1997) argues that such public award ceremonies are not
only important in terms of individual recognition, but also because they
promote to professionals, local politicians and the wider community, positive

images of looked after children's success. Indeed, comments gathered from local authority personnel seemed to indicate that the introduction of awards ceremonies were helping to communicate positive messages of success.

> What I saw at the awards ceremony was wonderful. Some of those young people have come through very difficult times and have been very challenged themselves and have exceeded everyone's expectations. To have that acknowledged for them, and to show everyone else there what they were capable of, was excellent. We had the local newspapers along and people from the radio station and the young people were just so pleased. I just thought that was wonderful.
>
> *(Allborough: Education Officer)*

In Wentown, the local authority had conducted an awards ceremony for a number of years prior to the introduction of the project, although project funds were used to enhance the scale and profile of the event. However, project funds were also used in Wentown to introduce a novel manner of rewarding young people's achievement. A Rewards for Revision scheme was introduced to offer monetary rewards to young people in Year 11 who obtained GCSE examinations. Money was offered for every examination passed, with bonus amounts being allocated for grade points above predicted levels. The rationale behind the reward was that they would not only acknowledge achievement but it should also motivate young people to apply themselves to their revision programme. The scheme was relatively well known to young people in the study sample and some of these had been eligible for rewards, but they were unsure whether it had helped them to revise as they were only notified about the scheme shortly before sitting their exams. It is obviously important to ensure that such schemes are sympathetic to the timing of the school year, and the Project Lead Officer in Wentown has sought to remedy this problem by circulating information at the start of Year 11. Most of the remaining young people who had not yet taken GCSEs believed it was a good idea and reported that it might make them apply themselves better to their studies, although some believed they would not be affected by the promise of monetary rewards.

Foster carers interviewed in Wentown were all aware of the scheme and the majority welcomed it as a positive method of encouraging young people to succeed. Two carers were frustrated that they had not been consulted regarding involvement in the scheme and stated that they did not think the level of reward was appropriate. In one instance, this was due to a carer claiming that they did not have the financial means to provide equal rewards for their own children who were sitting exams; in another, it was due to a distaste for associating monetary gain with educational application.

> I actually felt that was wrong. I was quite annoyed by that actually. I've sort of taken a lot of effort to stress to [foster child] that he needs to be getting his exams because of the general value of education and the passport to further things like college and university that exams can give you. I think that's a much more important thing to work for than just some quick fix of a hundred quid or so. I'm not saying rewards are a bad thing but it doesn't always have to be a wedge of cash.
> *(Wentown: foster carer)*

Promoting resilience and self-esteem

As Jackson and Sachdev (2001) point out, research clearly indicates that looked after children are subject to numerous risk factors for educational failure. Such risk factors can, however, be mediated by the resilience of the young person. Resilience can be defined as the capacity to develop normally despite adversity (Smith and Carlson 1997) and appears to be associated with motivation to learn and academic engagement, as well as other, non-educational factors (Fergusson and Lynskey 1996; Finn and Rock 1997; Gilligan 1999). Strongly linked to the concept of resilience are notions of self-efficacy and self-esteem.

Self-efficacy is a belief that individuals can influence what happens to them in life and they are active agents in creating and following plans (Houston 1995). Individuals with a strong sense of self-efficacy appear to be more likely to apply themselves to tasks and persevere despite difficulties (Lee and

Bobko 1994). Self-esteem relates to an individual's feeling of their own worth and confidence that they can cope with life's challenges (Curry and Johnson 1990; Rutter 1987). There is a well-documented relationship between self efficacy/self-esteem and academic success; with higher levels of self-efficacy/esteem being associated with higher levels of attainment (Pajares and Schunk 2001; Rotheram 1987; Wiggins 1987). It is argued that this association may be due to individuals with higher self-esteem being more open to learning experiences. Those with a strong sense of their own worth may be more realistic about their achievements and weaknesses since they are not solely dependent upon the judgments of others and can risk being wrong and learning from their mistakes (Atkinson and Hornby 2002).

A number of project activities in the current study acknowledged the importance of the link between resilience/self-esteem and academic engagement and achievement. A range of strategies was employed to attempt to promote the resilience and self-esteem of looked after children.

Perhaps the most focussed of such project activities is found in Nettbury's decision to use project funding, combined with Quality Protects and Standards Fund resources, for a dedicated educational psychologist post for looked after children. The remit of this post was to develop strategies to support the educational and emotional health of looked after children and undertake focused work with them to promote resilience. The psychologist undertook a variety of small-group work with looked after children in the borough's high schools to determine their needs and identify appropriate support. Two young people in the Nettbury sample reported having contact with the psychologist for two or three group sessions. Such initial meetings were appreciated by the young people concerned. The educational psychologist had also been involved in other activities such as consultation with foster and residential carers, to establish their requirements. They also developed training packages to enable them to better support the education of looked after children; and developed systems in the Educational Psychology Service to identify and deal appropriately with looked after children. A number of personnel in the Education Department in Nettbury believed this work would enable professionals to respond more effectively to young people's needs and, as such, had committed funding to continue the post.

> I've heard some anecdotal stuff that the young people
> she's been to see in our schools have benefited from the
> contact. She's also been raising awareness about the
> needs of looked after children within the EP
> [Educational Psychology] service and with the social work
> staff at [residential centre] so they can try to identify and
> address what might be educational problems for looked
> after children. It's all valuable stuff.
>
> *(Nettbury: Education Officer)*

The educational psychologist is to continue to work on issues of resilience promotion. It will be of interest to examine further the impact of this post in the continued evaluation programme.

Another way in which project activities in Nettbury aimed to promote the resilience of looked after children was through opportunities to develop leisure interests and activities. The development of such interests can offer marginalised young people opportunities to 'join or re-join the mainstream' (Smith and Carlson 1997) and may promote resilience by enabling young people to discover a positive pathway through, and out of, life in care (Gilligan 1999). Gilligan outlines a range of resilience-enhancing activities that appear to be of benefit to looked after children and young people, including involvement in cultural pursuits and sporting activities.

Closely tied to the notion of providing opportunities for young people to benefit from leisure and cultural activities is the recent governmental emphasis on the potential contribution of 'out of school hours learning' or 'study support' to school improvement (Department for Education and Employment 1997b). Study support has been defined as activities that are linked to schools and which aim to assist students' learning, raise achievement and/or promote positive personal and social change (Department for Education and Employment 1998). A large body of research from the United States indicates that school students' participation in extra-curricular activities is significantly related to a range of positive outcomes such as academic attainment, academic self-concept, application to homework and good attendance (Brown and Steinberg 1991; Camp 1990; Marsh 1992). Further evidence from the UK suggests that involvement in 'curriculum enriching' activities (such as sports, cultural pursuits, music, dance) is positively related to academic progress in areas such as reading performance and mathematics (Brooks and others 1997; Smith and others 1989) as well as to school conduct and relationships with peers (Posner and Vandell 1994). In addition, study support time involved in 'curriculum extension' activities (academic-related activities) appears to be linked with improved GCSE performance (Pocklington 1996; Tower Hamlets Study Support Project 1997).

In Nettbury and Wentown, project activities were directed towards improving the provision of study support for looked after children through both curriculum extension and enrichment schemes. Curriculum extension projects took the form of after-school homework clubs for looked after children. In Nettbury, a weekly after-school club for looked after children attending middle schools was established in a local library. The club is not intended to be exclusively for homework, but is run by library staff who arrange and supervise a variety of fun, educational activities as well as ensuring that children and young people have access to a range of books and resources that might support homework. In Wentown, a similar scheme has been set up in the form of a Saturday Club for looked after children in school years 5, 6 and 7 in a study centre based at the local football club. The focus of the club is on developing and supporting literacy, numeracy and information technology skills in a relaxed and entertaining environment. In both cases, feedback collected by the Project Lead Officers suggests that the location of the activities away from the school environment was valued by the children involved.

Due to timing, these clubs were not part of the external evaluation. However, a number of schemes that could be classed as curriculum-enriching activities had been running for a sufficient period to enable questions to be asked about their potential benefit. Project funding in Nettbury was used to initiate a pilot leisure pass scheme entitling looked after children, and their foster families, to free entrance to the local leisure centre. Feedback from young people and their carers indicated that the scheme was a success.

> Yes – I had one of the passes. It worked really well
> for me because I'm sporty so I really appreciated being
> able to go more often than I used to.
> *(16 year old, foster care)*

> Yes, because the way they've actually done it was
> excellent, because it's quite expensive for families,
> especially if they're fostering younger children, they've
> got to take their own and those whereas if it's done for
> the family it's really useful.
> *(Nettbury, foster carer)*

As a result of the pilot scheme, the provision of free leisure passes for looked after children has been included in the contract Nettbury holds with the company that runs the leisure centre on its behalf. Concessionary leisure cards are being issued to all looked after children from January 2004 (this would have taken place earlier but for the temporary closure of the leisure centre).

The Project Lead Officer in Nettbury also organised a week-long photography course for looked after children in the summer of 2002. The course was funded by the *Taking Care of Education* project and involved the Arts and Leisure Service, foster and residential carers, FE College and Kodak PLC. The young people who attended spoke enthusiastically about both the social and educational benefits of participating in this scheme.

> Yes. It was a great experience. Absolutely great. We were
> learning all aspects of photography taking the pictures,
> getting perspective, developing them. And it was just so
> much fun but also you were learning about the scientific
> principles behind taking and developing pictures. It was
> brilliant and I got a certificate and things at the end so it
> all adds up.
> *(16 year old, foster care)*

Hopefully, such opportunities for young people to engage in a wider range of learning opportunities will continue in Nettbury. The Arts and Leisure Service agreed to fund a similar course, in collaboration with a national gallery, during the half-term vacation of the 2003 Spring Term. Anecdotal evidence from staff suggests that this was equally as successful as the photography course. The Arts and Leisure service is also planning to develop a range of dance and drama activities for looked after children.

A Youth Participation Worker, jointly funded by the project and Comic Relief funds, has also been undertaking direct work with young people to increase their participation in youth activities and their involvement with the Nettbury Young People's Forum. The worker has also encouraged a number of looked after children to enrol on the Duke of Edinburgh's award scheme. Whilst personnel in both Education and Social Services departments appreciated the contribution of the Youth Participation Worker, young people in the sample were not aware of any activities associated with this role.

A final area of project activity in Nettbury intended to boost young people's self-esteem and resilience lies in a newly established mentoring scheme. Fully trained adult mentors are to provide support for 11–16-year-old looked after children in foster or residential placements, primarily those living outside the authority. The scheme has only just commenced, and young people and key personnel were therefore unable to comment on its efficacy, although all welcomed the idea in principle. If the mentoring scheme should prove successful, it is to be sustained by the wider Nettbury Mentoring Project.

Nettbury was not the only authority to initiate activities to promote the resilience of looked after children. In Wentown, a series of outward-bound residential weekends for looked after children were organised by the Project Lead Officer. The weekends were attended by around 8–10 young people and focused on team-building activities and fostering young people's personal development. The residential weekends were praised by a number of key personnel interviewed in Wentown who felt that they had an impact on young people's self-esteem which might well translate into improved educational performance.

> I think it's built their self-esteem. I think it's broadened
> their horizons in terms of what they could be capable of.
> I think it's got them talking about education in the
> broader sense. I think it's given them really positive
> experience in terms of activities and mixing with other
> children and adults.
> *(Wentown: Social Services Officer)*

The one young person who was part of the evaluation sample and had participated in the weekend also reported that they had greatly enjoyed the experience and would appreciate the opportunity to attend future events.

Another way to promote young people's resilience through involvement in wider learning opportunities in Wentown stems from the Project Lead Officer's involvement in the Local Government Association funded Teenagers to Work scheme. Her involvement extended the scope of this work-experience scheme to enable young people to produce a training video to use with social workers, designated teachers and carers. The video included interviews with 20 looked after children talking about their experiences of education whilst in the care system. The video project generated interest from central government's Social Exclusion Unit, and the Project Lead Officer and the young people were asked to go there to make a presentation as part of the Unit's fourth year celebrations. The young people who helped to produce the training video reported that they had greatly enjoyed this experience.

Encouraging school and college attendance

Obviously, an important element of motivating young people to pursue their education lies in encouraging them to actually attend a school or college to access available learning opportunities. Project activity in Allborough was directed towards promoting school and college attendance from residential centres.

In terms of work within residential centres, an Education Welfare Officer, funded by the *Taking Care of Education* project, provides support to residential staff both to improve young people's school attendance and maintain an overview of young people's educational progress. In addition to this post, Social Services funds – via the Quality Protects programme 'Education Representatives'– key workers with responsibility for supporting the education of looked after children in each of Allborough's residential centres. The representatives meet in a monthly forum, which includes the *Taking Care of Education* Project Lead Officer, the Education Welfare Officer for looked after children, the Senior Librarian for Allborough's schools, and an Advisory Teacher for looked after children. A major part of each meeting is dedicated to discussing school attendance issues, including effective strategies to encourage and maintain regular school attendance. Each residential centre now keeps attendance sheets to record whether young people attend school or college and these are brought to forum meetings to discuss progress made.

Young people in the project sample living in residential centres in Allborough had noticed that staff appeared to be giving more attention to their school attendance and believed this was encouraging more consistent attendance.

> Yes. I think they do that more now at [residential centre], yes. Like when I haven't been to school, they would encourage you to go and like they make you aware of what is going to happen if you didn't go. That you won't get anywhere in life and things.
> *(15 year old, residential care)*

Anecdotal evidence from staff within the local authority also suggested an improvement in attendance figures from residential children's homes.

> I have worked with social services for the last 20 years and I know how difficult it is, particularly for children in residential care certainly, getting them to school and I do feel through conversations with people that certainly seems to be an area that is improving.
> *(Allborough: Social Services Officer)*

In addition, project funding in Allborough was used to introduce a scheme to promote college attendance amongst looked after children. Young people were given the opportunity to earn £30 per week for regular attendance with bonus amounts being available at the end of each college term for a 100 per cent attendance record. The majority of young people in the Allborough follow-up sample (11, that is 65 per cent) were aware of the financial incentives tied to college attendance. Three of these young people were already in receipt of such funding and believed that it had encouraged them to go to college regularly.

> Yes. That £30 a week for attending. I think it is a very good incentive. Because it will make people get out of their beds. I've been attending better because I use the money to put in my savings. It is a really good incentive.
> *(18 year old, foster care)*

Amongst the eight young people who were aware of the scheme but were not yet in further education, three of these believed that it would encourage them to think more seriously about going to college, whilst five believed it would not serve as an added incentive as they were already committed to progressing to further education. All of these young people welcomed the idea and three believed it might encourage greater attendance once they had progressed to college.

A project activity in Wentown, which can in part be classed as aiming to ensure school or college attendance, concerns the funding of a dedicated worker relating to looked after children on the Wentown Vulnerable Pupils Panel (VPP). The VPP aims to identify and work with young people who are at risk of school exclusion or are persistently truanting. The dedicated worker liaises with looked after children to encourage them back into education and also acts as a point of liaison with other agencies involved in these young people's lives. This was not something the young people in the evaluation sample had experienced, but local authority staff believed the worker had experienced some success in enabling young people to participate in mainstream education. The next phase of the *Taking Care of Education* evaluation will monitor the work of the VPP more closely.

Summary

■ Individual and combined effects of pre-care disadvantage, distress in leaving home and entering the looked after system, and shortcomings in compensating for disadvantage are likely to de-motivate looked after children and contribute to educational failure. Determining factors that help to motivate and involve looked after children in education may therefore be a key when promoting educational success.

- The current study supports previous findings: receiving positive encouragements from significant others is the factor most frequently mentioned by young people when explaining their educational success.

- Award ceremonies celebrating the educational achievements of looked after young people was the project activity most mentioned and appreciated by young people.

- Financial incentives for obtaining GCSEs were seen positively by young people but it is uncertain how much an effect the scheme had on their motivation to revise and prepare for the exams.

- The three project authorities developed a range of activities and services aimed at promoting young people's resilience and self-esteem. These included group work with an educational psychologist, specific and long-term schemes aiming at developing and supporting leisure interests, and after-school homework clubs. Although evaluation was not carried out for each individual scheme, young people and key personnel commented positively on most initiatives.

- An education maintenance allowance was introduced in one of the project authorities in order to encourage young people to enter and to attend college. The scheme was well received by young people and appeared to be successful in promoting attendance; there is, however, no evidence that it has helped to increase the number of young people entering further education.

- One of the project authorities also employed a project-funded Education Welfare Officer to provide support to residential staff in both improving young people's school attendance and maintaining an overview of their educational progress. Monthly meetings of all the centre's educational representatives reinforce the support and training available.

8. The school experience

The importance of schools in the majority of children and young people's lives cannot be overstated. Schools have been described as second only to the family in the social, intellectual and behavioural development of children (Consortium on the School-based Promotion of Social Competence 1994) and teachers have more contact with children and young people than any other professionals (Gilligan 1998).

Schools obviously provide young people with the potential to access the curriculum and work towards obtaining examinations. Therefore, at the simplest level they have a key role to play in providing appropriate educational opportunities for looked after children. Research indicates that schools can also serve as an important protective and preventative resource for children experiencing social disadvantage (Rutter 1991) by enabling children to acquire constructive coping skills that allow them to develop normally in spite of adverse circumstances (Fergusson and Lynskey 1996; Smith and Carlson 1997). For many looked after children, school can represent a key element of stability during otherwise turbulent, and potentially traumatic, periods of family breakdown and entering or moving within the looked after system (Borland and others 1998).

Most looked after children attend school regularly and appear to value the importance of education (Shaw 1998; Social Exclusion Unit 2002). Therefore, they may well be able to access some of the beneficial effects of attending schools. However, it would be naive to assume that all schools follow best practice in motivating diverse groups of young people and enabling them to maximise their developmental potential. Variation in

examination pass rates and levels of attendance and exclusion across schools provides an indication that schools are diverse institutions with differential outcomes for young people with a similar social intake. Looked after children are no exception to this rule and variation is evident in the extent to which they are well-served by the schools they attend. A significant number of looked after children do not benefit from successful and stable school experiences due to reasons of exclusion, poor attendance, poorly managed transitions or delays in obtaining a school place, as well as problems that have endured throughout their earlier school careers (Department for Education and Employment/Department of Health 2000).

The Joint Guidance (Department for Education and Employment/ Department of Health, 2000) on the education of looked after children emphasises that these young people have the right to equal access to educational provision and opportunities, and that their individual needs must be sensitively and promptly met so that they can take advantage of those opportunities. This chapter outlines what the current project tells us about the ability of schools to maximise looked after children's opportunities to benefit from their school experience. The discussion is grouped around five main themes relating to:

■ general perceptions of the role of schools regarding looked after children
■ the role of teachers in the education of looked after children
■ the influence of peer relationships within the school setting
■ issues of attendance and exclusion
■ the use of Personal Education Plans (PEPs).

General perceptions of the role of schools in working with looked after children

During the years of statutory school age a vast proportion of young people's time is spent within schools. In spite of this, schools remain surprisingly detached from other child welfare agencies (Gilligan 1998; Lewis 1996). Whilst the recent promotion of Extended schools (Department for Education and Skills 2002a) may help to strengthen links between schools and social welfare agencies, the current research was undertaken before this initiative was likely to have had an impact. Interviews with key personnel across all three authorities revealed a prevalent perception that schools were disparate entities and there were major difficulties in working with individual schools to promote the education of looked after children.

Whilst most personnel agreed that the need to promote the educational opportunities of looked after children was a clear strategic priority for the key departments of Education and Social Services, many suspected that this priority may not be so salient within individual schools. The power of Local Education Authorities (LEAs) to achieve consistency across schools in certain policy areas was seen to have diminished since the 1988 Education Reform Act enabled schools to take responsibility for much of their budget. A number of personnel viewed schools as autonomous units with very different policies on discipline, exclusions, and levels of tolerance towards pupils presenting emotional and behavioural difficulties. This had inherent difficulties for achieving a coherent approach in promoting the educational needs of looked after children.

> Schools are so individual and we haven't got control over
> them, we can't make them all do things in the same way,
> so we can only do the best we can.
> *(Allborough: Education Officer)*

This perception was reflected in the project implementation plans across all three authorities. Apart from a limited range of training sessions for designated teachers, activities directed at school-level were noticeably absent from original plans. Reluctance to use the impetus of the *Taking Care of Education* project to effect school-based change is also evident in the efforts of Nettbury and Wentown to extend the availability of out-of-school-hours learning for looked after children. In both these authorities, the majority of primary and secondary schools already offer a wide range of after-school clubs and in some cases vacation activities are also available. However, project funding was directed towards establishing distinct clubs for looked after children in settings outside schools such as in libraries and sports clubs. The establishment of such homework and after-school clubs represents a laudable effort to ensure that looked after children have access to out-of-school-hours learning opportunities. Nonetheless, it could be argued that more effective involvement might result from collaborative work with schools to identify strategies to promote looked after children's attendance at mainstream clubs. This would represent a more inclusive approach with the potential to enhance young people's engagement with a number of aspects of school life, including developing friendships with their non-looked after peers. In addition, this approach would be more likely to lead to sustainable provision since it would not be tied to project funds.

In subsequent revisions of original project implementation plans, some efforts to work in partnership with schools did emerge in Allborough and Wentown. In Allborough, the Project Lead Officer successfully involved head teachers in negotiations surrounding the preparation of PEPs and appeared to have developed good working relationships with many schools. A number of personnel interviewed in Allborough believed that relationships with individual schools had been strengthened by having a Project Lead Officer with 'solid education credentials'. In Wentown, a work-shadowing scheme was established to enable teachers and social work staff to further their understanding of respective roles and promote awareness of the educational needs of looked after children. Although the scheme initially failed to run in 2003, this was due to limited involvement from Social Services staff rather than schools. In addition, both Allborough and Wentown decided to run training sessions for governors on the education of looked after children and have expressed a continuing commitment to the delivery of such training. These examples suggest that whilst it may require more effort to communicate and establish working relationships with a variety of individual schools, there is no reason to suppose that schools are unwilling partners in efforts to improve the education of looked after children.

The role of teachers in the education of looked after children

Research indicates that teachers can play a highly significant role in the development of looked after children, both in terms of encouraging academic success and providing emotional support to help children cope with distressing experiences (Gilligan, 2000). Educational success is likely to depend on the support of caring teaching staff who understand a young person's individual needs and circumstances and can look beyond any difficult presenting behaviour.

Some looked after children report receipt of additional educational support and encouragement from teachers who know they are looked after (Berridge and others 1996; Shaw 1998; Social Exclusion Unit 2002); and some studies indicate that a number of young people would prefer to confide their anxieties and worries to teaching staff than to social workers (Triseliotis and others 1995). Conversely, other young people report that teachers hold negative perceptions of looked after children that lead them to expect their educational attainment to be low (Biehal and others 1995; Jackson and Sachdev 2001). Indeed, other research indicates that teachers generally hold lower expectations of looked after children's educational attainment than do carers or social workers (Aldgate and others 1993; Francis 2000). However, in both these studies the researchers concluded that teachers' perceptions were based on a realistic reflection of the children's poor prospects rather than being a cause of them. In a study comparing teachers' perceptions of the educational ability of looked after children to those held for non-looked after children there were no apparent differences in assessments of ability, although looked after children were judged less likely to complete homework assignments (Elliot 2002).

In general, studies documenting young people's views of how teachers respond to looked after children provide some stark contrasts. Many positive examples of increased educational motivation due to additional support and encouragement from teachers are contrasted with reported instances of negative stereotyping, low expectations and a failure to understand issues associated with being looked after (Fletcher 1993; Shaw 1998; Harker and others 2003). The current study also found evidence of such diverse experiences.

The majority of young people provided highly positive comments about the supportive role that teachers and schools could play in their lives. When asked to identify individuals who had helped to support their educational progress, teachers were the most frequently mentioned group of individuals at both original and follow-up interviews. Providing support for children to achieve academically was seen as an important function of the teaching role.

Teachers were described as giving additional academic assistance to looked after children who had fallen behind in their studies, or were having difficulties concentrating on work due to problems associated with being looked after. They were also seen to promote self-belief in children's ability by encouraging them to believe that they could succeed academically.

> My head of year and my English teacher. I have a real
> bad problem with English, I couldn't like write essays and
> stuff … and it was putting me down and I didn't like it so
> I sort of gave up and I wouldn't write essays, but my
> English teacher said 'I won't let it go, I am going to get
> you doing this, and you're going to do well in English.'
> He is really good 'cos he lets me go to him and chill out.
> Like if I get worked up one day I can take a lesson out
> and try the work later.
> *(16 year old, foster care)*

Teachers were mentioned not only for providing support with studies. Many children described teachers as providers of emotional support and appreciated the opportunity to discuss worries and anxieties relating to being looked after with a trusted and respected adult.

> I never stopped going to school, even when I was being
> moved from pillar to post. School was the only place I felt
> at home. My friends knew what was going on and so did
> the teachers and they all really helped me. I suppose I
> was a bit weird really 'cos some people don't want to get
> up in the morning to go, but I was the opposite, first one
> in and never used to want to come home at the end.
> *(16 year old, foster care)*

A small number of young people felt that teachers had in some way served to hinder their educational progress. Although only six young people at original and four young people at follow-up interviews held such views, their comments serve to indicate that not all young people benefit from inclusive and supportive teaching practice. Comments about teaching staff hindering progress concerned issues of low expectations and negative stereotyping and a lack of understanding of what it meant to be looked after. It is worth noting that whilst positive comments about teaching staff were relatively evenly distributed across all three authorities, the pattern of negative comments differed slightly according to the authority by which young people were looked after. At both original and follow-up interviews all comments relating to teachers holding negative views and low expectations of young people came from the Wentown sample. These young people believed they had suffered from teachers holding negative stereotypes that looked after children were more likely to exhibit behaviour problems and have lower academic attainment than non-looked after children. One young person recalled having been placed in a lower set due to behavioural problems, although the young person attributed their removal to the teacher's negative perceptions of looked after children.

> Some teachers who I'd say that they didn't really like me because I was in care – they thought I was a troublemaker. Like [teacher], she had to choose between either me or [classmate] to kick out because, fair enough we were sometimes a pain together, but I do think she chose me because she thought I'd get lower grades 'cos I wasn't in a stable family.
> *(18 year old, independent living)*

The interviews that took place with teaching staff in Wentown suggested that some staff held negative views of looked after children.

> I know from the background about her parents that one didn't read or write and the other one was completely innumerate so it's not surprising that the poor child has learning difficulties. I suppose her placement now is far more literate than her previous background but of course there is so much going on in her mind that I don't know how much academically she can absorb ...
> I must say that I think you should be very careful in your study including young people like her. Apart from the fact that one has to be very careful with these children, my concerns about this particular child we've talked about is that her concepts are so limited that I'm not sure

she'd know what she was agreeing to in order to take part. OK you say you explain things fully first and get consent, so if she did volunteer and it was done that way and she knew what she was doing that is fine – but my suspicions are that she didn't have the foggiest of what she was doing. I am just thinking that maybe a caring parent would decide that this child isn't capable of making informed judgements.

(Wentown: primary schoolteacher)

The young person in question did manage to complete both original and follow-up interviews with ease and appeared to have a good understanding of the implications of taking part in the research. She also believed that she had made good academic progress since transferring to secondary school. This perception was supported by the young person's carers, who reported that she was indeed receiving good grades at school and had received a number of commendations during the current academic year. Such observations would certainly not have been predicted from the strikingly pessimistic views of the young person's primary school teacher. It may be that traumatic effects surrounding this young person's entry to the looked after system (a case involving sexual abuse) had caused a decline in this young person's ability to focus and concentrate in school. However, it is worrying to observe that a teacher was quick to assume that the special educational needs of this young person were a potentially insurmountable consequence of their background that could not be redressed by subsequent intervention.

In Allborough and Nettbury, young people did not report teachers holding negative views of them; but they did complain of teachers showing limited awareness of the potential impact that worries and anxieties associated with living away from home and being looked after might have on young people's ability to apply themselves to their studies.

Most of my teachers tried to help, but some of them didn't seem to understand how many worries I had and why I couldn't concentrate.

(17 year old, foster care)

In some cases this may have been due to teachers not actually being aware that a young person was looked after. Some young people wished for their looked after status to be relatively confidential but this could be problematic. Two young people reported that class teachers' lack of awareness of their looked after status had resulted in embarrassment when their absences due to care review meetings were queried in front of classmates.

> One of the teachers last year really embarrassed me because I had a six-month review thing and I was late to school. I went in after the lesson started and he said 'how come you're late?' and he sort of embarrassed me in front of the class. I couldn't think what to say and again he goes 'so why are you late?' and he shouted it out. So I went 'oh, I had an appointment' but it wasn't enough and he goes 'what sort of an appointment?' and I was like 'erm, my mum will send in a note tomorrow'. So [foster carer] wrote in a letter explaining everything – well not like the situation but just to say she's in foster care, can you not bring it up in front of the class and stuff.
> *(12 year old, foster care)*

The role of the designated teacher

Government guidance on the education of children in public care introduced the concept of designated teachers within all LEA-maintained schools. Such teachers are intended to act as the key link within the school for looked after children, and to act as the main channel of communication with other professionals regarding any looked after child. Although this initiative can be seen to be government-driven, in all three authorities project activity was to some degree directed towards this area, mainly through contributions to training for designated teachers. Therefore, it was of interest to establish young people's awareness of, and attitude towards, designated teachers.

Young people were asked if they were aware of the concept of designated teachers for looked after children within schools. Where young people claimed they had not heard of the term 'designated teacher' (or 'looked after link teacher' in the Wentown sample) a brief definition of the designated teacher role, based on information in the government guidance, was given to them and they were again asked whether they had any knowledge of such a role. Those young people who were aware of the role were asked to describe any contact they may have had with a designated teacher and for their assessment of the benefits of providing designated teachers for looked after children.

It emerged that 24 young people (44 per cent) had heard of the designated teacher role, while the remaining 31 young people (56 per cent) reported that they had no knowledge of it. Of the young people who had heard of the designated teacher, only six had experienced some form of contact with the designated teacher: two in Allborough, three in Nettbury and one in Wentown. Three young people commented on receiving pastoral support from their designated teacher, but in each case the teacher concerned was already cast in a pastoral role for that young person, either as form tutor or head of year. Hence, young people were unable to clarify whether they received additional support due to their looked after status.

> Yes, 'cos it's my head of year so I have contact with him anyway. He'll ask me in for a chat about how I'm getting on and stuff and talk about what I can do to improve – but I don't know if he sees me more 'cos I'm looked after, I think he just tries to help out most of the kids and get them to do better.
> *(16 year old, foster care)*

One young person cited an example of a designated teacher apparently serving as an advocate during an incident that could have resulted in the young person being excluded.

> I don't have him for any lessons, but when I was in trouble it got reported to him and he got involved to try and help sort stuff out, and when my social worker has to do reports things will go to him. I don't have to see him on a regular basis though.
> *(15 year old, foster care)*

One young person reported knowing the designated teacher through their attendance at review meetings, and one through simple contact in lessons rather than anything relating to being looked after.

Questions on young people's perceptions of the value of the designated teacher role were asked of all young people. Those who reported they were not aware of the role were asked whether, based on the definition provided, they felt that the idea was in principle likely to be helpful to young people who were looked after. Figures 8.1 and 8.2 display young people's views according to their awareness of the designated teacher role.

Figure 8.1: Percentage of responses to questions on the benefits of designated teachers from young people who were aware of the role (frequency of young people displayed within bars)

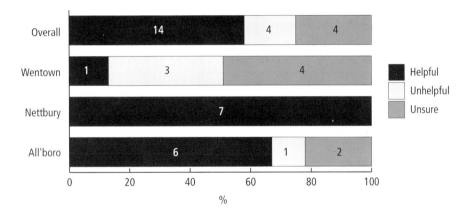

Figure 8.2: Percentage of responses to questions on the benefits of designated teachers from young people who were not aware of the role (frequency of young people displayed within bars)

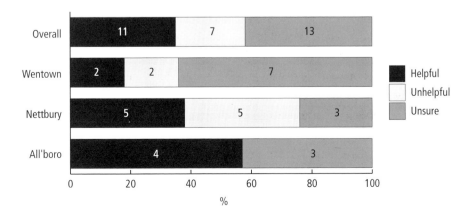

The majority of young people who were aware of the designated teacher role viewed it as a positive function. Understandably, most young people who had not heard of designated teachers before their interview were unsure as to whether they considered the role might be of use. Nevertheless, despite having been only briefly informed about the designated teacher role, a number of these young people were willing to forward their initial reaction as to the potential helpfulness of the role.

Most young people who perceived the role as helpful tended to believe that the designated teacher should serve some sort of pastoral support function and appreciated the notion that at least one individual within the school would be automatically aware of their looked after status.

> I think it's a good idea because if you know someone
> knows about your background and say you heard some
> bad news about your family or something so you can't
> concentrate on your lessons, it might be a good idea to
> talk to your designated teacher. You wouldn't have to like
> start from scratch, telling them about everything.
> *(16 year old, foster care)*

Other young people felt that the role would be supportive if it was used to oversee their educational progress and provide young people with advice and encouragement to assist their educational development.

> Yes, especially if they could spend a bit more time with
> you and give you some feedback on how they thought
> you were getting along.
> *(14 year old, foster care)*

All young people who viewed the role as helpful believed that an important function of the designated teacher was to ensure that relevant information about their progress was recorded and additional educational support, where necessary, was secured. A small number of young people believed that the role should be restricted to such general information collation and advocacy as opposed to a general support function. This was based upon a view that the designated teacher might not always be the most appropriate source of pastoral support for the young person.

> Yes, if it can help people to access support, but I'm not
> sure if they should take on a caring role because if you
> have worries and issues at school you tend to seek out a
> teacher you know and feel comfortable with and that
> might not always be that person.
> *(19 year old, independent living)*

Another common theme regarding why young people believed the
designated teacher could fulfil a useful function was the notion of a single
teacher being informed of the young person's care status and history. This
was seen as important in terms of reducing young people's perceptions that
their personal background could be common knowledge to a range of
teaching staff.

> It's good because it is uniting Education and the Social
> Services so it is easier for them to communicate, if you
> see what I mean, also if it is one designated teacher then
> the young person's personal history isn't being spread
> around from Social Services to lots of other teachers.
> *(18 year old, foster care)*

Conversely, for those young people who described the role as unhelpful, a
common theme was apparent in all of their responses. These young people
guarded their privacy strongly and did not believe it was appropriate for
information about their looked after status to be passed on to teaching staff
without their consent.

> I wouldn't like that. I don't see why people have to be told
> I'm in care. It's up to me if I want to tell people. I mean
> I'm sure they wouldn't be running around telling loads of
> people but say it's a teacher you don't like, I wouldn't want
> them to know about my home situation. It's not like I'm
> ashamed or anything, I just think it's private.
> *(15 year old, foster care)*

In addition to issues of privacy, four young people also felt that the
allocation of a designated teacher represented differential treatment to that
given to their non-looked after peers. The need for this was contested by
these four young people who wished to be treated in the same manner as
any other school student.

> No I think that's an awful idea. I preferred not to be
> known as someone in care so I wasn't singled out for any
> special support or treatment. I want to know that when
> I've done something I've earned it on merit not because
> people are saying 'Hasn't he done well for someone in
> care?'. No, I definitely wouldn't like the idea of having
> someone in school being told that I was in care.
> *(15 year old, living with relatives)*

Overall, a large proportion of young people in the follow-up sample (25, that
is 45 per cent) believed the designated teachers were likely to be helpful in
supporting young people's education. However, it should not be overlooked
that 20 per cent of the sample (11 young people) did not view the role as a
productive one and many of these young people were emphatic in their
belief that they did not appreciate a member of school staff having
knowledge of their care status without their consent. In addition, the exact
nature of the role that young people expected designated teachers to fulfil
was unclear. Whilst a number of young people felt that an information-
keeping function was appropriate, they did not necessarily wish to see the
designated teacher adopting a pastoral support role. That said, some young
people did express interest in the possibility of receiving pastoral support
from designated teachers, and indeed young people who had experienced
contact with a designated teacher expressed appreciation of the pastoral
support provided.

The influence of peer relationships within the school setting

Teachers are not the only individuals young people encounter in the school
setting. The majority of the school population is made up of students and
the influence of peers on children and young people's social behaviour and
educational performance is well documented. Peer pressure can exert both a
positive and negative influence on young people's academic attainment,
depending on the composition of the peer group (Gaviria and Raphael
2001; Hanushek and others 2001). Young people's academic attainment can

be influenced by that of other individuals within their friendship groups, with those whose friends have high academic achievement being more likely to succeed than those who mix in a group of low attainers (Robertson and Symons 1996).

Such observations resonated in the comments young people forwarded about the influence of peers on their educational experience. A number of those young people in the sample who believed they were doing well at school cited peers as a supportive factor.

> My friends are all doing well and it helps because if one of us falls down we pick one another up again so we're like a big team. Yeah, friends are important in supporting me.
> *(17 year old, foster care)*

In some instances, where young people's estimates of educational progress had improved at follow-up, this was attributed to a shift in friendship circles associated with increased motivation to attend school and concentrate on school work.

> My friends help now as well. Last year I was in with like the popular crowd and everyone was like nagging me, 'You should get on with your work at school, not go round with the class clowns' and I was 'Right, I've had enough.' So I sat down with these two girls who get on with their work in class and we sat there and we started talking and now we're like all best friends and I'm doing better.
> *(12 year old, foster care)*

Negative peer pressure was also apparent for young people who felt their education was not progressing well. Peers were the most frequently cited individuals described as hindering young people's educational progress. These young people described themselves as members of friendship circles that did not value education and there appeared to be an element of peer pressure in promoting disruptive behaviour.

> My friends don't help I suppose, mucking about and
> distracting me, stopping me from concentrating and that.
> I know it should be down to me to ignore them, but it is
> a laugh and they're my mates, you know, and it's hard.
> You can't really say 'Shut-up and listen,' they'd just laugh
> or start taking the mick big time.
> *(16 year old, foster care)*

Negative influence from peers can also take on a more directly damaging role where young people are bullied because of their looked after status or for other reasons. A number of previous studies cite examples of looked after children being bullied at school (Biehal and others 1995; Brodie 2001; Fletcher 1993) and the present study was no exception. Four young people reported having experienced bullying at school as a consequence of fellow students discovering they were in the care system. The lack of understanding shown and the level of taunting could serve to demoralise and demotivate.

> Last year I had some people saying bad things at school
> when they found out I was in foster care, like real nasty
> things, like 'You haven't got a mum and dad' or 'Your
> mum and dad wanted rid of you', and some saying rude
> racist things to me, and I got into a few fights because of
> it and that got me into trouble more than them at first.
> But then I told the teachers and they've kind of sorted it
> out and it's sort of stopped now.
> *(12 year old, foster care)*

Issues of attendance and exclusion

Poor school attendance is known to be a problem for a disproportionate number of the looked after population. Twelve per cent of looked after children missed more that 25 days of schooling over the academic year from 2001 to 2002 (Department of Health 2003b) and earlier work by the Audit Commission discovered that 40 per cent of looked after children were absent from school for reasons other than illness during a one-day attendance census (Audit Commission 1994). A recent survey of young people looked after by local authorities in England found that 17 per cent of young people reported regular truanting from school (Meltzer and others 2003).

The current study discovered lower rates of self-reported truancy, but nonetheless 9 per cent of the sample at the original interview and 7 per cent of the sample at follow-up interview described themselves as persistent truants. The slight reduction in reported truancy rates may be partly due to project activities that arose in Allborough to promote greater school attendance from residential centres as well as amongst young people attending further education colleges. Young people within the Allborough sample certainly indicated that they had received more encouragement to attend school or college due to project related-activities.

Looked after children are over-represented in exclusion figures and are 10 times more likely to be permanently excluded than non-looked after children (Department of Health 2003b). Permanent exclusions not only result in disrupted schooling due to problems of transition to new schools, but have the potential to lead to periods of missed schooling when delays in identifying alternative school placements are experienced. Missed schooling can also be experienced as a result of a series of fixed-term exclusions. Although it is difficult to estimate whether looked after children are over-represented in fixed-term exclusion rates as government statistics concentrate purely on the permanent exclusion rate, limited evidence suggests that they may also be more likely to suffer from fixed-term exclusions than the general pupil group. It is difficult to determine whether the higher rates of exclusion amongst looked after children are due to schools being more disposed to exclude this category of young people or that the combined effects of the turbulent lives of some young people and inadequate support to enable them to adapt and adjust to their situations result in behavioural problems. Research suggests that looked after children who are excluded frequently perceive that school exclusion was a justified response to their behaviour (Brodie 2001).

A total of 20 young people in the current sample had experienced some form of school exclusion throughout their care history. The majority of these were fixed-term exclusions with only seven young people reporting permanent exclusions. This is a smaller number than is often perceived. All instances of permanent exclusions were reported at original interviews and there were no further permanent exclusions reported for the intervening period between original and follow-up interviews. The most recent government returns also show, significantly, that there were no permanent exclusions of children looked after for at least one year in any of the project authorities. This could suggest that by the time of the follow-up interviews young people were being better supported to maintain their school careers, or that schools were becoming more inclusive and reluctant to exclude young people – possibly as a result of changes in government policy regarding exclusions. There was some indication that this may be the case in Allborough, where a young person reported that a potential exclusion episode had been avoided through improved dialogue between their school and carers. Likewise, in Nettbury, key local authority personnel reported that Nettbury schools were becoming more inclusive and exclusion for looked after children was no longer an issue for the authority.

In Wentown, there were two main areas of concern raised around issues of school exclusion by young people, teachers and carers alike. Firstly, although exclusion rates in Wentown schools had fallen for the whole school population (Department for Education and Skills, 2002b) and the looked after population alike, reservations were expressed that at secondary level this was due to a tendency to redirect difficult young people onto vocational schemes rather than reflecting greater success with maintaining young people in mainstream schools.

> It would affect the Government figures so what happens is people who get moved on to other institutions would at one time be called exclusions but now it is just part of the 'inclusive process'. So if someone is not doing well there is a project for pupils who may in the past have got an exclusion so it is a 'No no you can't permanently exclude you just pass them onto a project,' the category doesn't exist anymore so there is a vast improvement in this area but nothing has changed!
> *(Wentown: secondary school teacher)*

Where young people were offered vocational schemes they would continue to be registered at their original school and hence exclusion could be avoided. Whilst a number of local authority staff praised the innovative work of the Special Projects Group and commended the motivation of the staff connected with it, some concerns were expressed that the provision might represent an easy alternative to dealing with a challenging young person, rather than a genuine desire to best meet their educational needs.

> I'm not sure whether the young people who get involved with PRUs or Projects whether they do get reintegrated into mainstream. I think a lot of it still hinges around the mantra of corporate parenting of, is it good enough for my child? Some of the alternative provision is hugely imaginative but I fear they would fall at that basic hurdle of, well, if this was my child would I accept this as good enough? I think not.
>
> *(Wentown: Social Services Officer)*

A second area of concern in Wentown concerned the application of unofficial or informal exclusion episodes. Although research instigated by the Project Lead Officer in Wentown had indicated that such exclusions did not arise, the current study did find some evidence from interviews with carers and teachers that this practice may be happening. Carers spoke of schools contacting them to say they had sent young people home for the day, or asking them to come and collect young people to withdraw them from school when they were exhibiting problematic behaviour. Such practice was also confirmed by a Wentown teacher, who was reluctant to describe the practice as an exclusion, but nonetheless confirmed that young people could be asked to withdraw from school for a period.

> We've had one or two occasions where we've had to call [foster carer] to come into school and we've made a decision that he needs to be taken out. It's not truanting or anything like that, no. It's us working with [foster carer]. We did have situations where it maybe would have been an exclusion but we work very closely with the carer. We've just made the decision on two occasions, that maybe the best thing for him is to go home, talk his problems through, and then come back to school, next day or a couple of days late.
>
> *(Wentown: secondary school teacher)*

It is unclear whether the rationale behind such practice is to protect young people from building up a record of exclusion episodes, or to promote a more inclusive impression of a school by deflating exclusion rates. However, it is clear that such practice can result in disrupted schooling for some looked after children and young people. Other research has found that while 'cooling-off time' can be supportive in the short-term, it is important that it takes place as part of a clear plan through which issues in the young person's learning and behaviour are being comprehensively addressed (Brodie 2001).

The use of Personal Education Plans (PEPs)

As well as introducing the concept of designated teachers, the Joint Guidance also contained the statutory requirement that all looked after children of compulsory school age have a Personal Education Plan (PEP). In all three authorities, project activity was to some degree directed towards ensuring that looked after children had PEPs: through contributions to training for designated teachers and social workers, developing guidance on PEP completion for social workers, and reviewing the quality of PEPs produced.

The current research applied a similar line of questioning, examining young people's awareness of PEPs, as that used investigating designated teacher issues. Young people were asked if they had ever heard of PEPs, and where they claimed not, a brief definition was provided and their response checked. Those young people who were aware of PEPs were asked whether they actually had a PEP and, if so, how useful they were. Young people who had not previously heard of PEPs were then asked whether they thought the idea seemed helpful.

It emerged that 23 young people (42 per cent) had heard of PEPs: 4 in Allborough, 7 in Nettbury and 12 in Wentown. The remaining 32 young people (58 per cent) reported that they had no knowledge of them prior to their interview. Of the young people who had heard of PEPs only 16 reported having had a PEP: 3 in Allborough, 3 in Nettbury and 10 in

Wentown. Figure 8.3 shows how young people who were aware of PEPs felt about the usefulness of the plans.

Figure 8.3: Percentage of responses to questions on the benefits of PEPs from young people who were aware of PEPs (frequency of young people displayed within bars)

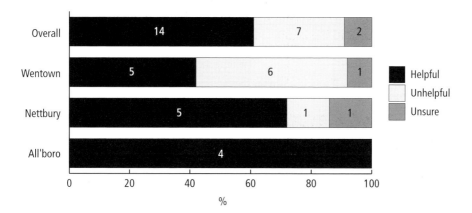

Most of the small group of young people who were aware of PEPs believed they were a positive development. Whilst this pattern of response is apparent in Nettbury and Allborough, in Wentown most young people viewed PEPs as adding little support to their educational progress. It is worth noting that five of the six young people in Wentown who did not find PEPs helpful actually had a PEP. One of these young people revealed that they had been informed that they had had a PEP some six months after it had been developed without any opportunity for their own input to the plan. The remaining young people reported minimal involvement in developing the PEP and believed the plan was simply a paper exercise representing an additional form to complete without any commitment to follow through the recommendations contained within.

> No. It didn't make any difference, no one really followed what went into it.
> *(16 year old, placed with relatives)*

> No. I just don't think it means anything, it's a bit
> of paper. It wasn't like it was used after we made it.
> *(15 year old, foster care)*

The young person in Nettbury who did not feel PEPs were helpful also reported having a PEP without anyone following up on any recommendations contained within it.

The remaining five young people in Wentown who had PEPs believed they were helpful, as did all of the young people with PEPs in Allborough and one of the young people in Nettbury to whom it applied. These young people tended to describe being actively involved in the development of their PEP.

> Yes. I was involved in deciding what went into that with
> my social worker and my tutor. We had a chat about how
> do I think I'm getting on in lessons and things like that
> and what I need to do to do better and what they would
> do for me and things.
> *(14 year old, foster care)*

The resulting document was seen to be helpful in terms of setting young people realistic targets that they could work towards. Young people reported that such targets were effective and, in their view, their application to their studies had improved.

> Yeah, it is helping. You know there's a target there and
> you know you've got to work to it. Like I put down to try
> to stop skiving, well not so much skiving as not going into
> the lessons. Then I mean I've done like, I think it's five
> or six weeks left to go and I've done three full weeks.
> *(15 year old, residential care)*

The notion of having targets to work towards was also noted by young people who did not have a PEP but, nonetheless, believed their use was likely to benefit young people's education. In addition, a number of young people mentioned that PEPs were likely to be beneficial if they were developed collaboratively by involving young people, social workers, teachers and carers.

> Yes, although I'm answering without experience, I think
> that it is always going to be a good idea to get people to
> think about goals and targets – both teachers, young
> people, carers, etc. – so that there is something to work
> towards. The young person can work towards better
> results, attendance or whatever and the adults in their
> lives have their own targets about how they can support
> that goal. Seems to me that can only be a good thing.
> *(18 year old, independent living)*

The 32 young people who had not heard of PEPs prior to interview were also
asked whether they thought a PEP could be a useful aid in supporting their
educational progress. Figure 8.4 displays their responses to this question.

Figure 8.4: Percentage of responses to questions on the benefits of PEPs from young
people who were not aware of PEPs (frequency of young people displayed within bars)

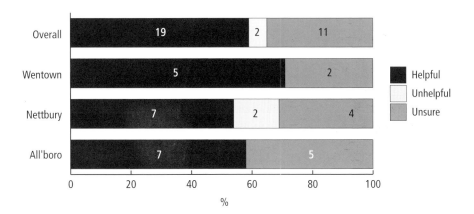

The majority of young people who had not heard of PEPs prior to their
interview welcomed the idea as presented to them by the research team.
They felt that making an explicit commitment to specific educational goals
would motivate them.

> Yeah, especially the target bit because if you're like me
> say, because I've got a target, a personal one, and only I
> know it – but you can too now – and it's to try and ignore

anything in class because I get easily distracted.
Sometimes if someone's being stupid and making a
stupid comment, sometimes I'll add to it or go along with
it. Now I'm trying to steer clear of that, which is good,
and I'm sort of doing it but I think if I had it written out
somewhere and people knew about it, it might make me
try harder.

(12 year old, foster care)

Those young people who did not think that PEPs were likely to be of benefit to them did not wish to be subject to planning measures that were not applied to the wider school population. The remaining young people who had not heard of PEPs before their interview were unsure as to their potential effectiveness given their limited knowledge.

Although the level of awareness of PEPs is disappointing across all three authorities, it is perhaps most surprising in Nettbury. In Allborough and Wentown, local authority personnel readily acknowledged that their rate of PEP completion was lower than desired, therefore it is perhaps unsurprising to find that a number of young people were not aware of PEPs. However, in Nettbury a considerable amount of the Project Lead Officer's time was directed towards encouraging social workers to complete PEPs in collaboration with teaching staff and young people themselves. This resulted in 100 per cent of Nettbury's school-age looked after population having a PEP on record by July 2002. This is impressive, but our findings suggest that many young people may not have been consulted regarding the content of their PEP, or even have been informed of its existence. Although there were some instances of young people describing involvement in the development of a PEP, these cases were in a minority. This raises serious questions about the value of the PEP where young people do not actively participate in its planning and development; hence the targets and support strategies contained in the PEP may not be relevant to the young person and it will be difficult to work towards the goals set if the individual does not know what these are. In striving to fulfil government objectives that all young people have PEPs, the principle of using the document as a meaningful tool to assist young people's progress may have been overlooked, so transforming the completion of PEPs into a futile bureaucratic exercise.

Young people themselves appeared well aware of the potential benefit of thoughtfully constructed PEPs. Those young people who had PEPs tended to believe that the educational targets outlined were relevant to them and served as added motivation in applying themselves to their studies. Those young people without knowledge of PEPs also expressed interest in the notion of having tangible educational targets. The idea of expressing a written commitment to making progress in their education was thought likely to improve the possibility that young people will honour such aims, particularly when they know that others are aware of the targets they have set.

The relevance of targets within the PEP appears to be enhanced through active involvement of young people in determining the contents. Unfortunately, such involvement was absent in some cases and this could lead young people to believe that the PEP was of little value. It also appears important that young people should perceive that the PEP is taken seriously and that recommendations contained within it are followed through and targets are reassessed to establish whether progress is being made. Half of the young people in Wentown who had PEPs believed the plans were of little use as no one had shown any interest in their contents once they were produced.

Summary

- Teachers have more contact with children and young people than any other professionals and research indicates that schools can serve as an important protective and preventative resource for children experiencing social disadvantage.

- The level of school autonomy created by the introduction of the 1988 Education Reform Act is seen to create pragmatic difficulties in working with individual schools to promote the education of looked after children.

- A number of successful project activities indicate that whilst it may require more effort to communicate and establish working relationships with a variety of individual schools, there is no reason to suppose that schools are unwilling partners in efforts to improve the education of looked after children.

■ Young people taking part in the evaluation project identified teachers as the most common source of both academic and pastoral support.

■ A minority of young people in the sample believed that teachers had somewhat hindered their educational progress. Negative comments related to low expectations, negative stereotyping and a lack of understanding of what it meant to be looked after.

■ A majority of young people were not aware of the existence of designated teachers; and the nature of the role young people expected designated teachers to fulfil was unclear.

■ Although generally positive, young people's views about the role of the designated teacher were mixed: positive comments centred on the fact that one teacher can centralise personal information and provide specific and informed support; negative comments referred to the lack of privacy with regard to care status and the provision of differential treatment for looked after children.

■ In terms of peer interaction, the present study's findings are broadly in line with previous research. Young people's academic attainment can be influenced by that of other individuals within their friendship groups, with those whose friends have high academic achievement being more likely to succeed than those who mix in groups of low attainers.

■ Reports from the young people interviewed and recent government returns indicate that there has been a marked reduction of the number of exclusions in all three project-authorities since the beginning of the project. However, there are some indications that those positive results might be partly due to changes in administrative procedures and recording method rather than to actual improvements in practice.

■ The slight reduction in reported school and college truancy rates may be partly due to project activities. One authority has placed a strong emphasis on promoting attendance amongst young people placed in residential centres and this has been clearly confirmed by participants of the evaluation sample.

■ A majority of the young people interviewed are aware of the potential benefits of PEPs and are specifically positive about setting clear individual targets. However, the present study indicates that PEPs are devalued because of the lack of young people's involvement in the process.

9. The care experience

A large body of research evidence highlights a link between children's home background and their educational attainment (Marjoribanks 1979; McCallum and Dernie 2001; Mortimore and Blackstone 1982). Family circumstances, including social class and parental interest in and attitudes towards education, are considered to account for much of the variation in children's educational achievement (Cox 2000; MacCallum 1996). Poor housing conditions, including having nowhere to do homework, are cited as affecting young people's ability to study. Social class appears to influence the availability of educational resources within the home environment and research indicates a positive relationship between levels of educational resources at home and educational success (Roscigno and Ainsworth-Darnell 1999; Teachman 1987).

Educational resources in the family settings include not only material provisions such as quiet study space, academic texts, information and communication technology, but also the availability of interested parents who show interest in young people's progress and encourage achievement. The social class and educational ability of parents may influence the degree to which they become involved in their children's education. Parents from poorer socio-economic backgrounds tend to exhibit less involvement in their children's education (Vincent and others 2000) and those who leave formal education at age 16 tend to report less confidence in helping young people with homework, communicating with teaching staff and participating in school activities (Williams and others 2002).

Given the established links between home background and educational support, Jackson and Sachdev (2001) comment that it is surprising that until recently little research or policy interest has concentrated upon the educational influence of the care environment. It must be acknowledged that since a large number children entering the looked after system are from disadvantaged backgrounds (Bebbington and Miles 1989; Borland and others 1998; Jackson and Martin 1998) they will already be at risk of underachievement due to a previous history of poor educational support. However, evidence indicates that the care environment and social work input may actually limit young people's educational opportunities. This is unfortunate, given the potential of the care experience to provide educational support that may help compensate for previous disadvantage.

Similarly, social workers have been criticised for failing to give education sufficient priority and to appreciate its importance to young people's life chances. Indeed, some commentators argue that social work has lost sight of the fact that, after the family, school can be the most powerful developmental influence in young people's lives (Gilligan 1998). Previous research suggests that social workers tend to view the educational needs of looked after children as a lower priority than placement issues, maintaining family relationships and dealing with emotional and/or physical needs (Fletcher-Campbell and Hall 1990; Francis 2000). This can be all too obvious to young people themselves, who note social workers' tendency to focus on physical needs (Harker and others 2003).

This chapter reports the views of young people, carers and key local authority personnel regarding the level of educational support available within care placements. Information gathered throughout the course of the project enables us to establish whether project activities have influenced the manner in which young people's educational progress is supported in foster and residential care settings. It then examines the perceptions of young people and foster carers about the ways in which social workers can help to support young people's educational progress.

The care environment

Research that has examined the educational support provided by the care environment has tended to focus more on residential than on foster care. A number of studies have reported that children and young people in residential care can experience difficulties in finding quiet study space to complete homework activities or revision exercises (Buchanan 1993; Fletcher 1993; Social Exclusion Unit 2002). Even where quiet study space is available, residential units do not always provide young people with basic books and reference materials to assist with homework activities and access to computers can be limited (Berridge and others 1996). There are reports that some residential homes tacitly support a culture of non-attendance at school (Biehal and others 1995) and residential staff have been uncertain how to tackle issues of non-attendance due to a lack of clear policies relating to attendance issues (Berridge and Brodie 1998). The educational background of residential staff can also influence their confidence in communicating with schools (Berridge and others 1996) and offering educational support to young people (Bald and others 1995). A recent survey by the Social Exclusion Unit found that limited numbers of young people reported receiving help with homework or other study support from residential carers (Social Exclusion Unit 2002).

There is little research examining the provision of educational resources in foster care settings, although recent findings suggest there may be a wide variation in the availability of educational supports (Harker and others 2003). Some evidence suggests that the educational attainment of children in foster placements tends to be better than for those in residential care, but this may be due to residential units dealing with more problematic children and young people (Borland and others 1998). There is an apparent link between the provision of support and encouragement for young people's educational progress by foster carers and their educational attainment (Heath and others 1994; Jackson and Martin 1998; Martin and Jackson 2002). Such support can include successful liaison with schools and Social Services to advocate young people's educational needs, as well as help with homework and learning skills development (Quinton and others 1996). However, as with residential care, not all foster carers possess the confidence and ability to support young people's education in such ways. Foster carers are drawn from all areas of the educational spectrum and, as such, a significant proportion have no formal qualifications (Triseliotis and others 1998). This is likely to impact upon their confidence in communicating with teachers and other professionals, as well as their ability to support young people's homework.

It would appear that the primary carers of children and young people who are looked after may not always be expected or equipped to provide optimum support for young people's educational progress (Social Exclusion Unit 2003). The recent introduction of national minimum standards for both residential (Department of Health 2002a) and foster care (Department of Health 2002b) emphasises the importance of carers supporting young people's educational progress. The standards include the need for carers to provide quiet study space, key books and resources to support education, as well as encourage attainment and school attendance and assist with homework activities. The introduction of the minimum standards is too recent for the current evaluation to assess their impact. However, the numerous *Taking Care of Education* project activities in each authority were designed to improve the capacity of care placements to support young people's educational progress. These activities, combined with government initiatives focusing on the education of looked after children, may well have begun to make a difference to how young people's education is supported within care settings.

Educational resources in care placements

The young person's interview schedule included a checklist to assess whether certain supportive factors were available to them in their current care placements. The checklist contained 12 items and was administered at both original and follow-up interviews. The checklist included both provision of material resources (for example, quiet study space and key books) and educational encouragement (for example, having someone taking an interest in education). Table 9.1 displays the items included on the checklist and the percentage of young people reporting their availability at both original and follow-up interviews.

Table 9.1: Percentage of young people in follow-up sample who reported availability of educational supports in care placements at original (T1) and follow-up (T2) interview

| | Percentage reporting availability | | | | | | | |
| | Allborough | | Nettbury | | Wentown | | Overall | |
Supportive factor	T1	T2	T1	T2	T1	T2	T1	T2
Quiet space to study in	94	100	90	95	89	100	91	98
Interested adult	94	94	85	90	95	90	91	91
Newspapers/magazines	81	88	70	100	67	79	72	89
Key books	75	82	65	90	72	89	70	88
Access to a local library	63	71	65	100	58	90	62	88
School-event attendance	75	94	65	85	74	79	71	86
Computer access	75	76	70	75	38	84	61	79
Funds for leisure activities	88	77	60	75	50	79	65	77
Educational outings	63	59	45	75	39	79	48	71
Funds to buy books	75	41	60	85	59	74	64	68
Internet access	38	47	25	70	28	74	29	64
Info on educational rights	13	24	15	40	6	47	11	38

Overall, Table 9.1 makes for encouraging reading. The reported provision of all forms of support within care placements has improved over time and, with the exception of information on educational rights, over 60 per cent of young people reported access to all forms of support. In terms of individual authorities, whilst all three can be seen to have improved over time there is some variation in the degree of improvement. Young people in Allborough had reported the highest levels of availability for most supports at original interview but appear to report a lower level of improvement at follow-up compared to other authorities. Young people in the Wentown sample reported the highest levels of availability in most areas at follow-up, but had reported the lowest levels at the original interview stage. Rates of change between authorities are particularly pronounced for certain types of support. The proportion of young people with access to computers has dramatically increased in Wentown from only 38 per cent at original interview to 84 per cent at follow-up. Similarly positive trends are apparent in Wentown and Nettbury. The level of improvement in terms of young people having information on their educational rights is also greatest in Wentown. Wentown shows a lower level of change in someone attending school events than either Allborough or Nettbury. Allborough is the only authority where there is a reduction in the reported availability of some supports, namely funding for leisure activities, opportunities for educational outings and funds for young people to buy their own books.

The distribution of the sample within the three authorities prevented a detailed analysis of the types of support available according to placement types in each authority. Nonetheless, it is possible to examine changes according to placement types for the sample as a whole. Table 9.2 displays the reported provision of educational supports in each placement type.

Table 9.2: Percentage of reported availability of educational supports according to care placement type at original (T1) and follow-up (T2) interview

Supportive factor	Foster T1	Foster T2	Residential T1	Residential T2	Relatives T1	Relatives T2	Independent T1	Independent T2
Quiet space to study in	87	100	100	100	91	100	80	89
Interested adult	90	100	78	100	91	91	80	67
Newspapers/magazines	72	88	89	100	64	82	60	78
Key books	66	94	78	84	64	82	80	78
Access to a local library	57	77	56	100	82	91	60	89
School event attendance	83	88	67	100	82	91	40	56
Computer access	69	94	67	67	46	64	40	56
Funds for leisure activities	62	88	67	67	46	82	80	33
Educational outings	55	71	56	67	36	73	20	56
Funds to buy books	61	59	78	50	55	64	80	67
Internet access	38	65	11	67	27	55	20	44
Info on educational rights	17	24	100	67	27	28	20	22

It appears that the most consistent pattern of reported improvement in availability of educational supports is found in foster, residential and relative placements. Young people in independent living tended to report reduced availability of a number of provisions at follow-up interview. Project activities designed to improve educational resources in care placements were targeted at foster and residential care, so it is encouraging to see that young people appear to be aware that improvements have occurred. At follow-up, young people in foster and residential care reported similar, if not a greater number of, supports as young people living with relatives. These findings raise interesting issues in terms of ensuring parity of support across different types of placement, and also highlight the need for local authorities to consider the distinct needs of young people according to their placement.

Interviews with young people and their carers enabled us to link reported improvements in educational supports to specific project activities. The following sections examine how project activities may have impacted upon foster and residential care settings.

Improved resources in foster placements

Encouragingly, young people in foster care in all three authorities reported an increase in the availability of most educational resources at follow-up interview. The most marked improvements arose in providing access to a computer, providing key books and improving opportunities to join and use a local library, all of which can be linked to project activities.

In Wentown, an activity that was acknowledged and appreciated by young people and their carers was the scheme to provide foster children with a personal computer that had internet access. This is likely to explain much of the improvement in 'computer access' and 'internet access' amongst young people in foster care in the sample.

Five young people in the Wentown sample had received a computer and the majority believed this was of great benefit to their education.

> Yes. I've got one here. It's a really great help for me to do my work on. Definitely very good.
> *(Wentown: 15 year old, foster care)*

Carers in Wentown also extolled the virtue of the computer scheme and had
noticed an impact on young people's willingness to complete homework
assignments and confidence in their ability to produce good quality work.

> I actually feel that it has helped her to become more
> confident and she has typed-up some of her essays. She's
> actually typed-up quite a few and saved them on disc and
> taken them away, so she's obviously learnt quite a few
> skills along the way.
> *(Wentown: foster carer)*

One young person stated that whilst they appreciated being given the
computer it had little impact on their education as she only used it to play
games. The young person's carer confirmed this, but still believed the
computer was having a positive educational impact. The young person
concerned had developed a dislike for reading but her enthusiasm for
computer games meant that she had needed to read and understand
complex instructions, thus developing her reading skills.

The *Book of My Own* scheme in Nettbury had enabled young people to
redeem book tokens at a local book store, and was much appreciated by
seven young people in the sample who were aware of the scheme. However,
this scheme highlights some of the difficulties faced by the projects in
ensuring their target audience was reached: despite the Nettbury scheme
being aimed at all looked after children, the majority of the sample claimed
they had not received a book token. Tokens were distributed to foster and
residential carers who could redeem them by taking young people to the
local bookstore, although only around 65 per cent of carers redeemed their
vouchers. The fact that a significant number of young people were not given
the opportunity to purchase books may indicate that some carers in Nettbury
were not placing sufficient emphasis on supporting young people's literacy
skills. A similar finding was observed in Wentown, where GCSE and National
Curriculum Key Stage revision guides had been offered in writing to foster
carers of looked after children. Whilst this may have been likely to impact on
the availability of key books, none of the young people in the Wentown
sample were aware of the scheme and local authority staff were unsure of the
take-up rate of this offer.

Schemes in Allborough and Nettbury to promote young people's involvement with the library service also applied to young people in foster placements. Information packs about the library service were forwarded to all foster children in Nettbury and internet vouchers for Allborough libraries were likewise delivered to young people in foster placements. Although only limited numbers of young people in the sample reported awareness of these schemes, they did appreciate their availability and had made use of their local library.

Improvements in opportunities to enjoy leisure activities may also be project-related. As previously noted in Chapter 7, the provision of leisure cards for looked after children had occurred in Allborough and Nettbury, vacation photography and arts courses had taken place in Nettbury and outward bound residential weekends in Wentown. Positive comments regarding leisure card schemes were forwarded by young people and their carers alike and there was some suggestion that these schemes enabled carers to become more involved in promoting young people's leisure interests. It was also appreciated that the leisure passes enabled carers and their families to benefit from reduced rates and felt this provided opportunities for the entire family to participate in enjoyable activities that could help build and strengthen relationships with young people.

Vacation photography and arts courses in Nettbury were also much appreciated by young people, as discussed in Chapter 7. Again, there was some evidence from interviews with foster carers in Nettbury that these events had a continuing effect in terms of young people's career aspirations and carers were able to use this to encourage educational progress.

> She did the summer course on photography and just absolutely loved it. As the upshot of that she's now decided to knuckle down because she wants to go to college next year to do photography. What she doesn't know – she thinks she's got to start saving after Christmas – is that I've managed to get her a second-hand manual camera. At first I thought it would have to be new, but I've got a friend who's a professional photographer and he said 'If you're only going to be spending about £140 you have to buy second hand.' But then he did all the

> donkey work for me to make sure it was a good one and
> he's said when she starts a course next September, she
> will be one of the best equipped, it will be one of the
> most professional ones there. So she's getting that for
> Christmas but she has no idea yet.
> *(Nettbury: foster carer)*

This quote emphasises the added impact that project initiatives might have if their effects can be reinforced by supportive carers who are sensitive to the need to promote young people's developing interests and use whatever levers they can to reinforce the importance of education.

Training activities designed to enable foster and residential staff to support young people's education more effectively took place as part of project activities in Allborough and Nettbury (such training already occurred in Wentown). In Allborough, whilst training for residential staff was widely believed to have facilitated a greater focus on education in residential centres, activities aimed at foster carers were seen as more challenging. A series of Foster Carer Information Exchanges had taken place in Allborough and, although it was felt that the sessions were a valuable method of promoting an educational ethos amongst foster carers, the limited number of foster carers attending was cause for concern. In Nettbury, *Reading Roadshows* and *Numeracy Roadshows* achieved about a 50 per cent attendance rate. Those carers who attended believed such events had enhanced their confidence and ability to support young people's education.

> The Foster Carers Information Exchange was really good
> for helping carers have some confidence – telling them
> that they have the right to query a school, and challenge
> them about decisions they might take. I know, not just
> myself, but other carers did appreciate having things like
> that cleared up and knowing what we should be doing to
> support young people. I already do that, but if I hadn't
> done it in the past then it would have really helped, it
> just confirmed that I am perfectly within my rights.
> *(Allborough: foster carer)*

> I though the roadshow thing was very good. I think they
> teach reading skills in such a different way now in schools
> that it was really helpful to have this professional group
> telling us what they knew about the best methods to get
> kids' reading skills up to scratch. It certainly gave me
> some good ideas and I got books and things to bring
> home. A really good use of my time actually.
> *(Nettbury: foster carer)*

Nonetheless, foster carers themselves were aware of the limited numbers who attended these sessions and some expressed concern that there was an element of 'preaching to the converted'. Carers commented that their attendance at the events illustrated to a degree that they were already committed to supporting young people's education, but wondered whether those who did not attend might be similarly motivated. Likewise, local authority personnel were concerned that the reluctance of some foster carers to attend training sessions might reflect a lack of commitment to promoting an educational ethos to young people. However, comments gathered from foster carers who did not attend training sessions suggested that other factors might be at play. Some carers commented that the young people they cared for were doing well educationally and this lessened their perceived need to attend training sessions.

> No I haven't been to anything. The thing is we haven't
> really got a problem. I probably would have gone had we
> had a problem with them but they both get up in the
> morning and go to school quite happily, so we don't
> really feel that it's what we really need at the moment.
> *(Allborough: foster carer)*

Other carers believed that they were already fully able to support young people's progress and as such would not benefit from additional training.

> I think I was working the day it was on, but to be honest,
> I'm not sure if I would have gone anyway. I've always
> promoted the importance of school to the children I've
> looked after – made sure they go in, do their homework,
> check they've got the books and things they need. So for

> me, it wasn't something that I really needed, I don't think
> it would have taught me anything I don't already know or
> made me do anything I don't already do.
> *(Nettbury: foster carer)*

In Wentown, at the time of the most recent interviews with foster carers, the *Taking Care of Education* project had not specifically targeted resources towards training on educational issues for foster carers, due to the fact that other training was already available. Some carers indicated that additional training in this area would be beneficial.

> It has been many years since I have been to school and I
> am not up on some things, I have got to say, I feel quite
> ashamed because half the things these children do I
> wouldn't be able to, I wouldn't know where to start.
> *(Wentown: foster carer)*

> I mean it's what? 40-odd years since I went to school and
> so much has changed. You know, they don't even add up
> and subtract the way we used to at school.
> *(Wentown: foster carer)*

The ability of foster carers to support basic learning skills is being addressed in Wentown. For example, the Project Lead Officer has introduced a scheme entitled *Books R Me through 2003* that involves the provision of a year calendar for foster carers based on the broad theme of literacy, learning and books, as well as a series of National Literacy Association reading roadshows and workshops taking place throughout the year. At the time of the most recent interviews with Wentown foster carers, this scheme was not yet underway but it will be of interest to monitor the development of this training in Wentown as the *Taking Care of Education* evaluation proceeds.

The comments from all three authorities indicate a need to highlight to carers the importance of ongoing professional development with regard to the education of looked after children. There may also be a need for greater consultation with carers. In one authority, it was suggested that training schemes could be made compulsory, but other staff were resistant to this idea largely due to the desire to retain local authority foster care staff. There was a perception that although a large core of loyal foster carers existed, there was a risk that they may be lured away by professional fostering agencies if the authority became over-prescriptive regarding their roles and training requirements. Against this it might be argued that potential carers might be attracted by the offer of more professional training. Part of the long-term solution, however, may be to ensure there is a focus on supporting young people's education in initial foster-care training programmes, as well as in later training events. At the time of initial interviews, none of the foster carers in the sample believed that promoting the educational needs of looked after children had been emphasised in their original training.

Improved resources in residential care

Young people in residential care reported either 'improved' or 'stable' provision of all forms of support except funds to purchase books and information regarding educational rights and entitlements. The most marked improvements arose in areas of having someone to show interest in educational progress and attend school events, access to a local library, availability of newspapers and magazines, and internet access.

Improvements in having someone taking an interest in young people's educational progress and attending school events is likely to have been influenced by project activities, particularly those arising in Allborough. A project-funded Education Welfare Officer had been working closely with staff in Allborough's residential centres to assist them in developing effective strategies to promote young people's school attendance and to maintain an overview of young people's educational progress. Each of the residential centres has an Education Representative, who ensures that wall charts in each centre display forthcoming school events and the worker allocated to attend each, as well as information on exclusion and admission procedures and a list of Education Welfare Officers allocated to each school. In addition, attendance sheets are maintained to record whether young people attend school or college. Education Representatives also meet in a monthly forum to discuss good practice in promoting school and college attendance and motivating young people.

Young people in Allborough agreed that staff appeared to be giving more attention to their school attendance and to supporting their education more generally.

> They have sat down with me and asked me what I was
> doing, how it was going and I've told them what I needed
> to do and things so that they could help me more.
> *(Allborough: 15 year old, residential care)*

Such comments at follow-up interviews contrasted with the negative views expressed at original interviews by carers and young people, namely that residential homes did not promote a culture of school attendance or always enable staff to show an active interest in young people's progress. Residential staff in Allborough acknowledged that improvements were related to the work of the *Taking Care of Education* project and the contribution of the Education Welfare Officer.

Improved access to local libraries is likely to be related to project schemes in Allborough and Nettbury, whereby Project Lead Officers established good links with the local authority library service, resulting in information packs about the libraries being provided for all children in residential homes. In Allborough, such activity is also likely to have impacted upon the reported levels of internet access as vouchers were distributed to entitle young people to free internet usage in local libraries. Internet use may also have improved due to schemes to enhance the computing capacity of residential homes. Although most homes did have a computer available at original interviews, these were not always configured for internet use. Project funding in Nettbury and Wentown had led to older computers being upgraded, or new computers being bought, thus facilitating internet access.

The increased availability of magazines and newspapers is also connected to project activities. In Allborough, the relationship with the Library Service resulted in regular deliveries of magazines and newspapers to residential units. This relationship also brought about deliveries of books to the centres on at least a termly basis and is likely to have contributed to improvements in the availability of key books. In Nettbury and Wentown, project funds had also been used to establish or improve a library resource within residential centres. However, the improvement in reported availability of key books was not as pronounced as in other areas. This may have been due to delays in establishing library facilities in Nettbury's children's homes. Despite the enthusiasm of the Library Services Officer charged with progressing the scheme, the children's homes' libraries had not been established within the desired timescale. Unfortunately, this delay was attributed to reluctance on the part of residential staff to involve young people in the purchase of books. Residential staff had claimed that current groups of residents could not be trusted to visit local bookstores as they would be inclined to shoplift. Despite attempts to persuade staff that this risk would be acceptable, they resisted pressure to involve young people and eventually a compromise was reached whereby residential staff were to select the books on young people's behalf. This is a disconcerting finding and suggests that some residential staff in Nettbury may hold negative attitudes about looked after children. Whilst one cannot establish whether perceptions about the young people's shoplifting tendencies would prove accurate, what is certain is that an opportunity to exhibit trust and involve young people in identifying resources to engage them in reading activities has been wasted.

General support for education in care settings

As well as examining how specific project activities might have influenced the degree of educational support available in care settings, interviews with young people also enabled us to identify more general examples of how the care environment might support their educational progress.

We have already noted in Chapter 4 that a key explanation offered by young people in relation to improvements in educational progress or maintenance of good progress was the encouragement and support provided by carers. Where carers had emphasised the importance of education and actively encouraged and acknowledged achievement, young people believed this had a significant impact on their educational progress. Similar findings emerged when questioning young people about the general impact of being looked after upon their educational progress. Where young people believed being looked after had a positive impact on their education this was related to increased opportunities to obtain educational support from both foster and residential carers.

> It's like at home you've only got your mum and dad and
> here you've got two or three, maybe four staff on in one
> night. When you're at home it's mum cleaning up, dads'
> at work, you don't get any help with homework but here
> we've got the staff available and even if they've got other
> jobs to do, like one's probably on the phone some of the
> time, one's doing paperwork and one is doing something
> else, there's still someone left who can help.
> *(Allborough: 15 year old, residential care)*

Some young people's perceptions had altered between interviews and a
change had occurred from thinking that being looked after had little impact
on their education to viewing it as having a beneficial effect. Such change
tended to be associated with being in a stable, supportive care placement.

> Last time I didn't think it had made a difference because
> I hadn't been living with [foster carer] for that long, but
> now I've been here for over two years and now I'm in
> year 10, [foster carer] is sitting down with me more and
> helps me more with homework and things.
> *(Wentown: 14 year old, foster care)*

Likewise, six young people who changed from reporting that being looked
after had a negative effect on their education to believing it had made things
better, explained their altered perceptions in terms of the duration of their
current placement. All of the young people had remained within the same
placement since their original interview (with the exception of one young
person who had moved to independent living two months prior to follow-up)
and believed that this had enabled them to benefit from educational support
available, as well as enabling them to feel secure enough to concentrate on
their education.

> I think it is better because I have been here [current
> placement] for two years now. But I think if I had been
> moving around, how it was when I was younger, I would
> have been worse off still because I wouldn't have been
> able to settle myself down and concentrate.
> *(15 year old, foster care)*

Placement stability was also proposed as justification for seven young people who changed from reporting that being looked after had improved their education to seeing it as having no effect. Six of these young people were in stable foster placements with no reported moves between interviews, whilst one young person had moved from residential to foster care 12 months before their follow-up interview. Whilst there was no reduction in the provision of educational support for these young people, the constant level of support had begun to be viewed as a natural aspect of their lives and was no longer seen as making a significant impact.

> I think last time I might have said better because I'd not been here that long so maybe it was more of a contrast to what I'd had at home. Whereas now, I mean I've been here for nearly two years so it just feels normal to be getting supported and stuff.
> *(Nettbury: 16 year old, foster care)*

However, placement stability was not always a necessary condition for perceiving being looked after as having a positive impact on education. Eight of the young people reporting a positive impact had experienced at least one placement move between interviews. Despite such change, these young people felt that being looked after had increased the range of individuals taking an interest in their education and this was beneficial to them.

Although the majority of young people reported that being looked after had a positive impact on their educational progress, 12 young people reported negative effects at both interview stages. Whilst no young people felt they were currently in care placements that offered little support for education, many believed that their past experiences in placements that lacked an educational focus had such a detrimental effect on their education that they had failed to recover from falling behind.

Such findings serve to emphasise the pivotal role that carers can play in supporting and encouraging young people's educational progress. This was reinforced by comments forwarded regarding key adults who might support young people's education. Carers featured highly amongst the comments about supportive individuals, with 28 positive comments being forwarded regarding the manner in which they encouraged and supported achievement. Emphasis was placed on the importance of encouragement for educational success in the form of verbal praise and material rewards, as well as generally showing interest in young people's education. Communicating expectations of success and celebrating young people's achievements, as well as showing disappointment should their effort and commitment wane, were seen as vital components in supporting young people's progress. Only three young people provided negative comments about carers at follow-up interview and these comments focussed on an absence of support and encouragement for educational progress throughout a young person's care history.

Young people's perceptions of social workers' support for education

The positive views young people held regarding carers were not replicated in their perceptions of social workers. In original interviews with young people, social workers were the individuals most frequently cited as hindering educational progress. Frequent reference was made to being moved within the looked after system without there being any apparent awareness of the young person's needs or the impact such movement might have on their educational progress. Although problems with placement availability are not necessarily social workers' fault, some children were disappointed with the level of interest social workers exhibited towards their education. It was felt that priority was given to meeting immediate physical and emotional needs with little emphasis on long-term developmental needs and educational opportunities.

> Social workers don't care about education. They just see you more like an animal that's got to be fed, watered, clothed and sheltered somewhere. Once they get that bit sorted it's just let's pass the buck to someone else.
> *(16 year old, foster care)*

Only four young people (two in Nettbury, one in Allborough and one in Wentown) mentioned at the original interviews that social workers had supported their educational progress. In all these cases, comments related to social workers taking an interest in young people's school work and, in some cases, offering assistance with homework.

> Yes. My social worker. She talks to me, like she explains things, so I understand them, like homework and things.
> *(Allborough: 13 year old, foster care)*

At follow-up interviews it was encouraging to discover that the number of positive comments about social workers had increased to 12. The greater appreciation of social workers' contribution occurred mainly in Wentown and Nettbury, with the frequency of comments about supportive social workers remaining constant in Allborough. Young people appeared to have noticed that social workers were taking more active interest in their educational progress.

> My latest social worker really helps support me. She's just like [foster carer]. Every time she comes she's like 'How are you getting on at school?' That's the first question she asks except for like 'How are you?' and I'm like 'Oh fine' but then I have to rush upstairs and get my studies down and show her and stuff like that. She's really nice. I've had her about a year now I suppose … all of my social workers have been good but I think she takes more interest in school.
> *(Nettbury: 12 year old, foster care)*

Some of the increase in positive comments related to young people moving to become the responsibility of leaving-care teams and perceiving that there was more support available there for educational issues. Four of the comments relating to social workers concerned leaving-care workers.

> My leaving-care worker was really encouraging and helped with sorting out the financial side for me with going off to uni and things. They seem a lot more clued up about education on the leaving care side of things.
> *(Nettbury: 18 year old, independent living)*

At the same time, social workers continued to feature relatively frequently at follow-up interview in comments from young people in Nettbury and

Wentown regarding individuals who had hindered educational progress.
Eight young people cited ways in which they felt social workers represented
barriers to their education. The majority of comments related back to issues
raised at original interview and concerned placement changes accompanied
by insufficient awareness of the young person's needs.

> Well, there was all the moving around at the start bit without
> much thought as to how that was going to affect me, so I
> don't really like the whole business of being in care.
> *(Wentown: 15 year old, placed with relatives)*

Some young people provided more current examples of how social workers
could be perceived as hindering educational progress. In Nettbury, three
young people in further education were disappointed that social workers had
promised them personal computers and these had failed to materialise.
Although this was not seen as a direct hindrance, it was seen to be an
example of raising young people's expectations and subsequently breaking
promises.

> It's not very bad but my social worker told me that Social
> Services would buy me a computer so I can develop my
> knowledge but then they didn't buy it after they told me
> they would. I wouldn't have minded not having one but
> after they told me it would be coming I started looking
> forward to it.
> *(Nettbury: 16 year old, foster care)*

It also appeared that difficulties could be encountered when young people's
educational achievement was high. Young people with the opportunity to
progress to university could find themselves uncertain about their financial
situation and the level of support they might expect to receive from the local
authority.

> To me it seemed as if they'd never come across the
> situation of having someone in care who wanted to go to
> university and they didn't know what to do because
> they'd just never considered what their policy might be.
> To me that suggests they've got very low expectations,
> which OK might be based on the fact that no one's done

it before, but that shouldn't stop you thinking that one of
these days some young people might come out with good
enough grades to go and you need to plan what you can
do for them. There's all these things like this project that
are supposed to help people like me get a better
education but if they don't seem to expect you to get as
far as university it's sending out a bit of a mixed message.
(18 year old, independent living)

It is worth noting that the majority of negative comments made about social
workers hindering progress related to broader organisational issues rather
than the view that individual social workers were not showing an interest in
young people's education. Failure to deliver on promises regarding personal
computers and a lack of strategies to deal with educational success cannot be
seen as the responsibility of individual workers. All comments at follow-up
interview regarding the individual practice of social workers were in fact
positive examples of how they were showing interest in young people's
educational progress. As we will see from the following section regarding
carers' perceptions of social workers, a similar pattern emerged with
individual staff being viewed positively but the organisation of Social Services
departments sometimes being seen as a barrier to providing effective support
for young people's education.

Carers' perceptions of social workers support for education

Interviews with foster carers at both initial and follow-up stages also provided
some insight into how social workers could directly support young people's
education, as well as assist foster carers in their role. The majority of
comments that were made about individual social workers' practice were
positive. Foster carers appreciated the professionalism of social work staff
and their commitment to supporting the development of the young people
for whom they were responsible.

> I suppose it can be difficult for them to have a really
> good overview and push the education side, because I
> would say in one respect that they've got such a big
> caseload they don't have time. However, having said that
> I've also experienced the very professional social worker
> who's managed to do it all and has been absolutely
> brilliant.
> *(Nettbury: foster carer)*

> [Foster child]'s social worker is just excellent. If there's a
> problem with school and I need anything sorted I just
> have to get on the phone and ask. Even when they're not
> there they always get back to me quickly and their advice
> is really useful. I think of it like a team effort now really
> and I think we work very well together.
> *(Wentown: foster carer)*

In addition, a number of carers commented that they felt the presence of
the *Taking Care of Education* project had promoted the significance of the
educational needs of looked after children and was helping to emphasise
that social workers should be displaying an active interest in young people's
educational progress.

However, foster carers across all three authorities reported a range of issues
associated with Social Services more generally that served as barriers to the
effective promotion of young people's educational opportunities.

Communication problems

The most frequently mentioned barrier concerned trying to contact social
workers and other Social Services staff to request advice and assistance
regarding young people's education. Foster carers in Nettbury and Wentown
mentioned at both interview phases that they were not always able to contact
social workers by telephone and their calls were not returned.

> Trying to get through to them on the phone can be a
> nightmare and then once you do get past the
> switchboards the chances of them actually being in the
> office are very slim. I appreciate that they've got other
> cases to deal with and it's not a desk job, but when you
> leave a message you do expect someone to get back to
> you rather than you having to keep chasing and chasing.
> *(Nettbury: foster carer)*

Even where contact was possible there were some concerns that the quality
of information and advice were insufficient.

> Social Services, I don't feel that they help, their advice isn't
> always enough. They often just say 'Speak to a teacher'
> when obviously I've done that, but it isn't always enough.
> Sometimes you need practical help from their end and
> they can't give it to you or they don't know how to.
> *(Wentown: foster carer)*

Staff shortages

During the initial phase of interviews a number of carers commented that
staff shortages in Social Services departments meant that young people did
not always have an allocated case worker, or a consistent worker over a
significant period of time. This could result in problems when seeking advise
regarding educational issues.

> I am not saying it was Social Services' fault but at the time
> they were going through a hard patch of X amount of
> social workers leaving, they didn't have the new social
> workers coming in to assign to the children. If and when
> I had to phone up Social Services, if they put another
> social worker on to talk to me, they didn't know [foster
> child's] case. So I just had to soldier on, on my own.
> *(Wentown: foster carer)*

The same themes recurred with carers who took part in a follow-up interview. Staff shortages and the use of short-term agency workers could impede young people's education. Some carers wished to see more formal systems in place to ensure that even temporary staff were expected to maintain an overview of children's educational progress.

> They've had an awful lot of temps come in and they don't really know the children, they're in for six months and then they're gone. So it's really left to the foster carers to fight for these children to get them into the schools whereas my argument is that some carers can do it and some can't. I personally feel that. I think it would help if there were guidelines actually written down that they have to adhere to with every child, with a checklist of all they should be asking about that young person's education and managers should be checking on this.
> *(Nettbury: foster carer)*

Indeed, one carer in Nettbury believed that a shortage of social workers had seriously affected the ability of existing staff to adequately support young people's education and that social work practice had worsened over the course of the project. They believed that staff shortages had rendered the caseload of current staff too excessive to enable many of them to maintain a holistic view of children's development and a detailed overview of their educational progress.

> They've all got their heads down and they're all running around like headless chickens sometimes and if they're not a person that's well organised, they're losing it, they're just doing the fundamentals and the children are losing out.
> *(Nettbury: foster carer)*

Financial needs

Some carers were unsure of the authority's willingness to provide additional educational tutoring for looked after children. Whilst it appeared that such support could be accessed, this could take a considerable amount of time to arrange and was not viewed as a widely available opportunity. One carer in Allborough expressed frustration over delays in arranging additional maths tuition for a young person who had fallen behind in her studies as a consequence of leaving home and entering the care system.

> There was more hesitation and they took three months to sort it out. I was willing to pay for it in the time waiting around for them to decide, luckily they said yes in the end, but it took them three months to sort it out. I don't think that's on. I think that all children in care should just be entitled to that without hesitation because it's what every parent would do if their kids are struggling and they could afford it, so Social Services should be able to get the funding. I had to ask and push for it, it wasn't offered. So I worry about foster carers that aren't asking and their children are struggling.
> *(Allborough: foster carer)*

In addition, one of the foster carers in Nettbury confirmed the comments of the young person who was progressing to university regarding the difficulty and uncertainty experienced in determining the level of financial assistance Social Services might be able to provide to support them. This is a matter of concern; financial difficulties are an impediment to many students in higher education and care leavers have enough problems to deal with as it is.

Ensuring educational provision

There was some indication that identifying school placements for looked after children entering, or moving within, the looked after system did not always take place according to the correct timescales. Two carers, one in Allborough and one in Nettbury, reported examples at follow-up interviews of young people being without school placements.

> I've got a child at the minute who's not even in school
> and she's not been excluded, I mean that needs
> addressing. She's been moved here but she did really well
> in her SATs last year and now she's not in school and
> that's ridiculous as far as I'm concerned. It's too far here
> from the school that she used to go to and I reckon that's
> an excuse for them to accept that. She's been out from
> the start of September which is six weeks and she doesn't
> get any schooling at all at the moment. I don't know
> what's going on, I've only got her for two weeks so I
> haven't really pushed it.
> *(Allborough: foster carer)*

In Nettbury, a foster carer reported her concerns that there was not always adequate emphasis placed upon identifying school and care placements in a coordinated way.

The carer concerned had learnt that a young person was about to be placed without a school placement.

> On the Tuesday I found out that she didn't have a school
> place so I called them up and said this child is meant to
> be coming to my care on Friday and unless she's got a
> place at the school it's not happening. I felt awful doing
> it but I knew I had to. My link worker was very supportive
> and they rang up Nettbury Social Services and went
> through all the details and I actually had confirmation on
> the Friday that yes, she had a place. So it was fine but it
> took a lot of effort sorting it out. But that shouldn't be
> the case, I shouldn't be put in that position.
> *(Nettbury: foster carer)*

Summary

- Research indicates a positive relationship between levels of educational resources at home and educational success. Educational resources in the family settings include not only material provisions such as quiet study space, academic texts, information and communication technology, but also the availability of interested parents who show interest in young people's progress and encourage achievement.

- Research evidence also shows that the care environment does not always function positively to compensate for earlier disadvantage, and that social workers tend to view the educational needs of looked after children as a lower priority than placement issues, maintaining family relationships and dealing with emotional and physical needs.

- Overall, improvements in the level of educational support available in care placements are noticeable in all three authorities and can mostly be attributed to a number of project activities. Support available for young people living independently is, however, still relatively limited.

- Most project activities aiming at improving educational resources and raising awareness of the importance of supporting and encouraging young people appear to have been very well perceived by those who had benefited or had been involved. However, the relative low attendance and take-up of project activities highlighted a number of barriers to engaging with carers.

- The young people interviewed highlighted the importance of receiving encouragements for educational success as well as having someone showing an interest in their education. Showing expectations of success and celebrating young people's achievements were seen as vital components in supporting their progress.

- The level of support available was often linked to living in a stable environment but placement moves were not seen by young people as detrimental to their education if they received a similar or enhanced level of support in subsequent placements.

- In the initial phase of interviews with young people, social workers were the individuals most frequently mentioned as hindering educational progress.

- Negative comments were often related to the lack of an educational perspective when changes of care placements were arranged and to the lack of financial support for young people going on to further or higher education.

- The follow-up interviews revealed some improvements, as it was felt that some social workers showed more interest in young people's education.

- Carers were positive about individual social workers and acknowledged the difficulties associated with their workload.

- Many carers also believed that the *Taking Care of Education* project had promoted the profile of the educational needs of looked after children and was helping to emphasise that social workers should be displaying an active interest in young people's educational progress.

- However, a significant number of foster carers across all three authorities also reported a range of issues associated with the Social Services system that served as barriers to the effective promotion of young people's educational opportunities. Issues can be grouped in four interrelated categories: communication; staff shortage; financial needs; and ensuring educational provision. There was no significant sign of improvement at follow-up interviews.

10. Conclusion

The main aim of the *Taking Care of Education* project was to influence local authority policy and working practice in such a way that it might improve the educational opportunities and outcomes for looked after children. It has been introduced in a context where there is much greater awareness of the additional challenges looked after children encounter at school and beyond, in further and higher education and employment. At the same time, despite a growing research base, there has been a lack of information about the relationship that exists between specific interventions and outcomes for children and young people, and about the best ways in which to develop a culture within local authorities that can effectively promote the educational welfare of looked after children. This evaluation has sought to develop this evidence base. In this final chapter, the intention is to draw together some of the key issues from the evaluation, and also to consider their implications for practice, policy and research. As one of the first major evaluations concerned with the education of looked after children, many useful lessons have been learned.

Educational progress and achievement

A critical question for the evaluation was the extent to which the *Taking Care of Education* project had succeeded in making a difference for looked after children. An obvious first step in answering this lies in determining whether any change had actually occurred in looked after children's educational experiences and outcomes over the three-year period. Encouragingly, the answer to this question is yes. Some positive change appears to have arisen in the education of those children involved in the evaluation sample, both in terms of their own subjective ratings and observations and the views of key adults in their lives. It was also reassuring to discover that the majority of young people in the follow-up sample were still engaged in education.

Government returns were one of the key sources of information in tracking children's progress. These suggested that, for the three authorities concerned, there was some evidence that educational outcomes for looked after children have improved over the past three years at certain Key Stages of the National Curriculum and that such improvement is greater than that apparent in national trends. However, some comment is required with regard to such government returns as a source. While these are undoubtedly important in understanding national trends, analysis of such statistics for individual local authorities is weakened by the fact that the limited numbers involved can frequently render percentage ratings meaningless. Aiming to establish whether significant change has occurred in annual outcomes is an impossible task where the number of children included in cohorts can be as few as three or four. Local analysis of statistics is therefore extremely important.

Nevertheless, at Key Stage 4, where GCSE or GNVQ examinations are involved, there were enough young people in each cohort across all three authorities to justify the use of percentage ratings. At this level, educational outcomes in Nettbury show the most consistent record of improvement, with looked after children's performance improving to reach a similar level of performance to non-looked after children. In Allborough, outcomes for looked after children also improved in 2001/2002, despite a dip in performance for 2000/2001. In Wentown, performance at this level fell to below national levels in 2001/2002, although the proportion of young people gaining five GCSEs at grades A to C is actually above national levels in 2000/2001 and 2001/2002.

Even the interpretation of these statistics is not entirely straightforward. In particular, it must be noted that the cohorts that are being analysed in consecutive years are not always comparable. Within each authority, groups vary from year to year in terms of numbers with statements of special educational needs, those experiencing permanent exclusions, significant periods of absence and indeed rates of young people being entered for examinations. Whilst at a national level it may be possible to take these effects into account to determine whether significant change has arisen, this is not possible with the much smaller numbers involved at local authority level. Hence, whilst findings relating to outcome indicators may be suggestive they are far from conclusive.

At the same time, this apparent problem highlights the importance of recognising the heterogeneity of the looked after group and the importance of linking initiatives focused on looked after children with other dimensions of educational policy and practice. It is also important to examine these issues within the context of local patterns of schooling – for example, numbers of looked after children present in schools, and the different kinds of school that exist in a local authority. Evaluation and research in this area also need to make better links between the experiences of looked after children and the significance of factors such as gender and ethnicity. These issues will be taken forward in the next phase of the *Taking Care of Education* evaluation.

The evaluation also examined other outcome measures for the sample group of young people. Overall, these indicated positive change for looked after children to a degree that was often more substantial than previous evidence might suggest. Significant increases over time in ratings of self-esteem and decreases in *Strengths and Difficulty Questionnaire* (SDQ) ratings at follow-up interview suggest that young people's psychological well-being and resilience has improved over the course of the project. Young people's reported perceptions of educational progress were also significantly higher by the time of follow-up interviews.

The general pattern of improvements observed on standardised measures and young people's subjective assessments of their progress is in keeping with patterns of improvement regarding GCSE attainment levels. This latter point is interesting in terms of indicating the importance of listening to and taking seriously young people's own views of their educational progress, and ensuring that these are integrated into planning for looked after young people. The most pronounced improvements in self-esteem, SDQ ratings and perceptions of progress were observed in Nettbury, with Allborough also showing a slightly higher level of improvement than that observed in Wentown.

The impact of project activities: support from carers and the care environment

This brings us to the question of how far project activities contributed to individual outcomes. This is far from easy, and multiple factors are likely to be involved in explaining any improvements.

There were many differences in project implementation styles and chosen project activities across the three authorities. This would be expected in the light of the different degrees and types of activity directed towards the education of looked after children prior to the project's introduction, and differences in the contexts in which Project Lead Officers were operating. Nettbury was the authority that directed the highest degree of project activity towards promoting the resilience and self-esteem of looked after children, and in general included the highest number of project activities that might be classed as directly supporting young people's education. This could explain the higher degree of improvement in measures of psychological well-being which in turn may be associated with educational progress. Equally, however, project implementation in Wentown involved more activities intended to promote young people's resilience and directly support their education than in Allborough. If such discrete project activities were directly linked to improvements in psychological well-being and educational progress, one might have expected higher ratings in Wentown than Allborough.

The most significant explanatory factor forwarded for positive progress by the young people themselves was the support and encouragement provided by foster and residential carers. This corresponds to other research (see, for example, Jackson and Martin 1998), but has not previously been expressed quite so clearly by a group of young people currently within the care system. The communication of an educational ethos within care placements and the perception that carers were interested in and willing to support young people's education was seen as a major factor in enabling young people to succeed. This suggests strongly that social workers and others need to ensure, when identifying placements for young people, that appropriate educational support is available and, where this does not appear to be the case, that arrangements are altered accordingly. This could mean providing additional training and support for carers in relation to the educational needs of individual young people. It will also be important to monitor the ongoing needs of young people and carers in terms of support – for example, as a young person moves from primary into secondary school.

The majority of young people in the follow-up sample had remained in such supportive placements for at least two years and many commented that this level of stability had enhanced their educational progress. That said, stability of placement is likely to be of most relevance where young people benefit from a rewarding and enriching placement. Young people who had experienced placement change viewed this as a positive factor if they moved to a more educationally and generally supportive placement. The awareness of educational issues demonstrated by social workers is also an issue during this process of change. In addition, it is only when such stability is in place that young people are in a position to access the curriculum and benefit from support available from teaching staff. This is, after all, an avenue of support that is only available to those young people who are encouraged to attend school in the first place. This question of the relationship between 'stability' and educational outcomes is a complex one and is deserving of further investigation.

The availability of adequate educational support in care placements is also important in explaining improvements in outcomes for young people across the three authorities. The majority of positive comments at follow-up interview regarding educational support obtained from carers were provided by young people looked after in Nettbury, followed by those in Allborough, with those in Wentown giving fewest comments about supportive carers. This pattern is reflected in findings regarding GCSE attainment and young people's perspectives of educational progress, where greatest improvement occurs in Nettbury, followed by Allborough and then Wentown. Although the numbers of young people in the current study are too small to suggest a definite link, the current findings do imply that supportive care placements are a key factor in facilitating educational success for looked after children.

Differences in the proportion of young people providing positive comments about carers may be linked to the focus of the *Taking Care of Education* project in each authority. A good deal of project activity in Nettbury was directed towards the provision of training sessions for residential and foster carers to enable them to support young people's literacy and numeracy development. Information seminars for foster carers were also held in Allborough and a great deal of work was focused on enabling residential carers to support and encourage young people's educational achievements. In both these authorities, encouraging carers to attend these events proved challenging. In Wentown, less work was directed at carers as part of the project; though there was some activity arising in Wentown's residential centres, including identification of education representatives and the provision of study support packs to help staff develop young people's literacy skills.

It may be that rather than being influenced by project-related training activities, carers' practice has remained constant and improvements are largely due to a considerable number of the sample remaining in a constant placement over the course of the project and being better able to benefit from available support. Pre-existing practice within the local authorities is also likely to have been important. In terms of the development of practice, it would appear that a key issue for local authorities is the extent to which educational issues are *routinely* highlighted during induction and ongoing professional training, in addition to events specifically focused on the education of looked after children.

Project activities also appeared to have a direct impact on young people's opportunity to access a range of material resources within their care placements, and these were valued by young people and carers alike. The availability of computers had been enhanced by project activity in Wentown whereby children in foster care were provided with computers, while schemes such as a *Book of My Own* in Nettbury, and library deliveries to residential centres in Allborough had increased opportunities to encourage and enable children to read. Although there remain some areas where the availability of resources could be improved, the overall impression is a positive one. In general, young people appeared to appreciate the increased provision of such resources although it is difficult to determine a definite link between availability of resources and improved educational outcomes.

The impact of project activities: support from school and teachers

A significant number of young people also said that teaching staff and schools in general had enabled them to make good educational progress. Teachers featured strongly in response to questions about individuals who help make a difference to young people's progress. This point highlights the need to ensure that the contribution of teachers and schools is fully included and properly understood in research and evaluation concerning the education of looked after children. Too often, research in the area of the education of looked after children has failed to reflect the reality of the schooling experience of young people themselves. There is also a danger that assumptions can be made about the views of teachers and other education professionals.

Schools, rather than teachers, were directly mentioned as a factor in maintaining educational progress where commendation systems were in place. This again serves to illustrate young people's desire to have their efforts and achievements acknowledged and is in keeping with the finding that awards ceremonies were so widely appreciated. Young people themselves are obviously well aware of the central role that schools and colleges can play in their lives. It is, therefore, perhaps unfortunate that so little project activity directly involved them in project-related activities.

The desire to have achievement acknowledged was also evident in comments relating to Personal Education Plans (PEPs). A number of young people reported that they would – or already did in the case of those who had PEPs – appreciate the opportunity to develop realistic targets which enabled progress towards a given objective to be tracked and recognised. In terms of the overall reaction to PEPs and designated teachers, the response of young people was mixed. Whilst the majority appreciated the potential benefits of such government-driven initiatives, their comments also remind us of the individuality of looked after children and young people. A number of the sample resisted the notion of policy and practice that singled them out from their non-looked after peers. This indicates the necessity to acknowledge the diversity of the looked after group and note that policy and practice initiatives that appeal to some young people may not be universally welcomed by, or appropriate for, all.

The findings covering awareness of PEPs and designated teachers indicate that the majority of young people are not yet aware of such initiatives. This is perhaps of more cause for concern in relation to PEPs as all looked after children and young people are meant to have such a plan. There is some indication that plans are being developed without young people's knowledge and this is likely to undermine the potential for such documents to support young people's education. In terms of designated teachers, there are some contradictory findings in terms of whether the role should involve a pastoral support function. Whilst some young people would welcome opportunities to access general support from a designated teacher, others acknowledge that this is potentially problematic if young people do not relate well to their designated teacher. This would suggest that the flexibility contained within the government guidance, to acknowledge that a support function may not always be appropriate, is sensible.

There is also a need for more thought to be given to ways in which activities for looked after children can be integrated into existing out-of-school activities. On the one hand, it is understandable that certain authorities felt the need to compensate for the limited uptake of out-of-school-hours learning amongst the looked after group. On the other hand, it might have been more advantageous to begin to question why mainstream activities were not being used and begin to address this rather than establishing separate groups away from the school setting. This would of course have involved a much higher degree of liaison with individual schools, foster and residential carers, and young people themselves to determine what might make out-of-school-hours learning a more viable option for looked after children. This approach also has practical advantages in view of the small numbers of looked after children within any single school, or indeed year group, across a local authority. There is a danger that schools are considered as distant entities that are somewhat divorced from the corporate body of the authority in terms of looked after children (Gilligan 1998; Lewis 1996).

Barriers to educational progress

Whilst it is encouraging to report positive findings for the majority of the follow-up sample, it should not be overlooked that some young people continue to report being looked after as having a detrimental effect on their educational progress. It is somewhat disheartening to observe that explanations given for this repeat many of the themes observed at original interview, and those outlined in previous research into the under-achievement of looked after children: placement instability, the distress of entering the looked after system, the lack of someone showing interest and encouragement – especially amongst social workers – and negative stereotyping of looked after children.

Comments regarding the absence of support and encouragement from carers appear to indicate that ongoing efforts need to be made in communicating the importance of supporting young people's educational opportunities. Some young people continue to perceive that negative stereotypes of young people in public care are held by certain professionals they interact with, as well as their non-looked after peers. This suggests that the *Taking Care of Education* project may need to carry out further work to promote positive images of young people who are looked after, images which stress their individuality and educate others regarding the diversity of reasons why young people might enter the care system.

In interpreting the findings from the follow-up sample, it is also necessary to acknowledge that the sample may be biased towards those young people who have had relatively positive experiences whilst being looked after. Those young people who were lost to the sample tended to provide more negative ratings on measures of psychological well-being and self-esteem and estimates of educational progress. These young people had also experienced more exclusion episodes and may have experienced greater placement change than those who were retained for the follow-up sample. Hence we cannot avoid the possibility that less positive findings would have emerged if all young people had continued to the follow-up sample. Nonetheless, for the 56 young people who were willing for us to gain insight from their experiences over a two-year period, there are indications of positive change.

Whilst a simple explanation of why such change may have arisen is difficult to forward, and the individuality of the young people concerned should not be overlooked, there does appear to be some consensus regarding a key element in promoting educational progress. The notion of encouraging and acknowledging young people's progress is constantly repeated in young people's explanations of why their education is going well, be this encouragement from carers, teachers and social workers, or through corporate events like awards ceremonies. The most commonly cited examples of support and encouragement related to carers, and many young people felt they had benefited from a care placement that enabled them to feel secure and settled and that promoted an educational ethos. The absence of such support was a central feature of explanations forwarded by young people whose achievement is less positive. Carers also appreciated working with social workers who could provide information on educational issues and, in line with previous research, were reliable and easy to contact.

There is nothing new or surprising in the discovery that young people believe obtaining effective support, encouragement and acknowledgement of their efforts is central to educational success. Indeed, the current findings echo the observations of previous research on factors that promote educational achievement for looked after children (see for example Harker and others 2003; Martin and Jackson 2002; Jackson and Martin 1998). Such observations do not run counter to basic motivational forces assumed to contribute to achievement for all children, or indeed for adults. In the 'adult world' it seems obvious, for instance, that employees will not work to their full potential without recognition of their efforts. There seems to be no reason why this should be any different for looked after children.

Developing a 'corporate' approach

The *Taking Care of Education* project may well have contributed to the generally positive outcomes for young people in the evaluation sample through the provision of direct support for young people, improved resources in care placements and training sessions for carers. However, it is possible that such activities may have only a short-term impact for a limited number of young people. The question of what aspects of the project will continue to influence policy and practice in the local authority is therefore important.

The underlying aim of the project was to promote sustainable change through influencing corporate policy and practice to such an extent that promoting the educational opportunities of looked after children became embedded within everyday practice. The multiple strands of information contributing to the *Taking Care of Education* evaluation enabled us to provide a detailed account of the processes involved in attempting to develop this 'whole authority' approach. Certainly, key personnel across all three authorities appreciated the significant role the project had played in enabling them to emphasise the importance of a corporate response. A number of elements that appeared of particular relevance to achieving this were identified.

Perhaps the most significant of these included the provision of the Project Lead Officer post. The availability of a dedicated staff member to develop and disseminate whole authority policy statements and principles of corporate responsibility was seen as a key feature in raising awareness of the educational needs of looked after children throughout the authority. The dedicated post was also seen to ensure that promoting the educational opportunities of looked after children remained a high profile issue whose importance was continually re-emphasised throughout a variety of departments. Even with the impetus stemming from the Quality Protects initiative and the Joint Guidance (Department for Education and Employment/Department of Health 2000), there were concerns that where staff were working to prioritise a wide range of issues, the education of looked after children could become peripheral. Inevitably, wider organisational issues such as staff shortage also affected the degree of continuity surrounding practice in this area. The Project Lead Officer role was offered the necessary 'protected time' required to oversee the work of a range of departments and services and ensure that the importance of a corporate response to the education of looked after children was constantly stressed. In keeping with previous research (Coles and others 2000; Harker and others 2003) the importance of the Project Lead Officer adopting a relatively senior position within the authority also seemed of relevance in the current study.

The development of corporate principles and policy statements to extend educational opportunities for looked after children was not seen as sufficient in promoting a whole authority response. A number of personnel believed that, whilst senior and middle management understood the aims of the project and the importance of the issues, some operational staff were less aware of the need to adopt a holistic approach to the education of looked after children. Policy statements and principles were not believed to have been fully translated or embedded into the practice of individual service teams. Measuring the amount and quality of inter-professional practice also proved difficult.

Some project activities tried to address these issues, and training was an important part of this. Training events were held in two authorities that involved social workers, residential staff and designated teachers, and these were positively viewed in terms of the impact they were expected to have had upon staff practice. Problems were encountered with respect to attendance, and there was particular concern at the absence of designated teachers from many such events. Local authorities also sometimes felt they were relatively powerless in such matters where individual schools were concerned. However, one authority had successfully engaged head-teachers as willing participants in inter-professional work. It should also be noted that low attendance rates at training events may not indicate that teaching staff do not wish to partake in inter-professional work but simply that additional effort, or alternative means, of involving such staff may be required. Wentown's experience in relation to work-shadowing suggests that perseverance can pay in building-up interest in such activities. Certainly, other evidence attests to the difficulties teaching staff face in obtaining cover to attend joint training events (Baginsky 2003).

Given similar difficulties in encouraging foster carers to attend training events, it appears that the provision of inter-professional training, while a key part of the development of practice, is a significant challenge to authorities. In two of the project authorities there are plans to move towards a system where training events are organised for small, local inter-professional groups of foster carers, social workers and designated teachers. It will be of interest to follow the development of such groups and their impact upon joint working and communication between foster carers and other professionals.

Perhaps the most challenging aspect of inter-professional practice which none of the authorities had fully managed to address concerned information sharing issues. Developing data sharing protocols and systems to facilitate joint access to information about the care and education of looked after children proved to be more complex than initially anticipated. Barriers existed in the form of anxieties about the kind of information that could be shared, the ethical issues and poor quality of data collected and recorded by different services, rather than from technical difficulties. It is therefore important that a correct understanding of data protection and confidentiality procedures is properly disseminated within local authorities, and that work continues in the development of confidentiality statements and principles to which individual staff and departments can sign up. However, these difficulties are far from being uncommon in projects taking an inter-professional approach, and it may be important for the authorities to learn from other initiatives relating to children and young people that are underway in their local areas.

The *Taking Care of Education* project has benefited from a significant investment of financial resources, and from the appointment of Project Lead Officers with the specific task of developing the work of the corporate parent in regard to the education of looked after children. It is gratifying that evaluation has been recognised as an important element in understanding the benefits of the project. Inevitably, some activities appear to have worked more effectively than others and it is clear that some of the issues known to disadvantage looked after children, for example lack of support and low expectations, are frequently resistant to even the most determined efforts. At the same time, many encouraging findings have emerged, most notably in terms of improved outcomes for young people, acknowledgement of positive support provided by carers and teachers, improved educational environments and a heightened awareness and understanding of educational issues as they relate to looked after children. The evaluation has been successful in developing understanding of the interplay of the different actors and organisational elements which serve to influence the educational outcomes for the looked after group. We have also highlighted the importance of the views of young people themselves about their educational experiences. It is clear that further work is required in terms of the extent to which the promotion of corporate responsibility for the education of looked after children, as well as specific activities targeted at young people, make a difference to educational experiences and outcomes. These issues will continue to be explored as the project and evaluation continue into a second phase.

Summary

- The *Taking Care of Education* project provided funding for three local authorities to develop their work in relation to the education of looked after children and young people. It is important to note that all three had a strong foundation from which to work.

- The evaluation found evidence that progress had been made in regard to looked after young people's educational outcomes in each of the authorities. It also identified a number of difficulties associated with measuring these outcomes and assessing how far improvements could be attributed to project activities. Considerable care is required in interpreting local authority statistics relating to educational outcomes for looked after children and young people.

- Supportive care placements were identified as central to educational progress. This suggests that ensuring carers understand the importance of education and receive training about how to respond to educational issues is an important part of developing an educationally supportive culture for local authorities.

- The three local authorities made considerable efforts to improve the educational environment for looked after children and young people. Schemes such as those involving the provision of computers were appreciated by young people and carers alike and appeared to make a positive, and practical, contribution to young people's schooling.

- Young people recognised the importance of schools and colleges to their lives and futures. They appreciated having their achievements at school celebrated, and commendations and award ceremonies were important elements in this.

- Young people had varying views on the role of Personal Education Plans and designated teachers. However, the research highlighted the need to involve young people in these plans. It is also important that staff understand the purpose and function of PEPs.

- Social workers can play a positive role in encouraging young people educationally, but this appeared to happen relatively rarely. Carers also highlighted some of the difficulties associated with obtaining advice and help on educational issues from social workers.

- The education of looked after children and young people is an issue that still appears to require a 'champion' who can coordinate work in this area. The importance of the Project Lead Officers in fulfilling this role was identified in all three local authorities.

- The sharing of information relating to looked after children continued to present challenges for all three authorities, despite considerable efforts on the part of the Project Lead Officers. The evaluation highlighted the magnitude of this task, and suggested that while its resolution may be beyond the scope of a time-limited project, the emphasis of *Taking Care of Education* on a whole authority approach was important in taking work in this area forward.

References

Alderman, M K (1999) *Motivation for achievement*. Lawrence Erlbaum

Aldgate, J and others (1993) Social work and the education of children in foster care, *Adoption and Fostering*, 17, 3, 25–35

Arblaster, L, Conway, J, Foreman, A and Hawtin, M (1996) *Asking the impossible? Inter-agency working to address the housing, health and social care needs of people in ordinary housing*. The Policy Press

Atkinson, M and Hornby, G (2002) *Mental health handbook for schools*. RoutledgeFalmer

Atkinson, M and others (2001) *Multi-agency working: an audit of activity*. National Foundation for Educational Research

Atkinson, M and others (2002) *Multi-agency working: detailed study*. National Foundation for Educational Research

Audit Commission (1994) *Seen but not heard: co-ordinating child health and social services for children in need*. HMSO

Baginsky, M (2003) *Responsibility without power? Local education authorities and child protection*. NSPCC

Bald, J, Bean, J and Meegan, F (1995) *A book of my own*. Who Cares? Trust

Bebbington, A R and Miles, J (1989) The background of children who enter local authority care, *British Journal of Social Work*, 19, 349–368

Berridge, D and Brodie, I (1998) *Children's homes revisited*. Jessica Kingsley

Berridge, D and Cleaver, H (1987) *Foster home breakdown*. Basil Blackwell

Berridge, D and others (1996) *Hello – Is anybody listening? The education of young people in residential care*. University of Luton

Biehal, N and others (1995) *Moving on: young people and leaving care schemes*. HMSO

Blyth, E (2001) The impact of the first term of the New Labour government on social work practice in Britain: The interface between education policy and social work, *British Journal of Social Work*, 31, 563–577

Borland, M (1996) *Review of Statements of Functions and Objectives in Residential Child Care*. Scottish Office Central Research Unit

Borland, M 'Educating accommodated children' *in* Hill, M and Iwaniec, D *eds* (2000) *Child Welfare, Policy and Practice*. Jessica Kingsley

Borland, M and others (1998) *Education and care away from home*. Scottish Council for Research in Education

Brodie, I (2001) *Children's homes and school exclusion: redefining the problem*. Jessica Kingsley

Brooks, G, Schagen, I and Nastat, P (1997) *Trends in reading at eight: A report on the 1995 survey of reading attainment in Year 3 in England and Wales*. National Foundation for Educational Research

Brophy, J (1987) Synthesis of research on strategies for motivating students to learn, *Educational Leadership*, October, 40–48

Brown, B B and Steinberg, L (1991) *Non-instructional influences on adolescent engagement and achievement: Final report, Project 2 (ED340641)*. University of Wisconsin-Madison, National Centre on Effective Secondary Schools

Bullock, R, Little, M and Millham, S (1994) Children's return from state care to education, *Oxford Review of Education*, 20, 3, 307–316

Buchanan, A (1993) Life under the Children Act 1989, *Adoption and Fostering*, 17, 3, 35–38

Camp, W G (1990) Participation in student activities and achievement: a covariance structural analysis, *Journal of Educational Research*, 83, 5, 272–278

Carlen, P, Gleeson, D and Wardhaugh, J (1992) *Truancy: the politics of compulsory schooling*. Open University Press

Cheeseborough, S (2002) *The educational attainment of people who have been in care: findings from the 1970 British Cohort Study*. London School of Economics

Cheung, S Y and Heath, A (1994) After care: the education and occupation of adults who have been in care and at home, *Oxford Review of Education*, 20, 3, 317–327

Children and Young People's Unit (2000) *The Children's Fund*. Children and Young People's Unit

Cigno, K and Gore, J (1998) *An evaluation of the multi-agency children's centre, Walker Street, Hull*. University of Hull

Coles, B, England, J and Rugg, J (2000) Spaced out? Young people in social housing estates: social exclusion and multi-agency work, Journal of Youth Studies, 3, 1, 21–35

Consortium on the School-based Promotion of Social Competence 'The school-based promotion of social competence: theory, research, practice and policy' *in* Haggerty, R and others *eds* (1994) *Stress, risk and resilience in children and adolescents: processes, mechanisms and interventions*. Cambridge University Press

Cox, T (2000) *Combating educational disadvantage: meeting the needs of vulnerable children*. Falmer Press

Curry, E and Johnson, N (1990) *Beyond self-esteem: developing a general sense of human value*. National Association for Education of Young Children

Department for Education and Employment (1997a) *Education Action Zones: an introduction*. Department for Education and Employment

Department for Education and Employment (1997b) *Excellence in schools*. The Stationery Office

Department for Education and Employment (1998) *Guidance for LEAs on Education Development Plans*. Department for Education and Employment

Department for Education and Employment (1999a) *Excellence in cities*. Department for Education and Employment

Department for Education and Employment (1999b) *Extending opportunity: a national framework for study support*. Department for Education and Employment

Department for Education and Employment (1999c) *Sure Start: making a difference for children and families*. Department for Education and Employment

Department for Education and Employment (2000) *Connexions: The best start in life for every young person*. Department for Education and Employment

Department for Education and Employment/Department of Health (2000) *Guidance on the education of children in public care*. HMSO

Department for Education and Skills (2001) *Schools achieving success (White Paper)*. The Stationery Office

Department for Education and Skills (2002a) *Extended schools: providing opportunities and services for all*. Department for Education and Skills

Department for Education and Skills (2002b) *Permanent exclusions from schools and exclusion appeals in England 2001/2002*. Department for Education and Skills

Department for Education and Skills (2003) *School Admissions Code of Practice*. Department for Education and Skills

Department of Health (1998) *Quality Protects: framework for action*. HMSO

Department of Health (1999) *The Quality Protects programme: transforming children's services 2000/2001*. Department of Health

Department of Health (2001a) *Children (Leaving Care) Act 2000*. HMSO

Department of Health (2001b) *The Children Act Report 2000*. HMSO

Department of Health (2001c) *Explanatory notes to Children (Leaving Care) Act 2000*. The Stationery Office

Department of Health (2001d) *The Quality Protects programme: transforming children's services 2002/2003*. Department of Health

Department of Health (2002a) *Children's homes: National Minimum Standards: children's homes regulations*. The Stationery Office

Department of Health (2002b) *Fostering services: National Minimum Standards: fostering services regulations*. The Stationery Office

Department of Health (2003a) *Children looked after by local authorities, year ending 31 March 2002 (England)*. HMSO

Department of Health (2003b) *Outcome indicators for looked after children, year ending 30 September 2002*. HMSO

Department of Health (2003c) *The Quality Protects programme: Transforming children's services 2003/2004*. Department of Health

Department of Social Security (1999) *Opportunity for all: Tackling poverty and social exclusion*. The Stationery Office

Dubow, E (2001) Predictors of future expectations of inner city children: a 9 month prospective study, *Journal of Early Adolescence*, 21, 1 (Feb), 5–28

Dyson, A, Lin and M, Millward, A (1998) *Effective communication between schools, LEAs and health and social services in the field of special educational needs*. Research Report RR60, Department for Education and Employment

Elliot, A (2002) The educational expectations of looked after children, *Adoption and Fostering*, 26, 3, 58–68

Essen, J, Lambert, L and Head, J (1976) School attainment of children who have been in care, *Child Care, Health and Development*, 2, 339 – 351

Evans, R (2000) *The Education and Progress of Children in Public Care*. PhD Thesis, University of Warwick, Institute of Education

Ferguson, T (1966) *Children in care and after*. Oxford University Press

Fergusson, D and Lynskey, M (1996) Adolescent resiliency to family adversity, *Journal of Child Psychology and Psychiatry*, 37, 281–292

Finn, J D and Rock, D A (1997) Academic success amongst students at risk of school failure, *Journal of Applied Psychology*, 82, 2, 231–234

Firth, H and Fletcher, B 'Developing equal chances: a whole authority approach' *in* Jackson, S ed (2001) *Nobody ever told us school mattered*. British Agencies for Adoption and Fostering

Firth, H and Horrocks, C 'No home, no school, no future: exclusions and children who are "looked after"' in Blyth, E and Milner, J eds (1996) *Exclusion from school: inter-professional issues for policy and practice*. Routledge

Fletcher, B (1993) *Not just an name*. Who Cares? Trust and National Consumer Council

Fletcher-Campbell, F (1997) *The education of children who are looked after*. National Foundation for Educational Research

Fletcher-Campbell, F and Archer, T (2003) *Achievement at Key Stage 4 of young people in public care*. National Foundation for Educational Research

Fletcher-Campbell, F and Hall, C (1990) *Changing schools, changing people: The education of children in care*. National Foundation for Educational Research

Francis, J (2000) Investing in children's futures: enhancing the educational arrangements of 'looked after' children, *Child and Family Social Work*, 24, 3, 241–260

Furnham, A and Rawles, R (1996) Job search strategies, attitudes to school and attributions about unemployment, *Journal of Adolescence*, 19, 4, 355–369

Galloway, D, Armstrong, D and Tomlinson, S (1994) *The assessment of special educational needs – whose problem?* Longman

Gatehouse, M and Ward, H (2002) *Information and information systems for looked after children (Annual Report 2001)* Loughborough University, Centre for Child and Family Research

Gaviria, A and Raphael, S (2001) School-based peer effects and juvenile behaviour, *The Review of Economics and Statistics*, 83, 2, 257–268

Gerwitz, S 'Education Action Zones: emblems of the third way?' *in* Dean, H and Woods, R eds (1999) *Social Policy Review 11*. Social Policy Association

Gilligan, R (1998) The importance of schools and teachers in child welfare, *Child and Family Social Work*, 3, 13–25

Gilligan, R (2000) Adversity, resilience and young people: the protective value of positive school and spare time experiences, *Children and Society*, 14, 37–47

Gilligan, R (1999) Enhancing the resilience of children and young people in public care by mentoring their talents and interests, *Child and Family Social Work*, 4, 3, 187–196 Goddard (2000)

Goddard, J (2000) Research review: the education of looked after children, *Child family social work*, 5, 1, 79-86

Goodenow, C (1993) The psychological sense of school membership among adolescents: scale development and educational correlates, *Psychology in the Schools*, 30, 79–90

Goodman, R (1999) The extended version of the Strengths and Difficulties Questionnaire as a guide to child psychiatric caseness and consequent burden, *Journal of Child Psychology and Psychiatry*, 40, 5, 791–799

Goodman, R (2001) Psychometric properties of the Strengths and Difficulties Questionnaire, *Journal of American Academic Child Adolescent Psychiatry*, 40, 11, 1337–1345

Goodman, R, Ford, T and Metzler, H (2003) Mental health problems of children in the community: 18 month follow up, *BMJ*, 324, 1496–1497

Gordon, D, Parker, R and Loughran, F (2000) *Disabled children in Britain: a re-analysis of the OPCS disability survey*. The Stationery Office

Gower, L (1999) *The educational outcomes of looked after children* MA Thesis, Anglia Polytechnic School of Education

Griffiths, C (1999) *Breaking their fall*. National Literacy Association

Hallett, C (1995) *Inter-agency co-ordination in child protection*. HMSO

Hanushek, E and others (2001) *Does peer ability affect student achievement? Working Papers No 8502*. Working Papers from National Bureau of Economic Research

Harker, R (2001) *Taking care of education: young people's experiences in three local authorities*. National Children's Bureau

Harker, R and others (2003) Who takes care of education? Looked after children's perceptions of support for educational progress, *Child and Family Social Work*, 8, 89–100

Hayden, C (1996) Primary age children excluded from school: a multi-agency focus for concern, *Children and Society*, 8, 3, 257–273

Hayden, C (1997) *Children excluded from primary school*. Open University Press

Heath, A F, Colton, M J and Aldgate, J (1994) Failure to escape: a longitudinal study of foster children's educational attainment, *British Journal of Social Work*, 24, 3, 241–260

H M Treasury (2003) *Every Child Matters* (CM 5860). The Stationery Office

Home Office (1998) *Crime and Disorder Act 1998: introductory guide*. Home Office

House of Commons Health Committee (1998) *Children looked after by local authorities. Volume 1: Report and Proceedings of the Committee*. The Stationery Office

Houston, D M (1995) Surviving a failure: efficacy and a laboratory based test of the hopelessness model of depression, *European Journal of Social Psychology*, 25, 545–558

Hudson, B (1987) Collaboration in social welfare, *Policy and Politics*, 15, 175–182

Hudson, B, Hardy, B, Henwood, M and Wistow, G (1997) Working across professional boundaries: primary health care and social care, *Public Money and Management*, Oct/Dec, 25–30

Jackson, S (1987) *The education of children in care*. Bristol papers in applied social studies No. 1, University of Bristol

Jackson, S and Martin, P Y (1998) Surviving the care system: education and resilience, *Journal of Adolescence*, 21, 569–583

Jackson, S and Sachdev, D (2001) *Better education, better futures*. Barnardo's

Jackson, S and Thomas, N (2001) *What works in creating stability for looked after children*. Barnardo's

Jackson, S and others (2002) *The costs and benefits of educating children in care* Institute of Education Cohort Studies Working Paper 4, Institute of Education

Leathard, A (1994) *Going inter-professional: working together for health and welfare*. Routledge

Lee, C and Bobko, P (1994) Self-efficacy beliefs: comparison of five measures, *Journal of Applied Psychology*, 79, 364–369

Lewis, M (1996) *Integrating services for children at risk: Denmark, France, Netherlands, United Kingdom (England and Wales)*. OECD Centre for Educational Research and Innovation

Lynes, D and Goddard, J (1995) *The view from the front: the user view of child care in Norfolk*. Norfolk In-Care Group, Norfolk County Council

Lumsden, L S (1994) *Student motivation to learn*. Eric Clearinghouse on Educational Management

Maguire, M, Maguire, S and Vincent, J (2001) *Implementation of the Education Maintenance Allowance pilots: The First Year* Research Report 255, Department for Education and Skills

Maguire, S, Maguire, M and Vincent, J (2002) *Implementation of the Education Maintenance Allowance Pilots: The Second Year* Research Report 333, Department for Education and Skills

Marjoribanks, K (1979) *Families and their learning environments*. Routledge and Kegan Paul

Marsh, H W (1992) Extracurricular activities: beneficial extension of the traditional curriculum or subversion of academic goals?, *Journal of Educational Psychology*, 84, 4, 553–562

Martin, P Y and Jackson, S (2002) Educational success for children in public care: advice from a group of high achievers, *Child and Family Social Work*, 7, 2, 121–130

McCallum, I (1996) The chosen ones?, *Education*, 187 ,3 ,12–13 (19 January)

McCallum, I and Demie, F (2001) Social class, ethnicity and educational performance, *Educational Research*, 43, 2, 147–159

Meece, J and McColskey, W (2001) *Student motivation: A guide for teachers and school improvement teams*. SERVE, University of North Carolina

Meltzer, H and others (2003) *The mental health of young people looked after by local authorities in England*. Office for National Statistics

Ministerial Task Force on Children's Safeguards (1998) *The Government's response to the Children's Safeguards Review (Cm 4105)*. The Stationery Office

Morgan, S (1999) *Care about education: a joint training curriculum for supporting children in public care*. National Children's Bureau

Morris, J (2000) *Having someone who cares? Barriers to change in the public care of children*. Joseph Rowntree Foundation and the National Children's Bureau

Mortimore, J and Blackstone, T (1982) *Education and disadvantage*. Heinemann

Office for Standards in Education (2002) *Raising achievement of children in public care*. Office for Standards in Education

Oliver, C and others (2001) *Figures and facts: Local authority variance on indicators concerning child protection and children looked after*. Thomas Coram Research Unit

Pajares, F and Schunk, D H (2001) 'Self-beliefs and school success: self-efficacy, self-concept, and school achievement' *in* Riding, R J and Rayner, S G *eds* (2001) *Self–perception: international perspectives on individual differences (volume 2)*. Ablex Publishing

Pisapia, J and Westfall, A (1994) *Developing resilient schools and resilient students*. Research Brief 19, Metropolitan Educational Research Consortium

Pocklington, K 'The evaluator's view' *in* Myers, K *ed* (1996) *School improvement in practice: Schools Make a Difference Project*. Falmer Press

Posner, J K and Vandell, D L (1994) Low income children's after-school care: are there beneficial effects of after-school programmes?, *Child Development*, 65, 2, 440–456

Pringle, M K (1965) *Deprivation and Education*. Longman

Quinton, D and others (1996) *Establishing permanent placements in middle childhood: Maudsley Adoption and Fostering Study Report for the Department of Health*. Department of Health

Rea Price, J and Pugh, G (1996) *Championing children*. Manchester City Council

Rees, J 'Making residential care educational care' *in* Jackson, S *ed* (2001) *Nobody ever told us school mattered*. British Agencies for Adoption and Fostering

Roaf, C (2002) *Coordinating services for included children*. Open University Press

Roaf, C and Lloyd, C (1995) *Multi-agency work with young people in difficulty: Findings No. 68*. Joseph Rowntree Foundation

Robbins, D (2001) *Transforming children's services: An evaluation of local responses to the Quality Protects Programme Year 3*. Department of Health

Robertson, D and Symons, J (1996) *Do peer groups matter? Peer group versus schooling effects on academic attainment*. London School of Economics, Centre for Economic Performance

Roscignio, V and Ainsowrth-Darnell, J (1999) Race, cultural capital and educational resources: persistent inequalities and achievement returns, *Sociology of Education*, 72, 3, 158–178

Rosenberg, M (1979) *Conceiving the self*. Basic Books

Rotherham, M (1987) Children's social and academic competence, *Journal of Educational Research*, 80, 4, 206–211

Rutter, M (1987) Psychosocial resilience and protective mechanisms, *American Journal of Orthopsychiatry*, 57, 3, 316–331

Rutter, M (1991) Pathways from childhood to adult life: the role of schools, *Pastoral Care in Education*, September

Shaw, C (1998) *Remember my messages*. Who Cares? Trust

Sinclair, I and Gibbs, I (1998) *Children's Homes: A study in diversity*. Wiley

Sinclair, I, Wilson, K and Gibbs, I (2000) *Supporting foster placements*. Department of Health

Sloper, P and others (1999) *Real change not rhetoric: Putting research into practice in multi-agency services*. Policy Press

Smith, C and Carlson, G (1997) Stress, coping and resilience in children and youth, *Social Services Review*, 71, 231–256

Smith, D J and others (1989) *The school effect: A study of multi-racial comprehensives*. Policy Studies Institute

Social Exclusion Unit (1998) *Truancy and school exclusion Cm 3957*. Social Exclusion Unit

Social Exclusion Unit (2002) *Report on the education of children in care: Children and Young People's Questionnaire*. Social Exclusion Unit

Social Exclusion Unit (2003) *A better education for children in care: The issues*. Social Exclusion Unit

Social Services Inspectorate (2003) *Mid-year progress report and delivery forecast for social services 2002/2003*. Department of Health

Social Services Inspectorate/Office for Standards in Education (1995) *The education of children who are looked after by local authorities*. HMSO

St Clair, L and Osborne, A F (1987) The ability and behaviour of children who are 'in care' or separated from their parents, *Early Child Development and Care*, 28, 187–354

Stein, M, Rees, G and Frost, N (1994) *Running - the risk: young people on the streets of Britain today*. Children's Society

Stobbs, P (1995) *Making it work together: Advice on joint initiatives between Education and Social Services Departments*. National Children's Bureau

Sutton, P (1995) *Crossing the boundaries: a discussion of children's services plans*. National Children's Bureau

Teachman, J D (1987) Family background, educational resources, and educational attainment', *American Sociological Review*, 52, 4, 548–577

Tomlinson, T (1993) *Motivating students to learn*. McCutcheon Publishing Company

Tower Hamlets Study Support Project (1997) *Closing the gap: Tower Hamlets Study Support Project*. Tower Hamlets Study Support Project

Triseliotis, J, Borland, M and Hill, M (1998) *Fostering good relations: A study of foster care and foster carers in Scotland*. The Scottish Office

Triseliotis, J and others (1995) *Teenagers and the social work services*. HMSO

Utting, W (1997) *People like us: The report of the review of safeguards for children living away from home*. Department of Health

Vacha, E F and McLaughlin, T (1992) The social structural, family, school and personal characteristics of 'at-risk' students: policy recommendations for school personnel, *Journal of Education*, 174, 3, 9–25

Vernon, J and Sinclair, R (1998) *Maintaining children in school: The contribution of Social Services Departments*. Joseph Rowntree Foundation

Vincent, C, Ranson, S and Martin, J (2000) *Little polities: Schooling, governance and parent participation*. Economic and Social Research Council

Webb, R and Vulliamy, G (2001) Joining up the solutions: the rhetoric and practice of inter-agency cooperation, *Children and Society*, 15, 315–332

Wentzel, K P (1997) Student motivation in middle school, *Journal of Educational Psychology*, 89, 411–419

Wigfall, R and Moss, P (2001) *More than the sum of its parts: a study of a multi-agency child care network*. Joseph Rowntree Foundation and National Children's Bureau

Who Cares? Trust (1998) *Remember my messages*. Who Cares? Trust

Who Cares? Trust (2001) *Right to read*. Who Cares? Trust

Wiggins, J D (1987) Self-esteem, earned grades and television habits of students, *School Counsellor*, 35, 2, 128–133

Williams, B, Williams, J and Ullman, A (2002) *Parental involvement in education*. Department for Education and Skills

Wilson, A and Charlton, K (1997) *Making partnerships work: Practical guide for the public, private, voluntary and community sectors*. Joseph Rowntree Foundation

Wyman, P A and others (1992) Interviews with children who experienced major life stress: family and child attributes that predict resilient outcomes, *Journal of the American Academy of Child and Adolescent Psychiatry*, 31, 904–910